the
SOUND
of the
FUTURE

The Coming Age of Voice Technology

Tobias Dengel
with Karl Weber

PUBLICAFFAIRS
NEW YORK

To my mother, Gisela,
who gave me the confidence to try anything
and was always there when I needed to be lifted back up.

Immer positiv.
She left us much too soon.

———————————

PublicAffairs
Hachette Book Group
1290 Avenue of the Americas, New York, NY 10104
www.publicaffairsbooks.com
@Public_Affairs

Printed in the United States of America
First Edition: October 2023

Published by PublicAffairs, an imprint of Perseus Books, LLC, a subsidiary of Hachette Book Group, Inc. The PublicAffairs name and logo is a trademark of the Hachette Book Group.

The Hachette Speakers Bureau provides a wide range of authors for speaking events. To find out more, go to hachettespeakersbureau.com or email HachetteSpeakers@hbgusa.com.

PublicAffairs books may be purchased in bulk for business, educational, or promotional use. For more information, please contact your local bookseller or the Hachette Book Group Special Markets Department at special.markets@hbgusa.com.

The publisher is not responsible for websites (or their content) that are not owned by the publisher.

Print book interior design by Linda Mark.

Library of Congress Cataloging-in-Publication Data
Names: Dengel, Tobias, author.
Title: The sound of the future : the coming age of voice technology / Tobias Dengel with Karl Weber.
Description: First edition. | New York : PublicAffairs, 2023. | Includes bibliographical references and index. |
Identifiers: LCCN 2023005247 | ISBN 9781541702363 (hardcover) | ISBN 9781541702387 (ebook)
Subjects: LCSH: Voice computing.
Classification: LCC QA76.9.V65 D46 2023 | DDC 006.2/48392—dc23/eng/20230317
LC record available at https://lccn.loc.gov/2023005247

ISBNs: 9781541702363 (hardcover), 9781541702387 (ebook)

LSC-C

Printing 1, 2023

Contents

PART TWO
RISING TO THE CHALLENGE

PROLOGUE

The Power and Potential of Voice Technology

THOUGH I WORK WITH COMPANIES THROUGHOUT THE WORLD, there is one story about the transformative power of voice technology that never ceases to inspire me. It began in May 2018 when a student at the University of North Carolina named Anastasia Soule—a music lover and an avid runner—was in New Orleans to celebrate her twenty-first birthday with her family. With no warning, she began to feel odd symptoms—weakness and poor coordination. Within hours, they got worse: her fingers and toes tingled, and her body felt numb.

Soule tried to shake off the problem. As planned, she and her mother began seeing the sights of New Orleans—but she found herself asking her mom to stop every few minutes so she could sit and rest. This was not the Anastasia everyone had come to know—the vigorous woman friends described as "the picture of health," who'd recently qualified for that fall's Boston Marathon.

A few days later, Soule found herself in Tulane Medical Center, almost completely paralyzed from her shoulders down. She had contracted Guillain-Barré syndrome (GBS), a neurological disorder that affects approximately one person in 100,000. GBS causes the body's immune system to attack the nervous system, stripping the nerves of their protective myelin sheath. Little by little, the brain loses control of the electrical signals that normally connect the mind to the body. The individual who suffers with GBS becomes physically help-less and sometimes dies.

Luckily for her, Soule was surrounded by family and friends who cared about her deeply. One of these was Matt Kubota, her boyfriend at the time, who was a product designer at WillowTree, the company I cofounded. Anastasia's illness was Matt's first experience with some-one suffering from an extreme physical disability. Shocked by her plight, Matt discovered the extent to which people with paralysis are cut off from the world, unable even to speak with those they love.

The ability to communicate is a fundamental human function. When a person is seriously ill, lack of that ability can make medical treatment extremely difficult by limiting access to basic information about the patient's condition—Does she have any feeling in her limbs? Is she too hot or too cold, hungry or thirsty?

To deal with this problem, Soule's caregivers used a standard tool for such circumstances—a chart with letters of the alphabet. Her care-givers would hold up the chart and point to the letters one at a time. Soule would use head movements—a nod or a shake—to indicate which letter was correct, gradually spelling out the words that would express her meaning. After a few grueling hours like this, Matt hit on the idea of improving the system by listing the letters of the alphabet in order of frequency—E, T, A, O, I, N, and so on—rather than in alpha-betical order. This made it possible for Soule to spell most words a little more easily. But the process was still agonizingly slow and frustrating.

Naturally, Matt searched for a technological fix. But he found that there was no accessible, easy-to-use, voice-based tool that could enable victims of paralysis to communicate with others. A small indus-try had grown up around building custom-made devices that could allow people with little or no mobility to communicate, either in writing or through artificially generated speech. However, these devices were complicated, unwieldy, and extremely expensive, requiring an investment of $10,000 or more. One example was the voice-generating system used by scientist Stephen Hawking, who suffered from amyotrophic lateral sclerosis (ALS), often called Lou Gehrig's disease, which involved a specially programmed laptop computer attached to a customized set of switches. This kind of support was inaccessible for the vast majority of people who needed it.

Kubota decided, "There ought to be an app for that." He convinced his colleagues at WillowTree to join him in launching a pro bono project to develop a communication tool that people with disabilities could access easily, anytime, anywhere, and without having to spend thousands of dollars. The result was a voice-technology tool they ultimately dubbed Vocable AAC. (The acronym stands for *augmentative and alternative communication*, and it defines an entire category of voice tools and devices that can help people who have limited ability to communicate verbally with others.)[1]

Vocable enables even a person with acute paralysis to quickly and easily select words or phrases from a screen. Using speech-generating technology, those words or phrases are then spoken out loud to a caregiver or anyone else in the room. An additional software tool captures the words of the caregiver, converts them into written text, and makes them the basis of a continuing exchange. Thus, Vocable allows a paralyzed person to have close-to-normal conversations, communicating practical information—the presence or absence of pain, or the need for an extra blanket or a glass of water—that may be vitally important to caregivers, family, and friends, as well as allowing them to have conversations about feelings and emotions just as all of us do.

The service Vocable provides seems marvelously simple, almost miraculous. But creating it wasn't easy. It took Kubota, senior project manager Andrew (Drew) Miller, and a team of twenty contributors—four engineers, two designers, a researcher, a product architect, and several others—some eighteen months to build a smartphone app that could address the communication challenge faced by the seriously disabled.

One key to a solution lay in the fact that Soule, like many people who are otherwise paralyzed or have motor deficits, was still able to control the movement of her head. This meant that a software tool capable of tracking such movements should theoretically be able to convert that information into letters, words, or phrases selected from those presented on a screen—and then into speech, making conversational communication possible.

Kubota discovered a way to make this happen during one of Apple's annual Developers Conferences, where new technology tools are presented for adoption by outside software companies. At the 2018 conference, Kubota and a colleague heard about an update to Apple's year-old Face ID system, which uses twin cameras in a smartphone to create two complementary images of a face. More than 30,000 invisible infrared dots are then projected onto the image to create an ultra-detailed 3D map of the face that can be used to reliably identify a user, speeding and simplifying log-ins.

"When I saw that," Kubota recalls, "I slapped my coworker on the shoulder and said, 'Hey, we can use that data—and not just to unlock a phone.'"

Back at WillowTree headquarters, Kubota and his colleague Duncan Lewis analyzed how the Face ID technology was able to precisely track the movements of an individual's head and eyes. They found a way to use Apple's image-mapping system to model beams of light—"almost like twin lasers," Kubota says—as if they are projecting from an individual's eyes onto the smartphone or tablet screen in front of her face. The movements of those beams can be captured as they jump from one letter, one word, or one phrase to another. Within seconds, a message can be pieced together and then articulated using speech-generating technology, thereby giving a paralyzed person a voice.

This was a huge breakthrough. (It's an example of the multimodal thinking that I will explore in depth, illustrating how voice connects with other capabilities, such as sight, touch, and, in this case, head and eye movement, and often serves as a crucial tool for making the impossible possible.) But it was only the first step in crafting Vocable. Just as important—and complex—was developing the social and intellectual context that would make Vocable a practical communication tool for those living with paralysis or other communication disabilities. It required months of research, experimentation, feedback, and revision in collaboration with potential users of the app, medical professionals—doctors, nurses, therapists—and caregivers, family, and friends of those who are communication-impaired. Speech-language pathologists from Duke University offered their expertise to help guide the work of the WillowTree team.[2] Additional help was provided by other professionals, such as Adina Bradshaw, a speech-language pathologist at the Shepherd Center in Atlanta, where Anastasia Soule had moved to continue her recovery in June 2018.

These early tests and experiments helped define parameters such as the kinds of words and phrases that needed to be made available in the app. As a result, several categories of phrases were built into the program, grouped under headings like Basic Needs, Personal Care, Conversation, Environment, and Feelings.

However, it quickly became apparent that no one-size-fits-all set of words would serve the needs of every potential user. One member of the WillowTree team, product architect Kylie Kalik, happened to have a master's degree in health behavior and education, making her particularly sensitive to the social challenges involved in health care. She recalls, "We spoke with one therapist about using Vocable, and she told us she needs a different selection of words for every patient. Some just want to get straight to discussing their medical condition and the next steps in treatment. But one loves to start his session by talking about his favorite topic—race cars. And another always wants to take a few minutes to chat about his love of bourbon."[3]

Differences like these make us human—and make communication a deeply personal activity. To serve the wide range of emotional and intellectual needs that humans convey through voice, the development team made it possible for the list of phrases available to be augmented and customized over time to suit the needs of a particular user. Matt Kubota remembers hearing about one patient who was a die-hard fan of the Buffalo Bills NFL team. The patient's brother worked with the team at the hospital to develop a personalized list of words and phrases for Vocable that would allow the two men to share their reactions as they watched the games together—including a handful of choice expletives for use when necessary.[4]

Other forms of customization also proved to be essential. From conversations with users and caregivers, Kylie Kalik learned that it was important for patients to be able to adjust the speed and responsiveness of the head-tracking tool.

Someone who is recovering from a motor accident may have cognition and motor skills that are changing from week to week. The same with someone who has ALS. Depending on how their abilities evolve, Vocable may need to change over time to move more quickly or more slowly. Otherwise, the app may select a letter or word that the user didn't intend, or it may lose a word or phrase because it takes the user longer than expected to settle on it.

Through these kinds of iterative learning and steady improvements, the WillowTree team gradually transformed Vocable from a great idea into a practical, working tool. In March 2020, Vocable became available free of charge for use on a number of iOS and Android smartphones and tablets, largely eliminating the giant cost hurdles that once locked too many paralyzed individuals into spaces of isolation and silence. By mid-2021, the app was being used by thousands of individuals in forty-nine countries.[5]

Anastasia Soule has since recovered from GBS and has even begun to run again.[6] But a significant number of people around the world continue to need the kind of communication support that Vocable AAC provides. They include people who've experienced a stroke, those with conditions like ALS or multiple sclerosis, and those who've suffered spinal cord injuries (the last-named group estimated at around 17,500 annually in the United States alone).

Vocable is a powerful example of one way in which voice technology is transforming our world—in this case, by giving a voice to those who've been deprived of one. In the pages of this book, you'll discover many of the other dramatic changes being driven by voice tech, and you'll learn about how you and any organization you work for can participate in this revolution.

INTRODUCTION

*Unmistakable Signs of the Impending
Voice-Technology Wave*

IT MAY BE HARD TO IMAGINE NOW, BUT FOR SOME FIFTY years, one of the largest media businesses in the United States was the Yellow Pages. An awkward, unwieldy book printed on thin yellow paper arrived on millions of American doorsteps each year. It was a vital information source that the typical family consulted practically every day to find everything from plumbers to car repair shops to lawyers. It was your best and often your only source when you wanted to find a local business, a professional office, a government agency, a nonprofit organization, or any other entity with a phone number and an address. And companies paid heavily to appear in those Yellow Pages directories, published by AT&T and other phone companies. For many small businesses, a full- or half-page Yellow Pages ad was by far their biggest marketing expense and critical to driving customers to their company. With advertising revenues reaching a high of $14 billion per year, the Yellow Pages was an incredible cash cow, and AT&T's most profitable division by far.[1] The only costs of selling a Yellow Pages ad were the sales commission and the paper it was printed on. The unionized salespeople made a killing—a good sales rep could clear a quarter million dollars a year. And decade after decade, the profits kept rolling in.

Then came the internet.

The phone companies were not oblivious. By the mid-1990s, they had seen the move to online information sources coming. Their reasonable response was to build their own yellow-page websites. In 1996, yellowpages.com was launched, bringing the most trusted brand in information search online. (The site was purchased by two of the biggest phone companies in 2004.)[2] "Searches are moving online, but we've got this problem solved," or so the people running the phone companies thought. After all, if a Yellow Pages website had all the best information, and the phone companies could cross-promote it in their print Yellow Pages and other advertising, why wouldn't users go to the phone company site when they were looking for local merchants?

At the time, I was leading AOL Local, which included AOL Yellow Pages. We saw an immense opportunity to move these searches to our platform by offering a faster, more user-friendly search experience. Every year, we relentlessly focused on improving and simplifying the experience, especially how fast someone could find the best answer they were looking for. And every year, more and more searches migrated to platforms like AOL, Yahoo, and Google and away from the Yellow Pages, whether in its print or online forms.

By 2010, one of the largest media industries in the United States had been essentially wiped out. My kids have never seen a printed Yellow Pages book, and they'd never think of searching yellowpages.com to find a local business.

The executives behind both the print and the online versions of Yellow Pages missed one crucial insight: that user experience is king, and human beings will be inexorably drawn to solutions that make doing any given task faster and easier.

In the rearview mirror, this seismic event seems obvious. Yet for those of us involved at the time, it was a slow-moving collapse that took years to become apparent. A few early visionaries spoke about the potential of the internet to transform the advertising industry, impacting not just the Yellow Pages but newspapers, magazines, and other media as well. But change came slowly at first, and the prophets were dismissed as fearmongers—until their predictions came true, decimating businesses that had survived for generations.

When big technology shifts come, they don't just elevate a new class of companies focused on bringing that technology to life—like Google with internet search, Apple with digital photography, or Amazon with online shopping. They transform the entire economy, including almost every industry and every company. Yet such trends are difficult to perceive because they move slowly at first—and even when they are recognized, developing a strategic response is excruciatingly difficult. Just ask the executives at Yellow Pages companies, Kodak, and thousands of brick-and-mortar retailers, all of whom have been devastated by the digital technology revolutions of recent decades.

Here's another classic example. In the months after the iPhone was launched in 2008, it sparked what was then the fastest adoption of a new technology in history. The rise of the smartphone transformed one industry after another, driving changes that almost no one foresaw. When Steve Jobs announced that developers would now be able to build mobile applications and distribute them on the smartphone platform, how many people guessed that, within a decade, the taxi industry would be essentially wiped out by Uber and Lyft? How many guessed that the most powerful driver of consumer satisfaction in the banking industry would soon be the quality of a bank's mobile app? How many guessed that mobile apps would become the primary customer connection point for almost every consumer-facing business, from airlines to restaurants?

Few foresaw the scope and scale of the changes that mobile technology would bring. But those who did were in a position to take advantage of those changes and to reap the rewards.

The Sound of the Future is about a comparable technology shift that is now in its early stages. It's the emergence of a new kind of interface that will redefine how users interact with technology, much like the personal computer in the '80s, the internet in the '90s, and the smartphone in the 2000s. Just like those technologies, this new interface will have the potential to touch every person, every company, and every industry. Almost imperceptibly, this technology is already emerging all around us. Some industries have already felt the shift. In the years to come, as we learn to harness it, the world will experience a seismic shift—though many will recognize it only when they see it in their rearview mirrors.

The internet helped people find local businesses faster and more easily than the Yellow Pages; the ever-present smartphone made hundreds of activities more convenient than your laptop. In a parallel fashion, the technology I'll describe is one that will make virtually every interaction we have with our laptops, smartphones, and every other computing device twice as fast—or faster. It will make countless activities easier, and make others possible for the first time, which in turn will enable many companies to transform their business models, benefiting their customers, their employees, and their own bottom lines. It will relieve people suffering from illiteracy or disabilities by empowering them to participate easily in a range of activities that most people take for granted. And it has already begun to touch millions of us every day in our homes and on our mobile devices, making the world faster, more engaging, and simply *fun*.

You may be thinking that any single technology that can do all this would have to be an amazing breakthrough with its origins in the world's most advanced research centers—and you'd be right. The technology I'm describing does depend, in part, on the latest developments of artificial intelligence (AI), machine learning, and computing power. But it draws much of its magical-seeming power from the world's most ancient and ubiquitous human innovation—the 100,000-year-old "technology" known as human speech.

Voice, of course, is the most familiar and natural way of communicating, one that virtually all humans practice beginning in infancy. But it's a mode of interaction that, until recently, was rarely available when it comes to human-machine connections. For all the power of modern digital computers, we've been forced to communicate with them using keyboards, mice, and touch screens—all more or less awkward, slow, error-prone, decidedly unnatural, and, for some people and purposes, practically impossible. For the last 100-plus years, we've used our hands to communicate with machines via buttons, knobs, pedals, levers, and keyboards. Voice technology promises to liberate us from these clumsy tools and return us to the innate form of communication we humans have known for thousands of years. It's the *ultimate interface* that will make everything we do with technology easier, faster, more accurate, more fun, and in the end, more human. We will finally be able to communicate with machines in the same way we communicate with each other—via our voices.

I've written *The Sound of the Future* to explain how this transition is happening, why it matters, and what all of us—especially business leaders—can do to make the most of the enormous benefits it promises.

The most impactful technological revolutions are, at their core, interface revolutions. The rise of personal computing in the 1980s, the internet in the 1990s, and today's mobile world in the 2000s all hinged on the adoption of specific interfaces that hundreds of millions of users learned to use to connect with machines and with one another, from the QWERTY keyboard to the mouse and the smartphone touch screen. Each new interface increased the speed and ease with which people could access, interact with, and exchange information in all its myriad forms.

In one sense, voice is no different—it is simply the next new interface that people will use in their interactions with technology. In a few basic forms, such as the Alexa smart speaker or the GPT-powered customer-service software tool that can understand and respond to simple commands, it is already becoming familiar to millions. And yet voice is completely different from previous interface revolutions, because voice is *not* a technological interface but rather a *human* interface, one that virtually all humans on earth learn to use beginning in infancy and use naturally and intuitively every day of their lives. That's why I call it the *ultimate interface*.

THE TWO BIG PROBLEMS WITH VOICE TECH TODAY

Most people are already familiar with the earliest widespread applications of voice technology—so-called smart speakers like Amazon's Alexa and Apple's Siri. The odds are good that you already have one of these devices in your home or office. If so, you may feel skeptical about the idea that voice tech is poised to transform our world. After all, you might say, Alexa and Siri are useful for a few things—transcribing a text, checking the weather, turning on the lights. But that's hardly world-changing.

This is true enough. For most people, the current applications of voice tech are interesting, fun, and helpful, though not transformative. But there's a simple explanation for this, and it's one of the insights at the heart of this book. *Voice does contain the seeds of a potentially radical transformation of the relationship between human beings and technology—but those seeds have only* begun *to sprout, for reasons that reflect the typical pattern by which new technologies develop.*

As I'll detail in this book, the technologies underpinning the voice interface have been developed and are rapidly being perfected by a sprawling network of companies. Some of them are well-known technology giants like Amazon, Google, Microsoft, and Meta; others are start-ups or midsize companies known mainly by industry insiders, with names like OpenAI, Cerence, Vocera, Speechify, Fluent, Read-Speaker, Dashbot, SoundHound, and dozens more. Each of these companies is contributing pieces to a rapidly growing, increasingly flexible collection of voice tools that organizations in practically every industry can adopt to their own needs, from transforming customer service to streamlining a host of internal processes. In this book, I'll refer to this vast and steadily expanding set of voice tools by the name *voice technology*, or, more succinctly, *voice tech*.

The incredible speed with which voice tools are being developed and improved creates enormous opportunities for businesses—yet most organizations have barely begun to optimize their use of voice tech. As a result, many of the ways voice tech is being used today seem insignificant or limited. However, this is the story of any new technical wave. It takes years for entrepreneurs, designers, and engineers to shift their thinking to take full advantage of any new technological paradigm.

In fact, history shows that a new technology generally emerges incrementally from the old technology it is replacing—and as this happens, the most familiar uses of the old technology distort and limit our perceptions of the new. Early TV shows, for example, were simply radio programs with bare-bones video images added. It took years for broadcasters to evolve new models of televised entertainment, from the sitcoms of the 1960s to the reality shows of today. In the early days of the internet, the online version of *Time* magazine was a straightforward scan of the print edition; AOL was a narrowly constrained system that trapped online users within a limited range of activities and websites, great for sending email and checking scores and weather, but little else. The dynamic, all-encompassing nature of today's internet took years to evolve.

It's no wonder that, in the infancy of television, many people regarded it as a mere fad. (A 1951 article in the *Wall Street Journal* quoted a "New York movie mogul" as saying, "Video isn't able to hold on to the market it captures after the first six months," and added that one San Franciscan observed, "People soon get tired of staring at a plywood box every night.")[3]

Similarly, an executive at Time Inc. in 1995 would have been correct to point out that the online version of the magazine was much harder to read than the print version—and no advertising executive would have dreamed of pulling their ads from *Time* magazine and moving them to the internet. Even media insiders found it very difficult to imagine what the ultimate forms of these early, constrained new technologies would be.

Today, voice technology is in a comparable place. The basic voice-driven interfaces we commonly encounter are "walled garden" systems much as AOL was, offering voice-only experiences locked within the Alexa and Siri platforms, which users are unable to escape. Nonetheless, just like AOL, they have attracted considerable interest—in fact, smart speakers have enjoyed the fastest adoption rate of any new technology in human history (surpassing even the smartphone), which offers a powerful indication of the enormous potential appeal of voice as a mode of communication.[4] But ultimately today's voice assistants usually leave us disappointed and unfulfilled. Why? Because, for the most part, *we're simply doing voice wrong*. We are trying to replicate a human voice experience that involves both speaking with and listening to "assistants" like Alexa and Siri. But this approach completely misses the point.

What's the key attraction and the greatest benefit of voice technology? The overarching driver is the fact that we speak three times faster than we type, and we do so with purpose-driven fluency, rarely even having to devote conscious thought to the process. The beauty and power of voice is that it is the easiest, most natural, and most convenient way for us to communicate with our devices.

Yet as much as we want to talk to machines, we *don't* want to listen to them respond. The reason is that it takes twice as long to absorb words through listening as compared with reading, making it much harder to understand and retain information. When it comes to receiving information, reading is usually the best option. It's faster and more flexible, allowing us to refer back to items we may have missed or want to focus on. Thus, while it's quick and easy to tell Alexa to order us a pizza, it's awkward, slow, and frustrating to have to listen to Alexa responding with all the confirmation details regarding our choice of toppings, size, crust, and so on. It's much more efficient to see the order we just placed summarized on a screen, and then confirm it with a simple Yes.

So the entire paradigm of voice technology is backwards right now, all the way down to the convention by which we describe Alexa and Siri as "smart speakers." In reality, we want nothing to do with "smart speakers." What we want are "smart mics," whether on our phones, in our laptops, or in other devices throughout our homes and workplaces—listening tools that will allow the machines around us to react instantly to our instructions and desires. The current mismatch between what humans want from voice and what voice tech now delivers is the first big reason why voice has not yet transformed our world.

Today, the voice-tech industry is in the earliest stages of changing its approach to take full advantage of the inherent benefits the technology offers. Voice tools are evolving to employ what I call the *multimodal interface*—using not only voice but screens, keyboards, sounds, and haptics (touch-based cues) to connect humans and machines, depending on which communication mode is most appropriate for a particular use.

In their earliest implementations, these multimodal systems will follow the turn-based, *call-and-response* communication paradigm that humans are currently used to: we will tell our app what movie to buy tickets for, and subsequently get the confirmation of the order on our screens. Over time, however, we will be evolving to an even-larger breakthrough, in which machines will use multimodal methods to respond to us simultaneously, at the same time as we speak. In this world of *concurrent communication*, the device will communicate back to us while we talk: as we mention the name of a movie, its title will appear on screen, and when we ask for two tickets, a haptic tremor or an audible "bing" will instantly respond.

As these multimodal systems proliferate, the speed and usefulness of voice tech will become increasingly obvious, and the floodgates will open as countless activities are redesigned and reimagined to take full advantage of the benefits of voice.

There's a second big reason why voice tech has not yet transformed the world in the way I foresee. Most uses of voice tech today involve what are called voice assistants—often referred to as *voice bots*. These include not only the freestanding, multipurpose voice bots like Alexa and Siri, but single-purpose voice bots that usually provide service to customers of banks, airlines, retail stores, and many other businesses.

Voice bots are a natural step in the evolution of voice tech, and there's nothing inherently wrong with them. But the way most voice bots today are designed and used has unintentionally undermined user trust.

The trust we place in people or devices is based on two main elements: *affective trust*, which is based on subjective emotional factors and is usually formed in the first few seconds of interaction, and *cognitive trust*, which forms over time and is generally based on the answer to the question, "Does this person or device do what they promise to do?"

Today's voice bots undermine both dimensions of trust, largely because, again, designers are trying to imitate the human voice experience.

On the affective side, devices that try to replicate the emotional qualities of human beings have been shown to trigger the so-called *uncanny valley* response, first described in 1970 by Japanese researcher Masahiro Mori.[5] Mori found that as robots get more human-like, they actually become less engaging or trustworthy to humans—perhaps because, deep down, we sense that we are being tricked by something that is not human at all. As a result, we associate these experiences with corpses or zombies—nonhuman simulacra of humans that we find eerie and disturbing, and that we instinctively want to flee.

Mori's discovery has since been replicated in multiple experiments, as well as in numerous examples from entertainment and media. For example, it has been shown that people tend to consider cartoon characters (clearly not human) much more sympathetic than film characters designed to be human-like avatars (uncomfortably close to humans).[6] This helps to explain, for example, why the cartoon-like characters in the computer-animated film *Toy Story* (1995) have attracted a huge fan base, while the avatar-like characters in *The Polar Express* (2004), another computer-animated film, failed to connect with audiences. *Toy Story* was a box-office hit and inspired a series of popular sequels; *The Polar Express* was a flop and attracted critical reactions like this one from Stephanie Zacharek of *Salon*: "I could probably have tolerated the incessant jitteriness of 'The Polar Express' if the look of it didn't give me the creeps."[7]

The uncanny valley effect is triggered whenever machines are designed to mimic humans too closely. Thus, by attempting to make voice assistants like Alexa and Siri as human as possible, we are falling into the trap of alienating users rather than engaging them.

Equally important, today's voice bots often fail the test of cognitive trust as well. Most voice tools are not yet able to engage in complex, spontaneous, open-ended conversations as well as an average human. AI experts are working to improve this performance, and later in this book we'll examine how their efforts are beginning to bear fruit. But until the launch of OpenAI's ChatGPT 3.5 in November 2022, attempts to engage in free-form conversations usually fell apart after a series of short turns. Many voicebots still lack this capacity.

As a result, when we expect Siri to understand and respond to our requests with the accuracy and reliability of a human being, we are usually disappointed. If instead we were to view Siri as a machine designed to complete a limited number of simple tasks, our trust level would increase. As we'll be discussing in this book, the issue of trust is another challenge the voice-tech industry is now tackling head-on.

What's needed, then—and what's already underway—is a complete rethinking of what voice tech will look like in the years to come. It won't be voice bots. These are the AOLs of voice technology, which will serve merely as stepping stones to a much better result. As voice tech is unleashed from Alexa and Siri; incorporated into thousands of

apps, websites, and devices; and incorporated into multimodal interfaces that take full advantage of the best capabilities of voice trans-
mission from humans coupled with machine responses via screens,
sounds, and more, the ultimate interface will be born.

SIGNS OF THE COMING VOICE-TECH REVOLUTION

Is voice technology really the next big thing? One way to consider that
question is to look at what the tech giants are investing in. Virtually
without exception, today's biggest and smartest tech companies have
been placing giant bets on the future of voice.

Google's CEO Sundar Pichai describes it this way: "We have
invested the last decade in building the world's best natural language
processing technology." Microsoft's CEO Satya Nadella sees the advent
of voice as a transformative moment: "As an industry, we are on the
cusp of a new frontier that pairs the power of natural human language
with advanced machine intelligence." It's no secret that one of Microsoft's biggest plays in the space is its multibillion-dollar investment in
OpenAI, the developer of ChatGPT, and the implementation of that
technology in its search engine Bing. And Amazon's founder and chair-
man Jeff Bezos has committed more than 12,000 employees to developing voice technologies.

Other major tech players, including Alibaba, Apple, Baidu, IBM,
Oracle, Samsung, and Tencent, are also moving into voice at full speed,
deploying their internal R&D capabilities, working with outside partners, and acquiring voice-focused start-up companies—all with the
goal of creating and controlling the voice-driven platforms that they
believe will dominate the next age of technology.

Of course, the tech giants have been wrong before. They were
wrong in 2012, when the Consumer Electronics Show was buzzing
with 3D TVs. Some forecasters at the time were predicting that over
50 percent of US households would have a 3D TV by 2020. That might
have been a great change of pace for TV viewers stuck at home due to

COVID-19, but it didn't happen; in fact, to this day I have yet to see a single 3D TV installed in a home.

Two years later, the big rage was virtual reality, with hype fueled by the much-ballyhooed launch of Google Glass and Facebook's purchase of the VR firm Oculus for $2.3 billion before it had launched a single consumer product. But today, VR is still in search of its breakthrough application, and the metaverse—though it has been eagerly embraced by Mark Zuckerberg—remains largely a vague concept in most people's minds.

Since 2015, a lot of the buzz has been around blockchain, which was supposed to transform global business through its unique data-security features. But as of 2022, its original use case in cryptocurrency remains the only field that blockchain has deeply impacted—and even that application appears to be losing much of its appeal, with the 2022 collapse of numerous cryptocurrencies amid accusations of mismanagement and possible fraud.

These and other innovations attracted hundreds of billions of dollars' worth of investments and yet, so far, none of them has panned out. Why were some of the smartest minds in the world wrong about them? And how can we tell whether, this time, they're right about voice?

All of the technologies I just mentioned—3D TV, VR, blockchain—are impressive. They all have some practical uses and at least a handful of avid fans. But just because a few early adopters, hobbyists, or niche users adopt a technology doesn't mean the general public will. Most business leaders want and need to know about the technologies that will permeate the economy the way PCs, the internet, and smartphones have done.

Fortunately, a lot of thoughtful research has been done into the challenge of recognizing major tech trends before they are obvious. Experts like Amy Webb, founder of the Future Today Institute and author of *The Signals Are Talking*, have defined the most important indicators of a truly transformative tech trend as that it is driven by and responds to *basic human needs*; it *evolves as it emerges*; and it often appears originally as *a series of unconnected dots*, which only gradually cohere into a powerful, change-driving force.[8]

In the "misses" such as 3D TV, VR, and blockchain, these three defining indicators didn't apply. Most important, none of those failed innovations fulfilled *basic human needs*, as defined by questions like these:

- Where and how are people wasting their time (as they perceive it)?
- Where and how are people struggling to use technology?
- Where and how are people looking for accurate information and having difficulty finding it?
- Where and how are people stuck in trying to perform everyday tasks?
- Where and how is technology contributing to people's physical safety—or undermining it?
- Where and how is technology presenting usage barriers for people with special needs?
- Where and how do people feel a sense of trust and security when using technology?

Consider 3D television. What human need does that technology really meet? Yes, it's undeniably mind-blowing when you first experience it—which is why so many company executives fell in love with it. They fell into the trap of backing an impressive technology that was looking for a use case—rather than identifying a basic human need and meeting it with technology. The fact is that very few families are sitting around their living rooms wishing that their TV image was in 3D.

Voice is *different*. Voice offers compelling answers to every single one of Amy Webb's human-need questions laid out above. That's very rare. Even strong emerging technologies usually address only a few of these basic needs. Voice is *faster* than any other tech interface, with the potential to eliminate countless hours of wasted time. It's *more intuitive* than any other mode of communication. It provides the *simplest and most reliable* way of accessing information. It can make everyday tasks *vastly easier and more efficient.* It contributes significantly to *human safety and well-being.* And it makes the use of technology *more natural and comfortable* than ever before.

In addition, the development of voice matches the traits that Amy Webb describes. Voice is clearly evolving as it emerges from niche applications and voice-only bots like Alexa and Siri to become a widespread, eventually ubiquitous tool. Ultimately, voice will become the primary interface between humans and machines because it is faster, easier, more flexible, and more intuitive than any other way we have to communicate with machines. Voice makes it easier for us to tell machines what to do, and, when used correctly, gets us away from the awkward, laborious act of listening to machines telling us what to do. And as you'll see, the promise of voice is now rapidly being realized because of the many emerging voice tools that are now coming together to make voice technology not just practical, but truly transformational.

In Part One of this book, we'll consider the vital human needs that voice serves better than other technologies. This roster of valuable voice-based services will show why voice *should* be on the verge of becoming ubiquitous. But is it really happening? The answer is yes—and it's happening faster than most people may realize.

With relatively little fanfare, voice tech is already being used in various forms by an estimated 62 percent of American adults.[9] This makes it the fastest adoption of a new technology in history, even faster than the previous record holder, the smartphone.

That's an important early indicator, though by itself it doesn't prove that voice tech is on the verge of transforming the world. In his classic book *Crossing the Chasm,* Geoffrey Moore discusses how any new technology must succeed in bridging the gap that separates early users from the mainstream. This is where technologies often fail (once again, Google Glass and the Oculus Rift come to mind).

There is, however, critically important data suggesting that voice tech is indeed crossing the chasm. What's more, 80 percent of those now using voice tools describe themselves as satisfied or very satisfied with their performance.[10] Surveys also show that over 70 percent of consumers say they prefer using voice to conduct online searches whenever possible, rather than relying primarily on their keyboards.[11] These are revealing statistics, especially given the current imperfect state of voice technology. It shows how intuitively appealing the voice interface is and how users are drawn to its speed and convenience, even in a world where it is still far from perfect. Going back to the AOL comparison, it reminds us of how many users eagerly engaged with AOL even though they had to muddle through an excruciatingly slow and unstable user experience often mocked as the "world wide wait."

Today the uses of voice tools are rapidly expanding beyond the basics—checking sports scores or the weather, or dictating an email. A growing number of employees around the world are using voice tech on the job in some way, from warehouse workers locating items in stock to field technicians delivering and receiving reports from remote client sites. In fact, one study finds that 76 percent of businesses report they have experienced "quantifiable benefits" from voice-tech initiatives, such as incorporating voice bots into their processes.[12]

Voice tech is a global phenomenon, and growing even faster in countries other than the United States and in languages other than English. Voice bots are already being used by 1.4 billion people around the world—and 40 percent of those global users report they prefer using a voice interface to interacting with a live human being.[13] By 2024, the number of voice-empowered devices in the world is expected to exceed the global human population.[14]

These voice trends have been building for a decade—Siri launched in 2011 and Alexa in 2014. But many of us have failed to notice the trends and consider their implications. Similarly, it took about ten years for the earliest forms of the internet to achieve the success of the World Wide Web of 2000, and it took a decade for early interactive mobile experiences to give rise to the explosive growth of the smartphone. The signs suggest that voice is rapidly approaching a tipping point of ubiquity and popularity.

BARRIER-BUSTING BREAKTHROUGHS: CHATGPT AND BEYOND

The data I've just presented raises the question: Why is voice becoming such a powerful trend at this precise moment?

I'll delve deeply into the answer a little later in this book. But one huge driver is a series of technological improvements—the newly emerging tools I mentioned earlier. Technologies like automatic speech recognition (ASR) and natural language processing (NLP) have made huge strides in recent years. Leaps in AI and machine learning have accelerated the development of combined hardware/software systems that understand ordinary human speech, can speak back in colloquial language, and can interpret and follow voice orders with steadily increasing accuracy. ASR tools have made enormous progress in understanding spoken English, and in the right circumstances development companies like Google are achieving accuracy rates in the range of 97 to 99 percent. These tools are still far from perfect—but they're much closer to perfect than they were ten, five, or even two years ago.

Many of these developments have been happening quietly, unnoticed by most people except for hard-core technology specialists. But in November 2022, one breakthrough shook the world, garnering global headlines and reactions ranging from amazement and awe to near-apocalyptic dismay. This was the release of ChatGPT 3.5, a natural language chatbot, developed by the research lab OpenAI and fueled by the latest improvements in artificial intelligence, that is capable of startlingly realistic verbal interactions with human users.

Within two months, over 100 million users flocked to the ChatGPT website to experiment with this text-and-response tool. They quickly discovered its amazing array of capabilities. ChatGPT can engage in a highly believable written conversation on a wide range of topics. But it can also draft essays and stories, create a scene for a movie or TV show, compose song lyrics and poetry, and even write and debug a computer program. Having been trained on vast amounts of data and text content from the internet and other sources, ChatGPT can answer factual questions about history, science, culture, current events (at least through the year 2021), and countless other topics. Perhaps most impressive, it is able to remember the contents of earlier exchanges in the same conversation, meaning ChatGPT can conduct a lengthy dialogue without "losing the thread" of the core subject.

These capabilities exceed those demonstrated by previous tools for natural language generation—with powerful implications for the next generation of voice tech tools.

ChatGPT pushed AI research to the center of the global conversation. The *Atlantic* magazine dubbed it one of its "Breakthroughs of the Year," declaring that it "may change our mind about how we work, how we think, and what human creativity really is."[15] The *New York Times* called it "the best artificial intelligence chatbot ever released to the general public," and controversial CEO and tech entrepreneur Elon Musk called it "scary good," adding, "We are not far from dangerously strong AI."[16]

Others, while impressed by ChatGPT's capabilities, pointed out its flaws, among them its susceptibility to a phenomenon called *artificial intelligence hallucination*. This is the tendency to respond to prompts with answers that sound plausible but are factually false or nonsensical—for example, by writing paragraphs of technical information that mention research papers that never existed.[17] Hackers tested ChatGPT's limits and found it was disturbingly easy to get the chatbot to violate its pre-set rules against dangerous, racist, or abusive content. Reports of these limitations generated a backlash by people who declared ChatGPT unready for public use and decried its early release as irresponsible.[18]

The episode left many observers scratching their heads about what it means for the present and future status of AI—as well as for technologies like voice tech that rely on AI. The answer is that these types of generative AI technologies represent a massive technological breakthrough and create opportunities throughout the economy for dislocations, both positive and negative. Yes, ChatGPT is an amazing step forward in the development of natural language generation. But at the same time, it has significant flaws that must be addressed before it can be used for all the highly ambitious functions some have proposed (such as replacing Google when searching for information). After all, a data source that is correct (say) 95 percent of the time would be dangerous to rely on whenever accuracy really matters—which means, for most purposes, it would be useless.

But that leaves a host of specific, limited, but highly valuable purposes that ChatGPT and similar language-generation tools can safely and effectively perform in 2023. Many more such purposes will be added over the next five years. As I'll explain in Chapter 7, organizations like WillowTree are already using tools like ChatGPT to streamline basic tasks involved in creating powerful voice-tech systems—and doing so without posing any risks to customers, users, or anyone else. Future iterations of these tools will become even more useful—though as with all new technologies, there will be missteps along the way.

The lesson for businesspeople and others interested in understanding how AI-driven voice tech will impact their work: even today, AI continues to be a work in progress. But it's already remarkably powerful and extremely useful—provided you understand its limitations and apply it wisely to the tasks it is equipped to handle.

The true power of ChatGPT and similar tools will become apparent when they graduate from the current text-based call-and-response interface to a multimodal interface that provides a text, graphic, or voice response delivered largely concurrently with the user's input. When this happens, generative AI will be a core driver of fundamental changes in the nature of human-machine interaction.

The work of developing and refining AI tools like ChatGPT is the core of what those tech giants and hundreds of other companies have been spending many billions of dollars to achieve in their quest to shape the emerging era of voice. Continuing waves of innovations will arrive in the coming years, producing major economic and social changes, some of which are almost impossible to predict—just as no one predicted that the advent of the internet would be the end of the Yellow Pages industry, or that the iPhone would result in the transformation of the taxi industry via the launch of apps like Uber and Lyft.

History teaches another lesson about technological revolutions. Each new wave of tech has resulted in a winner-take-all competitive scrum, with a few brands emerging to control the market in each industry. This suggests that those who become leaders of the voice revolution over the next decade will be very difficult to displace.

Thus, the one thing we can be sure of is that, as the rush to make voice universal accelerates, the business stakes are high. The last thirty years of digital innovation have taught us that, over time, the best user experience consistently wins. The powerful advantages of voice, and the important human needs it serves, will help to make voice the favored interface of billions of users around the world. So the companies that do the best job of integrating voice tech into their systems will enjoy a huge advantage in the next phase of technological and economic development. Because every industry in the world will be impacted by this coming revolution, now is the time for business leaders to begin exploring the use cases and strategic implications of voice for their companies.

THE CHALLENGES AHEAD

As you can see, I'm convinced that voice tech is a major trend that will produce dramatic changes in our world. But there remain plenty of questions to be answered and challenges to be met in the years to come.

As with any technology wave, the exact timing of the voice-tech revolution is unknowable. There will likely be hurdles and retrenchments along the way, potentially not dissimilar to the "dot-bomb" bubble of the late 1990s, which sorted out winners and losers from that phase of the digital revolution. In the fall of 2022, a number of giant tech companies like Amazon laid off thousands of employees, including many in their voice divisions. This represents part of a natural, recurring cycle in tech innovation. When AOL imploded, it did not mean the end of the internet; when Motorola, Nokia, and BlackBerry phones disappeared, it was not the end of mobile. Instead, it represented a sorting-out of winning and losing models, which is a natural and inevitable process in a world of continual change.

In the years to come, the speed of the voice-tech revolution will be driven by the pace of further technology improvements, the agility with which innovators adopt new paradigms, and how quickly human behavior changes. Some industries will move more quickly than others; some use cases will emerge and flourish faster than the rest. Issues related to regulation, security, and privacy will play a role as well. In the chapters to come, I'll discuss each of these challenges and offer my thoughts as to how best to address them.

There will be successes and failures, winners and losers. We're already seeing interactive two-way conversations like those featured in the early versions of Alexa and Siri fade in prominence. They are being replaced by apps like Spotify and Waze, which provide mic buttons that allow users to communicate their needs, interests, and questions vocally as a natural part of the connection. Some of the ongoing experiments with voice tech will prove to be wildly successful; others will flop dramatically, maybe even becoming laughingstocks, as Microsoft's well-intentioned but awkwardly implemented support bot "Clippy" did.

In the chapters that follow, I'll provide details, examples, and recommendations that leaders can use to make smart decisions about implementing voice tech in their own companies. The goal will be to help you fully understand the potential benefits of voice, for your organization and for the people you serve, as well as the steps you can take, beginning today, to bring those benefits to life. We'll start with a deep dive into the human needs that voice tech can serve, which will help you grasp the truly impressive potential for voice to make life easier, safer, more efficient, more inclusive, and more fun, for billions of people around the world.

PART ONE

THE HUMAN NEEDS MET BY VOICE TECHNOLOGY

1

SPEED

*Increasing the Efficiency of Every
Human-Machine Interaction*

BACK IN 1965, PRINCETON ECONOMISTS WILLIAM BAUMOL
and William Bowen diagnosed the economic malady now called Baumol's cost disease.[1] They first wrote about the problem in connection with the performing arts, but eventually they showed that the same phenomenon applies to many kinds of labor-intensive activities, including those involved in education, government, law, and health care. All are areas in which costs have relentlessly and frustratingly continued to rise in recent decades—by contrast with other activities, especially the manufacture of products such as food, clothing, appliances, electronic devices, and automobiles, in which prices have tended to fall, often dramatically.

Why the difference? The sectors afflicted with Baumol's disease are ones in which the need for human labor has been relatively unaffected by automation. Machines have been able to drastically reduce the human time and labor involved in assembling a car, sewing a dress, or harvesting a field of grain. But there's been no way to shorten the time it takes for a nurse to interview a patient or a lawyer to draft comments to a contract. The result, then, is that labor-intensive sectors tend to show little or no gain in productivity, leading to a seemingly inevitable upward cost spiral in those fields.

Until today, that is. Voice technology coupled with AI tools is the first digital breakthrough with the potential to significantly reduce the impact of Baumol's disease in industries like health care, where efficiency gains have been limited or nonexistent for decades. Whenever human labor is used to capture, explain, or share information, voice technology can make the activity far more efficient. As I've noted, humans can speak three times faster than they type. Therefore, using voice inputs to capture data, take notes, fill out forms, manage service issues, respond to basic questions, make and change appointments, and handle an endless list of other routine tasks can save millions of employees countless hours per year—often in increments of just a few seconds or minutes at a time. The cumulative result will be a vast productivity premium and cost reduction across virtually every industry, including those most heavily impacted by Baumol's disease.

When considering the promise of voice, it is critically important to understand the importance of even marginal improvements in speed/ efficiency. Seconds matter, particularly where technology is involved. Users of computers, smartphones, and other digital devices are extraordinarily impatient. For example, research shows that, when the time to load a web page increases from one second to three seconds, the likelihood of a user abandoning the site increases by 32 percent.[2] Similar effects are noted when it takes more than a few seconds to search for a specific piece of information or complete an online purchase. Interface designers understand this, which is why they are relentlessly focused on taking out friction points and improving users' ability to get the jobs they want done as easily and quickly as possible.

These differences in seconds can bring entire industries to their knees, as illustrated by the Yellow Pages example. The online versions of the Yellow Pages proved to be no match for the search power of Google, and speed was a major factor. In 2002, how much faster was Google than Verizon's SuperPages.com? Our experiments at AOL at the time showed that the entire process of finding a plumber on Google—typing Google's URL, selecting the location, and describing the nature of the search (e.g., "plumbers in Arlington, VA")—would take a user about fifteen seconds. This accelerated over time as search engines integrated with the browser, so you could type a search directly into the URL bar and the system knew your location. As a result, by about 2007, a user could just type "plumbers" and get a list of local plumbers in five seconds or less. By contrast, it took at least thirty seconds to do the same thing on SuperPages.com, due to the cumbersome ads and the less friendly navigation process. That original fifteen-second difference—which eventually grew into a twenty-five-second difference—ultimately spelled doom to the Yellow Pages empire, and triumph for Google.

The leaders of Google took this lesson to heart. To this day, Alphabet remains relentlessly focused on speed. That's why they have never put ads on Google's home page, even though it is arguably the most valuable page on the internet and could drive millions of dollars' worth of ad revenue per day to Google. Billions of people rely on that search engine, in large part because the service it provides is so blazingly fast.

Another great example is Amazon. Why has Amazon become dominant in online commerce? Its pricing isn't always better than competitors'; it's often worse. Until recently, Amazon used the same delivery and package-tracking systems as its competitors. But Amazon has one huge advantage, represented by the service patent it has vigorously enforced and defended for years—its system for one-click checkout. Millions of consumers choose Amazon over every other shopping engine because it has all our checkout and shipping information available via one-click checkout, saving us valuable seconds every time we shop.

Examples like these show why it's important to take very seriously the user-imposed dictate of speed. As you consider a specific use case for voice, you may be tempted to think, "Okay, I can see that using voice might save someone a couple of seconds. But that's not really a big deal." In fact, speed is a very big deal. Just ask the business leaders who bet their future on SuperPages.com.

The effect of speed on consumer behavior isn't the only reason why business leaders need to pay attention to voice. As Baumol and Bowen explained, differences in the amount of time required to perform specific tasks—even small differences—have a huge economic effect when multiplied by thousands, millions, or billions of repetitions.

Thus, speed makes work better in many ways, some of them obvious, others less so. It makes specific individual tasks faster and easier; it enables a particular application or system to serve more people more quickly, thereby benefiting both users and the organization that serves them; and it helps organizations increase productivity growth, offering the potential for increased revenue, profit, and shareholder value.

The numerous, varied impacts of speed on the way businesses operate help to explain why the single biggest impact of voice-generated speed will be in workplaces of almost every kind. Baumol's disease may not be completely cured by voice tech, but its painful impact on service-based industries will be dramatically reduced.

Speed is the ultimate weapon in business. In the years to come, voice will be a powerful tool used by countless businesses in the vital quest to do everything faster.

FROM SPEECH TO TEXT:
MAKING THE JOURNEY EASIER, BETTER, FASTER

"The Ballad of John Henry" tells the story of a legendary railroad worker, a "steel-driving man" who used hand drill, hammer, and muscle power to blast holes in bedrock when tunnels were being built through mountains. When the railroad company bought a new steam drill to speed up its work, John Henry went up against the device in a contest to see which was stronger, man or machine. John Henry was able to drive the drill fourteen feet into the rock in the same time the steam drill drove just nine feet. Man had bested machine—but it was a Pyrrhic victory, for soon afterward John Henry died of sheer exhaustion.

Historians say that, if there was a real John Henry, he may have fought his fatal battle during the building of the Chesapeake and Ohio Railway around 1870. It was almost a century and a half later, in 2016, when machines finally bested humans in another symbolic contest. This time, the battle was for supremacy in a very different activity—not steel-driving, but typing.

It happened when researchers from Stanford University, the University of Washington, and the Chinese internet company Baidu set up a competition between thirty-two human typists and a program called Deep Speech 2, using texts in both English and Mandarin to test the speed and accuracy of the transcribers. (Baidu and its Deep Speech 2 program are an example of the many companies and the dozens of tools that constitute the burgeoning field of voice tech, which is making the voice revolution possible.)

Prior to this, software programs using voice recognition for transcribing text from speech had been widely considered glitchy and error-prone, often misled or confused by slang expressions, unusual accents, and ambient noise. That's why human typists were still regarded as the gold standard for creating accurate transcriptions. The 2016 contest showed that a new era had arrived. Deep Speech 2 proved to be three times faster than the human typists—and its error rate was 20 percent lower (in English) and 63 percent lower (in Mandarin).[3]

Unlike John Henry, the human typists beaten by Deep Speech 2 will probably never enter popular lore. In these early decades of the twenty-first century, we are accustomed to having machines outcompete us in information- or data-driven activities where we once reigned supreme, from *Jeopardy!* to chess. And as I'll explain, in the few short years between 2016 and 2022, voice-powered transcription from speech to text has jumped from being a clumsy second-best choice to a preferred option used by growing numbers of people.

The arrival of voice tech is the culmination of a long journey. An early version of the speech-recognition technology at the core of modern transcription tools was first demonstrated by Bell Labs back in the 1950s. Developed as a tool to help toll operators process long-distance telephone calls more rapidly, "Audrey" was housed in a room-sized computer and was capable of recognizing how callers pronounced the nine digits from one to nine with 90 percent accuracy. It was an incredible innovation for its time, but Audrey was too costly and limited to be practical, and it was never put to use.

By the early 1970s, the Defense Department's legendary DARPA division had created a program called "Harpy" that was able to recognize over 1,000 spoken words—about as many as the average toddler. This was another big step forward, but still far too limited to be of much practical use.

A major breakthrough occurred in 1990, when Dragon Systems, then led by Dr. James Baker, released DragonDictate, the first commercially available, general-purpose speech-to-text tool. It was an impressive achievement, though it had at least one huge flaw: because the software was unable to cope with the continuous flow of sound that characterizes most human speech, users were forced to insert a noticeable pause between words when using DragonDictate. Not only did this slow down the dictation process, but it required users to adopt an unnatural, awkward style of speech that drastically reduced one of the core benefits of voice—its intuitive, natural ease of use.

This weakness was finally overcome in 1997 with the release of NaturallySpeaking 1.0 by Dragon Systems. Users could now dictate text about as fluidly to a machine as to a human typist, eliminating the pauses that had often caused them to lose track of what they were saying and made the entire process frustratingly clumsy and slow. The modern era of speech recognition, featuring steady advancements in flexibility, accuracy, and speed, was underway. To this day, Dragon Systems—now part of Nuance, since 2021 a division of tech giant

Microsoft—continues to play a leading role in the world of speech recognition and voice technology in general.

Today, automated tools for converting speech to text are on their
way to replacing traditional typing in a growing range of applications.
Microsoft Word, the world's most pervasive writing tool, now offers
"Dictate your documents with voice commands" as a routine feature.
Apple, Google, Amazon, and a host of smaller companies also offer
various voice-to-text tools, each with its strengths, weaknesses, and
most popular applications.

Is this a big deal? It depends on how you look at it. Typing as a
stand-alone profession is a dying field. Government statistics say that,
as of May 2020, fewer than 43,000 people were employed as "word
processors and typists" in the United States, and the number is steadily
shrinking.[4]

On the other hand, we've all become typists, all day, every day on
our laptops and smartphones. From assistants and receptionists to
C-suite-level executives, people use keyboarding to write emails, send
texts, post on social media, draft reports, create presentations, fill out
forms, and basically run their lives. And students from grade school
through PhD programs use their keyboards to take notes and to write
compositions, term papers, and dissertations.

Many teenagers of today are extraordinarily fast at typing on a
smartphone, whereas my father takes minutes to knock out even simple sentences with his two thumbs. But both are using a highly inefficient system to transmit information. Keyboarding text is simply slow,
error-prone, and awkward. Still, the world finds it largely unavoidable.
Many of us spend most of our working days with our fingers flying over
keyboards. This includes people who work at some highly skilled and
technical jobs, from medical transcriptionists and court reporters to
translators, advertising copywriters, and journalists.

The mature speech-to-text revolution will be a godsend for anyone who today spends a significant amount of time using a keyboard.
As the purely mechanical aspect of this work—namely, getting words

down on paper or on a screen—becomes automated through voice technology, professionals will be able to spend more of their time and energy on the more challenging, creative, and important aspects of their work: checking to ensure that crucial data points are correct and clearly explained; fine-tuning details of style such as word choice and sentence structure; and bringing purely human gifts such as empathy, imagination, and humor to their writing.

To understand how this can impact an entire industry, consider software development. The US alone has an estimated 3.9 million people working in software programming. You probably don't think of these relatively high-paid engineering and IT specialists as "typists"— yet that would be a reasonable description of much of their days, since many of these individuals spend up to 80 percent of their work time clicking away on keyboards, laboriously hand-typing commands. That leaves just 20 percent of their time for the higher-order work of conceptualizing, planning, and designing the programs.

That is now beginning to change, with voice coding becoming a growing phenomenon in the world of programming. Voice-tech companies like Serenade and Talon have developed specialized tools that allow coders to use voice (sometimes in combination with other input methods, such as eye-movement tracking) to enter the complex combinations of words, symbols, and numbers that make up software code.[5]

Making this possible was a complicated, fascinating challenge. General-purpose speech-recognition tools, which work fine when transcribing a typical business letter, legal document, or newspaper story, struggle to cope with the nuances of software languages like Java, C++, JavaScript, or Python. These coding languages involve a host of specialized commands, many of them modified versions of English words (with an extra letter added, for example), and a single character, symbol, or space that is omitted or misplaced can easily cause an entire program to crash.

To manage these difficulties, the developers have created ingenious tricks that help the software to understand precisely what the programmer has in mind as they dictate a line of code. For example, users of Talon's open-source tool for voice coding employ a unique alphabet code when they need to input a single letter—one that begins with "air, bat, cap" to stand for the letters A, B, and C (as opposed to the more familiar "Alpha, Bravo, Charlie" from the so-called NATO alphabet). The developers of Serenade, a similar open-source tool, started their process by studying reams of software code they'd written in recent months and extracting a list of fifty key commands that they translated into simple voice commands that their system could understand.

Thus, users of Talon and Serenade have some specialized skills to master before they can use these tools to fluently and quickly create code using voice. But when you are working on a task for six, eight, ten, or even twelve hours at a time—not unusual in the world of the programmer—the skills you employ soon become second nature. Talon founder Ryan Hileman found that, within a few weeks, he could enter code using Talon as fast as a typical professional typist—and that his productivity was even greater, because he no longer needed to take breaks to rest his hands.[6] Similarly, Matt Wiethoff, creator of Serenade, reports that there are still a handful of coding activities that can be done faster on a keyboard than with voice—but he adds that, as the software continues to be improved, those items are being steadily crossed off the list, one by one.[7]

Voice-based programming entered the industry mainstream in a big way in November 2022. That's when GitHub, the most popular work-sharing platform for programmer teams, announced that they were making voice-based programming available via their Copilot software, initially on an experimental basis. Thousands of programmers who use GitHub every day can now use voice commands to generate code, to navigate through programs, and even to create summaries of code functions.[8]

My company, WillowTree, employs hundreds of software developers, and we're beginning to embrace the potential of these tools. We've found that once developers have gone through the learning phase associated with any new tool, voice-powered software engineering can be a powerful driver of increased productivity. Our clients pay us for our time, so the ability to be more efficient with programming outputs is a critical competitive advantage in our field. We've found that an excellent software developer can work at multiple times the speed of a mediocre software developer. This delta will only increase now that we can supply that high-performing developer with the latest voice-driven efficiency tools.

The replacement of keyboarding with voice entry of coding commands will make the work of programmers easier, faster, and more accurate. As a result, the entire programming industry will become more economically productive. Those companies whose programmers don't embrace the voice revolution will be left behind.

Software coding isn't the only activity being made faster and more efficient by the voice-to-text revolution. Almost every industry employs people who are spending significant time transmitting information via keyboard. Over time, practically all of these roles will be transformed by using voice. As you walk around your company or organization, make a note of who is using a keyboard. Then begin to imagine a world where the significant majority of this work gets done via voice entry, at speeds two to three times faster.

Naturally, high-skilled, high-cost activities will migrate first. The world of medicine is a leading example. Physicians, nurses, therapists, and medical technicians spend a sizable chunk of their time entering text into devices—notes from patient interactions, test results, prescriptions, data needed for insurance claims, and so on. For almost half a century, hospitals, clinics, and other medical organizations have tried to improve the speed and efficiency of these tasks, first by employing human transcription services and then by using software-driven tools to convert spoken notes into text. In recent years, voice-to-text tools like DragonDictate have taken a big step upward in accuracy and reliability. Not only are the basic voice-recognition systems better than ever, but recent breakthroughs in AI have enabled the tools to use context clues to understand what the text actually means. This allows them to correct mistakes and prompt physicians for next steps in real time.

SAVING PRECIOUS SECONDS

We naturally crave the ability to complete tasks more quickly—especially routine, noncreative ones that are uninteresting in themselves. As Amy Webb noted in *The Signals Are Talking*, this desire to complete tasks faster and more easily is a prime driver of technology revolutions. This craving is particularly intense when it comes to the ways we interface with technology. And this makes voice tech especially important for any organization that competes in a consumer marketplace.

The speed and simplicity of voice technology have the potential to dramatically reduce the pervasive friction we all experience when it comes to tackling the tasks of daily life.

A simple, typical example: ordering two pizzas with two toppings on each using a typical non-voice-tech app like the one operated by Pizza Hut takes forty-five seconds to a minute. (By the way, that is one-third to one-fifth the time it took just a few years ago on the web.) Pretty good—but placing the same order using an AI-powered voice-tech app takes about ten seconds. That's thirty-five seconds in savings in a world where a delay of two seconds can cost you customers.

That difference is more than enough to turn the provider of that faster process into a clear winner in the marketplace. This is not lost on leading innovators like Domino's, who are investing heavily in AI research to continue improving their voice ordering tools. In fact, they consider such tech-based improvements to their customer service so central to their future that former CEO J. Patrick Doyle called Domino's "a tech company that happens to sell pizza."[9]

Fast-food giant McDonald's also understands the accelerating power of voice. In 2019, it acquired Apprente, a start-up voice-tech company dedicated to building "conversational agents" capable of handling automated voice-based ordering in multiple languages. The Apprente team became the core members of a new McDonald's unit known as McD Tech Labs, which is working to automate the thousands of drive-through restaurants the company operates around the world. The goal: service that is easier, more accurate, and above all faster for the millions of McDonald's fans.

The results have already been gratifying. As of early 2022, McDonald's reports an average reduction in ordering time of thirty seconds, which translates to a measurable increase in customer satisfaction. The company is now engaged in scaling its use of the voice-based technology to more than 14,000 locations across the United States.[10]

Fast-food outlets aren't the only restaurants that are turning to high-tech tools for increased speed. Over the last decade, apps have taken full-service restaurants by storm. In the era of COVID-19, countless restaurants eliminated traditional menus, which can carry infection and require frequent cleaning, and replaced them with apps. In these restaurants, the server typically comes to your table and enters your order into a mobile device. The device transmits the order to the kitchen automatically, which saves time and reduces error.

So far, so good—but this improved system is ripe for further disruption. Waitstaff can typically be seen hunting and pecking through multiple menus to get to each item on the app, and if a diner special-orders something, the job becomes even more complicated. Voice tech offers a solution. A restaurant customer can transmit their order orally to the server, with the information being captured by a voice-based app at the same time. If you take a step back and think about the fact that a computer can instantly understand and process an order the moment it leaves a customer's lips, the whole concept of an employee painstakingly translating those same sound waves into an online order via taps, swipes, and keystrokes seems patently outmoded.

This obvious opportunity to use voice tech to improve service speed and increase efficiency has generated significant interest among restaurateurs. A host of voice-tech companies are offering AI-enhanced tools for taking customer food orders, and many restaurant chains are beginning to use them. Some, like Applebee's and Marco's Pizza, provide automated smartphone lines that customers can use to place orders by speaking, which are then converted into text messages for delivery to the kitchen staff. (Ordering by phone can also allow customers to request their meals while driving to the restaurant, letting them begin eating within seconds after their arrival.) In other restaurants, on-site kiosks are made available where voice orders can be placed. Managers appreciate the fact that voice ordering makes it possible to operate with fewer workers, especially in the aftermath of the economic disruptions and staff shortages caused by COVID.

Voice ordering is not yet ready to transform the entire food-service sector. Some voice-ordering apps still experience error rates up to 15 percent, which is significant enough to cause concerns among some restaurant managers. High-end restaurants are likely to want to retain traditional waitstaff systems in order to provide a luxurious personal touch. And some industry leaders worry about specific customer groups that may not be ready to rely on an automated ordering system. Greg Levin, the president of the BJ's Restaurants chain, observes, "If you've got a special need—maybe a peanut allergy or have other food sensitivities— you're going to want to talk to somebody to get that comfort."[11]

Like most of the voice-tech industry, food ordering is a work in progress. But the speed advantages are undeniable, and as the technical capabilities of voice-based ordering tools continue to improve, their proliferation is all but inevitable.

The food-ordering example also suggests the broader applicability of voice tech for companies in almost every industry. Wherever possible, information should be entering the system for processing and response the moment it leaves the customer's mouth, without the need for a time-consuming process of data entry via keyboarding, swiping, and tapping.

SOLVING THE CUSTOMER SERVICE CHALLENGE

In the years to come, a range of business functions will be transformed by voice-generated speed. Customer service is one arena where this change is already underway.

Companies in a wide range of industries, from travel and financial services to consumer products and high technology, currently employ large teams of workers whose sole task is to respond to customer questions. Customer service is a critical differentiator for most companies, because unsatisfactory service makes a disproportionately negative impact on customers. Customers who experience bad service are more likely to leave online reviews than those who experience good service—and relationship experts have found that it takes five positive experiences to outweigh the emotional impact of a single negative experience. Improving your organization's overall level of consistent service quality is the only reliable way to beat these odds.

One key driver of customer dissatisfaction is hold time. In an effort to reduce long hold times, cost-constrained customer-service departments often resort to speedup measures like imposing time limits on calls and incentivizing staffers to maximize the number of queries handled per hour. This often leads to complex problems being given short shrift, generating still more complaints from unhappy customers.

Voice technology is the key to addressing these issues. Call centers throughout the world have begun implementing voice-tech-powered approaches to customer service, including chat and voice bots. Straightforward questions like "What's the balance in my bank account?" or "When will my package arrive?" can be handled via voice-driven automation, eliminating the tedium customers experience when they must endure long waits for an operator or use keyboards to laboriously tap out text messages. It also cuts service costs enormously by allowing companies to reduce the number of people required to field customer calls and text messages. And as I'll explain, these bot experiences are only the beginning—a preliminary step along the way to a much more efficient and trustworthy multimodal voice environment.

The latest breakthrough is that customers are beginning to "talk to their apps," rather than calling into a call center and wading through the automated systems that have been available for more than twenty years. As voice experiences become smarter through new capabilities supported by AI, customers are increasingly able to access nonroutine service support via voice tools directly on an app or website.

Financial services is one industry that is benefiting significantly from these developments. For example, customers of U.S. Bank can use its Smart Assistant voice bot to perform common transactions simply by saying a few words—for example, "Transfer $1,000 from savings to checking" or "Make a $300 payment on my auto loan." Other bank voice assistants can offer a range of personalized services—for example, by providing a snapshot of a customer's recent spending in a particular store, a list of automatic recurring charges, or a notification when there's a change in their credit rating.[12] Each time a new item is added to the list of services that voice-driven tools can provide, bank customers are saved precious minutes they'd otherwise spend waiting online or scrolling through pages on their phone or laptop looking for particular bits of data.

Of course, voice-driven customer-service tools save companies money by lessening the need to employ huge teams of people to handle basic requests. A call handled completely by an in-app voice tool reduces per-transaction costs by 70 to 95 percent as compared to traditional customer-service rep methods. Even more important, voice tools free up the service personnel who remain on staff to handle situations where creativity and a human touch are demanded, as when a customer calls with an unusually complicated problem like "I just made a mistake with my credit card bills—I paid my Amex business card the amount I owe on my personal Amex card, and vice versa. Can you switch where those payments are applied?" When skilled human beings can spend their days focusing on the trickiest challenges (because the routine ones have already been handled by voice-automated tools), their jobs become more interesting and enjoyable—and the overall level of customer satisfaction rises.

Voice tech is improving customer service in a variety of other ways—for example, through tools designed to enhance the performance of employees. *Conversation intelligence* is a new methodology that uses AI, speech recognition, and natural language processing to analyze sales calls, service calls, and other interactions between employees and customers. Traditional methods of monitoring and improving such interactions relied on live experts listening to a small fraction (perhaps 1 or 2 percent) of calls and offering feedback and coaching based on what they heard. Today, companies like Level AI, Observe.AI, Invoca, and Gong have developed software tools powered by artificial intelligence that can study thousands of audio interactions, live or recorded, and extract data to help answer a wide array of questions: What sorts of issues or problems are generating the most service calls? Which of our sales or service representatives are performing best, which ones are struggling, and what kinds of coaching can help close the gap? Which portions of service or sales calls represent key moments when crucial customer decisions are made, and how can our team members' strategies during those moments be optimized? The new conversation-intelligence tools can also support workers by listening in to live customer conversations, detecting when specific product or service questions are being asked, and instantly providing relevant backup information to the employee on the line.

For many companies, customer service has long been a crucial challenge. Today, the speed made possible by voice technology can finally turn this challenge into a potential competitive edge. If your organization has yet to employ in-app or on-website voice technology as a basic tool of customer service, you are passing up a major opportunity to save money while improving customer satisfaction.

BRINGING THE BENEFITS OF SPEED TO EVERY CORNER OF BUSINESS

Beyond customer service, voice technology is helping employees in many other business functions work better and faster. In the coming era of voice, countless workplace tasks will be made faster and more worry-free than ever, saving people millions of hours and vast amounts of stress.

Manufacturing is one arena where voice is beginning to have a major impact. The key breakthrough here has been two AI-driven innovations: being able to recognize the user's voice even in a high-noise environment, and the system instantly understanding and parsing the context of what it is being asked to do.

For example, Datch Systems is a voice-tech company that has developed an intelligent voice interface designed for companies in industries like energy, aerospace, and automotive, where activities from factory maintenance to customer-service calls create a steady flow of information that needs to be captured, organized, stored, and used intelligently. This is a job that can take 10 to 15 percent of the time of a typical worker, and it can be enormously frustrating when working with poorly designed software using the tiny keyboard on a smartphone in an industrial setting that may be poorly lit or dusty. Datch's voice-interface system offers an alternative that is easier, more accurate, and four times as fast.[13]

Entering work orders is a simple example where minutes are turned into seconds. Think about the task of entering a work order like "Hydraulic leak on lifting arm position 10 line 3 needs to be fixed ASAP." This might sound simple in itself—but imagine having to navigate to the right page and entry line on a complicated app or website and then type in the details without a single error, and to do it all in a manufacturing facility that may be noisy, dirty, or (just as challenging) ultra-clean. Instead, speaking that command into a system that understands what you say and knows where to send the message could save many minutes, not just for you but for the entire assembly line.

Other voice-based tools are bringing new levels of speed and efficiency to basic factory-floor activities. For instance, Fluent.ai has developed an embedded voice control system that allows workers to operate heavy machinery simply through spoken commands. The ability to manage tasks like these while keeping hands free and eyes focused on one's surroundings is a crucial asset for workers in a busy, ever-changing manufacturing environment.

BSH Home Appliances Group is a major European appliance manufacturer that has deployed Fluent.ai on its factory floor. Historically, workers had to press a button to advance appliances along the assembly line, taking valuable seconds to finish the job at their station, walk over to the button, and press it. Using headsets, they are able to continue their work on the assembly line right up to the point of completion, as well as noting defects or calling for assistance. Early returns see a 75 to 100 percent gain in efficiency per line, which is a very big deal in the world of manufacturing.[14]

Manufacturing is not the only business activity where voice tech is being deployed to save time. Singapore Airlines recently launched a system to voice-enable cabin sweeps between flights. The airline performs over 200 of these procedures a day, and improving their speed, efficiency, and performance has obvious benefits. Using Bluetooth-connected headsets and voice-tech tools that can understand and transmit spoken messages, service personnel are able to send reports such as "First Class Cabin complete," "Broken seat back at 23C," or "Need another case of water in middle galley" without stopping their work to type this information into a smartphone (likely via a series of menus, tabs, and screens) or scribble it on a paper form.

A parallel evolution has begun in the world of retail, with voice tech empowering speed breakthroughs on several fronts.

Retail giant Walmart is one of the pioneers in this movement. The company's innovation-incubation division, known as Store Nº8, has been deploying voice tools to make shopping faster and easier for customers. In 2019, it introduced Walmart Voice Order, which allowed customers to use voice tools like Siri to add items to their Walmart shopping list just by speaking. AI enables the service to learn from experience. Thus, when someone asks to have orange juice added to her cart, the app remembers that this customer routinely orders organic orange juice with no pulp, and adds it to the cart.[15]

Walmart has also created voice tools to help its employees work faster and smarter. In July 2020, Walmart debuted its employee-focused voice assistant "Ask Sam," which is used by workers at over 5,000 stores around the country. The app quickly provides basic data needed to serve customers better—product prices, store maps, sales information, and the like. It also quickly and efficiently handles issues like those usually managed by staffers in human resources or security, such as emergency lockdowns, weather alerts, safety procedures, and COVID-19 requirements. An employee can even keep track of a fellow worker's upcoming birthday by querying Ask Sam.[16] Every minute an employee saves by using Ask Sam is a minute freed up to provide personalized help to a customer in need.

Health care is yet another arena in which voice is already making many activities faster and more efficient. Radiologists, for example, who specialize in reading and interpreting X-ray images for diagnostic purposes, have been using voice-recognition technology to record their findings and transmit the results to patients and fellow professionals for close to a decade, cutting the average time for producing a report (according to one study) from 39 minutes to 3.6 minutes. The impact of this 10x improvement in timing cannot be overstated in terms of efficiency, quality of care, and the reduced anxiety suffered by patients and loved ones.

This practice is rapidly spreading to other medical specialists. Doctors of all kinds have long been using DragonDictate, the pioneering voice-transcription tool I mentioned earlier, to capture clinical notes in electronic medical records. This is much faster and, now, more accurate than typing. But even more important, it lets doctors focus on patients rather than a keyboard and a screen during a clinical consultation. Hands-free access to information also allows providers working in intensive care to keep doing their vital work while gathering essential data.

There have been limitations on the use of voice in medicine. Patient privacy has been one concern. Another has been the challenge of voice recognition in noisy, chaotic situations. And yet another is the fact that patients may often have difficulty speaking due in part to the medical conditions they are experiencing.[17] But improvements in voice technology are rapidly overcoming these barriers. Companies like Krisp have developed tools that use AI to mute background noise when communications apps are in use, making it possible for doctors and patients to share information even in an overcrowded emergency room. And another software tool, Voiceitt, offers speech recognition specifically designed to learn the unique vocal patterns of an individual with any of several speech disorders, bringing voice technology within reach of another medically challenged population.[18] Voice assistants are also being used in hospitals as the fastest and easiest way for patients to summon help—even if they are too weak, disoriented, or disabled to press a call button. S. Nicholas Desai, chief medical officer at Houston Methodist Sugar Land, calls this use of voice simply "the most natural way [to communicate] that the patient is already used to in their home or office."[19]

Thus, the use of voice to accelerate the delivery of badly needed services is now becoming the norm even in one of the most challenging settings—the world of health care.

IDENTIFYING THE OPPORTUNITIES FOR BUSINESSES

Time is money. Voice has the potential to save businesses of every kind countless hours of employee time—and that translates into billions of dollars for the bottom line.

To begin uncovering your company's opportunities to save time and money through the use of voice tech, start by analyzing all the time-consuming activities that take place in every department of your organization, from sales and marketing to human resources. Identify the places where time is spent on communication processes using traditional interfaces such as keyboards or touch screens. Then ask whether a voice app could be substituted that would be faster, easier, and more efficient. If you're not sure, check other organizations like your own to see what modes of communication they are using. You may be surprised to discover that a fast-moving company in your own industry has already pioneered a new voice tool—perhaps one that you could easily adopt.

Note that, over the past several years, a similar process of analyzing your business activities, defining potential alternatives, and benchmarking similar organizations has been applied by companies as part of conducting a digital transformation project, focused primarily on the integration of web-based and mobile capabilities in their business operations. While digital transformation continues to be important, the next big opportunity for many companies will be the voice transformation project.

As this comparison suggests, the emergence of voice tech isn't the first time that the arrival of a new interface has prompted reinvention on the part of business. Early users of smartphones and tablets will remember how their first experience with browsers on those devices was often miserable as they tried to navigate traditional full-sized websites on a much smaller screen.

Interface designers quickly recognized the problem. They developed the concept of *responsive design*, which held that all interactive experiences—between consumers and companies, between employees and employers, and between businesses that are partnering with one another—need to be optimized for every type and size of screen.

As the concept spread, the visual displays on smartphones got much better. However, in many cases, there was still an overwhelming amount of information being displayed—basically, the contents of the whole desktop website, just formatted for the small screen.

Further improvement and adaptation were needed. With mobile computing achieving ascendancy, designers realized, first, that use cases on mobile devices are fundamentally different from those on laptops and tablets; and second, that, for many use cases, usage on mobile devices surpassed usage on other devices.

Thus, the concept of *mobile-first design* was born. This held that users are more likely to be performing certain activities on a mobile device than on a laptop or tablet—which means that designing the interface with a smartphone in mind should take top priority.

Now a new stage in the evolution of responsive design is beginning—one that will take full advantage of the benefits of voice tech. As the new *voice-first design* paradigm emerges in the years to come, almost every app and website will be voice-powered. You can already see it happening through the proliferation of the mic button. Already widely available as an alternative to using the keyboard in texting and messaging, it is now showing up in apps themselves. The GPS app Waze has had a mic button at least since 2021—unsurprisingly, since entering queries or information while driving is an obvious use case for voice. Music player Spotify added their mic button in 2022—another obvious use case, centered on making search fast and hands-free.

Over the coming years, every process where information is being exchanged, data is being input, or questions are being asked will need to be reengineered to fit the voice-first design paradigm. Forward-thinking companies will begin to reassess every interaction they have with their employees, suppliers, and customers to optimize around the voice-first imperative of speed and to take advantage of the associated cost savings.

As with any new technology, there will be fits and starts, successes and failures. In 2019, the customer-relationship software giant Salesforce rolled out its Einstein Voice Assistant to help users rapidly enter data into the Salesforce platform. By the end of 2020, it had been shut down. Why? Mainly because it was a siloed, stand-alone voice experience, making it difficult for users to connect with everything else they were doing. Voice will continue to be a critical piece of Salesforce's strategy, just not on a stand-alone basis.[20]

There are still technical challenges, to be sure. Voice transcription, already vastly improved in recent years, still needs further improvement, especially in regard to challenging use cases like situations in which ambient noise is extensive. The ability of AI tools to manage a broad range of free-form conversations will continue to grow, making more complex interactions between users and devices possible. However, the biggest challenge may be updating and redesigning internal data systems to take full advantage of the voice paradigm. (It doesn't help much if store associates can use voice to ask for help with a customer's problem but you don't have a great database of relevant suggestions ready for your voice tool to supply.) I'll be offering advice on how to approach that problem in the second half of this book.

Challenges aside, the underlying message is clear: voice technology makes it possible to do a host of important things faster than ever before. In a world where time is increasingly the rarest and most precious resource we have, now is the moment to begin seeking—and seizing—the opportunities that voice tech creates.

2

SAFETY

Creating a Less Dangerous World

ONE OF THE TELLTALE SIGNS THAT A NEW TECHNOLOGY WILL become transformative is that use cases emerge that were not planned or even imagined during its initial development. For mobile, one example was ride-sharing. For voice, safety is on that list. Quite unexpectedly, everyone from the manufacturers of the most complex machinery in the world—airplanes—to quick-thinking individuals in danger are discovering that voice technology can be used to make many activities safer. And this discovery, in turn, is opening up new competitive and strategic possibilities for companies that take advantage of the potentialities of voice.

If the idea that voice technology can increase safety seems counterintuitive, consider the fact that there are people alive today who owe their survival to voice tech.

On December 10, 2019, eighteen-year-old Gael Salcedo was on his way to class at North Iowa Area Community College in Mason City, Iowa. It was a frigid winter morning, the temperature barely touching ten degrees Fahrenheit. Suddenly Gael's Jeep hit a patch of ice and skidded completely off the road. Within seconds, the car was window-deep in the Winnebago River—and sinking fast.

"Everything just went blurry," Gael recalls. "I didn't know where I was going and I didn't know what to do. I was just thinking, 'I'm going to die.'"

Badly disoriented, Gael had no idea where his smartphone was. But his survival instinct kicked in. "Hey, Siri," he yelled. "Call 911!" The automated assistant heard Gael's voice and responded instantly, sending his distress call and location data to the nearest emergency center.

Within a few minutes, firefighters were on the scene. The rising river current pinned shut the door on the driver's side of the car, making the rescue especially complicated. But working from the back compartment of the vehicle, Lieutenant Craig Warner managed to extricate Gael and help him get through the icy water to shore.

After being treated for shock at the hospital, Gael was released just three hours later—feeling lucky to be alive.[1]

When people think about voice technology, they understandably focus on the benefits it offers in terms of efficiency, productivity, and convenience. But there's an even more critical value that voice tech serves—namely, the need for personal safety. As the story of Gael Salcedo suggests, voice can make a hazardous activity like driving on an icy highway dramatically safer, saving lives in cases like Gael's and making sure that thousands of other potentially deadly accidents never occur in the first place.

What's more, stories like Gael's just scratch the surface of what voice tech can do to make our lives safer. People in hundreds of industries work with complicated, powerful machinery every day: transportation, military, health care, factories, warehousing, agriculture, and energy are just a few examples. For workers in these fields, voice technology offers practical advantages that can literally make the difference between life and death.

Today, voice-tech companies are busily creating tools to take full advantage of this unexpected capability. The years to come will likely see a flood of safety-oriented voice-tech applications, some of which we can barely imagine now. In this chapter, we'll look at some current examples and forecast others that may soon be under development.

HOW DANGERS ARISE—AND HOW VOICE PROVIDES PROTECTION

To understand how voice tech can help make the world a safer place, it's helpful to start by reflecting on where the dangers that threaten us come from.

Somewhat paradoxically, the technologies that have created the conveniences of modern life, such as the automobile, the airplane, factories, and industrial equipment, have also created new risks and dangers. Cars skid off highways as drivers text; airplanes crash when pilots can't manage the control systems; heavy machinery can malfunction when technicians are overwhelmed. All these examples represent new, technology-based threats to human beings. The sheer power of the equipment being used; the artificial ease of controlling it, which can lead to dangerous attention lapses; the complexity of the devices themselves, which can produce dangerous moments of confusion; and the speed of response required when an emergency involving a fast-moving piece of machinery is unfolding—all of these factors make modern technology risky to use.

There's another set of dangers posed by modern technology—those that relate to the incredible power of digital IT and communication tools to capture, save, manipulate, and transmit data. The dangers these data-management tools pose are not physical dangers that threaten life and limb. Instead, they are risks related to the theft or misuse of data by individual hackers, rogue employees, criminal networks, or malicious actors employed by enemy governments. Grouped under the general heading of *cybercrime*, these dangers include everything from malware attacks and identity fraud to the theft, sale, and misuse of financial, corporate, or government intelligence data. The cost to people and businesses is vast and growing. Experts project that cybercrime may cost the world over $10 trillion annually by 2025, with a typical security breach producing damages of over $4 million.[2]

Thus, even as people have benefited enormously from modern technologies, we've also had to continuously work to analyze and minimize the dangers they create.

Voice technology is poised to deliver safety breakthroughs in a myriad of ways. The reason is simple: most of the risks involved in modern technology are driven by the difficulties we often have when seeking to communicate with or control machines or digital devices. When powerful technology is being used, small flaws in the design of a user interface can be deadly: when the operator of a machine doesn't quickly and fully understand what is happening, or when it takes a few seconds too long to transmit clear instructions to the device through buttons, keyboards, levers, or pedals, emergencies can easily spin out of control.

Those who design and implement technology recognize these dangers. As machines have become increasingly integrated into daily life and work over the last several generations, engineers have gradually developed ways to make the powerful machines surrounding us safer, from power steering, power brakes, and seat belts in the cars we drive to warning lights, two-hand control devices, and emergency shutoff switches on the assembly lines where we operate powerful equipment. The advent of voice technology is adding an important new set of tools to this effort.

The story of Gael Salcedo shows how this change is already having an impact on our daily lives. Today's smartphones and computerized apps are increasingly being equipped with emergency features that use voice to add clarity and save precious seconds when emergencies are being dealt with. These tools make it possible for a user to summon emergency-rescue health-care assistance in seconds even when they are too disabled or disoriented to use keypad controls or other conventional devices.

The Apple iPhone, for example, has an Emergency SOS feature that can notify police or ambulance services without the user having to place a phone call. The phone itself can instantly transmit information about its location to rescue workers, saving precious moments and eliminating the risk of confusion over directions.[3]

Gael Salcedo is not the only person who is alive today because of voice tools like these. In December 2018, Nate Felix was off-roading with his dog in the Nevada desert when his Jeep flipped over in a dry lake bed. Nate was pinned under the vehicle, paralyzed by two broken vertebrae as well as intense fear. For a few minutes, he couldn't think of what to do. He began to wonder whether he would have to spend the night stuck under his car and imagined huddling with his dog to keep warm.

Then he remembered the voice assistant in his smartphone. Although he couldn't remember where the device was, he started yelling names of people for Siri to call. The first few efforts yielded nothing: "Cannot connect, cannot connect," was all he heard.

Finally, he thought to say, "Hey, Siri, call 911."

"Connecting," came the response.

A rescue team soon arrived and freed Nate from the wreckage using the jaws of life. The accident left him wheelchair-bound—but alive.[4]

In another case, three fishermen ran into life-threatening trouble as they worked the rough waters off Key Biscayne in May 2017. Their boat took on water and began sinking. They managed to get into their life jackets, but their wet hands prevented them from using the keypads on their phones. Voice made the difference: the fishermen used Siri to call 911, and the Coast Guard came to their rescue.[5]

The software engineers who originally developed voice technology were not focused primarily on safety. But incidents like these make it obvious how powerful voice can be as a safety tool. In response, new features and services are being implemented that take advantage of voice's ability to protect and save lives in the face of everyday emergencies.

For example, Visiting Angels is a Florida-based company that provides home-care service to seniors across the United States who may have physical or mental disabilities. In 2021, the company unveiled a new proprietary system called Constant Companion that uses a current smart speaker system (Amazon's Echo Dot, with voice assistant Alexa) to offer emergency protection to elders in need. When an accident or medical problem arises, the senior can summon help just by asking for it. This is a breakthrough for older folks who may struggle to use a conventional cell phone, especially if they suffer from dementia or other disabling conditions. Seniors also prefer the voice-activated system because it eliminates the need for wearable push-button devices that are easy to forget or misplace, and that make the wearers "feel old." The service works on its own network, separate from Amazon's, to ensure compliance with the privacy rules required by the Health Insurance Portability and Accountability Act (HIPAA). And beyond safety in times of emergency, Constant Companion's voice-tech system offers other benefits, from medicine reminders and daily phone check-ins (if requested) to music and audiobooks.[6]

Seniors aren't the only people being protected by the new voice-powered safety tools. A number of home-security services are now emerging that provide new levels of convenience and flexibility using voice. Alexa Guard, for example, listens for unusual sounds while you're away from home—the noise made by an intruder or a smoke detector—and can automatically alert you while also calling for rescue services. When you return home, you can simply announce, "I'm back," whereupon the system recognizes your voice and switches to a lower level of surveillance.

Another Alexa security service, rolled out in February 2021, is Alexa Greetings. It's especially appealing to people who live in high-crime areas or suffer from physical disabilities. When your doorbell sounds, the system asks the visitor why they're ringing and offers an appropriate response. For example, a delivery person will be told where to leave the package; a friend dropping by will be invited to leave a video note for the homeowner. If you're home at the time, you can use the Quick Replies feature to ask Alexa to use one of six preprogrammed responses to a doorbell chime, ranging from "Please leave a message" to "I'll be there in a minute." People nervous about possible intruders find intuitive, easy-to-use tools like these comforting, especially when they're home alone.

Voice tools can help with everyday security needs at work as well as at home. Again, modern technology is at the root of many of the dangers that we most need to guard against, such as the rising tide of cybercrime. Massive investments continue to flow into efforts to protect businesses from cybercrime, but these initiatives raise a strategic dilemma: the more companies harden their information systems by adding new layers of security, the more cumbersome and awkward they are to use. The all-too-frequent result: user abandonment and insecure work-arounds.

Voice-based user-authentication tools are playing an important role in this struggle. Innovators like the financial firm Charles Schwab are now using consumer voice authentication at scale, making investment accounts safer from fraud even while giving their legitimate owners easier, faster access. Callers with accounts are instructed to sign in by saying the passphrase, "At Schwab, my voice is my password." The sounds you utter are analyzed according to a proprietary algorithm that recognizes more than a hundred different physical characteristics, from the pitch of the tones you use to the way your accent affects the pronunciation of words. As Schwab explains, "Your voiceprint is uniquely yours," providing a secure method of identifying any single individual: "No more personal questions. No more PINs."[7]

Now, if you're a movie buff, the passphrase "At Schwab, my voice is my password" might ring a bell. In the 1992 thriller *Sneakers*, Robert Redford plays Martin Bishop, a security specialist leading a team whose mission is to recover a black box containing high-tech decryption technologies for the NSA. A turning point in the story involves Redford's team needing to fool a voice-recognition system to get access to a secret facility. They manage this by piecing together recorded fragments of speech spoken by someone with legitimate access to create a recording that says, "My name is Werner Brandes. My voice is my passport. Verify me."

In the movie, this clever trick works like a charm—which might lead you to wonder whether such a simple work-around could be used today to break into someone's Schwab account. The short answer is, it's extremely unlikely. Deceptive techniques like the one used in the movie, known as "spoofing," have spawned a host of defensive technological efforts. These anti-spoofing systems use AI to detect artifacts in doctored recordings that are inaudible to the unaided human ear.[8] Many voice-based systems also use techniques to ensure that voice transmissions are coming from a separately authenticated device (such as a phone). Most organizations that use voice recognition have incorporated such protective technologies into their systems, thus staying— at least for now—a couple of steps ahead of the would-be hackers. (In Part Two, we'll delve more deeply into the security challenges that users of voice technology, like all other digital tools, must constantly be aware of and work on.)

Voice authentication is also being used in a growing number of workplaces to protect the security of job sites, software apps, databases, and other valuable business assets. Remembering lengthy, complex passwords is a frustrating by-product of the digital age, but the use of biometric characteristics—especially voice recognition combined with other factors, such as facial and fingerprint recognition—is fast, intuitive, and easy, even as it makes systems exponentially more difficult to crack. Voice-tech companies like Verint are actively rolling out products like these, which are especially valuable to distributed workforces like stay-at-home employees of customer-service call centers. When employees are identified and granted access to resources based simply on voice and other biometric markers, security is transformed from an intrusive, inconvenient ritual into an easy, reliable process. And when voice commands make security controls faster and simpler to use—whether at work or at home—they are more likely to be engaged consistently rather than skipped "just this one time" . . . which can lead to calamitous security breaches.

REDUCING THE BIGGEST RISKS: MAKING FLYING SAFER

Some workplaces involve greater risks than others. Today's technology-driven society sometimes multiplies the risks we face by giving ordinary people control over once-incredible amounts of power, in forms that range from tractor trailers to jet airplanes. People carrying out professional occupations that involve significant risks on a daily basis will also benefit from the safety edge that voice provides—as will the society that depends on these well-trained, highly skilled, yet imperfect human beings.

When the Boeing 737 MAX airliner was rolled out in 2015, it featured a number of innovations, including distinctive split-tip winglets and airframe modifications that affected the jumbo jet's aerodynamic characteristics. A critical launch goal for Boeing was to enable commercial pilots to fly the new plane without needing new certifications, since retraining pilots is very expensive for airlines. To achieve that goal, the airliner's software included an array of ambitious new features, including many intended to increase safety by taking over control from the crew in certain situations. These included something called the Maneuvering Characteristics Augmentation System (MCAS), which was supposed to compensate for an excessive nose-up angle by adjusting the horizontal stabilizer to keep the aircraft from stalling—a complicated technical "hack" implemented by Boeing to avoid the larger cost involved in rewriting the program from the ground up.

The 737 MAX was a top seller right out of the gate. But what Boeing and its airline customers hadn't realized was that the software was being asked to do things the pilots didn't fully understand. As a result, pilots found themselves unable to interface in a timely fashion with the complex system in front of them. The ultimate result was two tragic crashes with 346 fatalities, forcing the grounding of the 737 MAX fleet and a fraud settlement that cost Boeing some $2.5 billion. Additional losses from cancelled aircraft orders, lowered stock value, and other damages have been estimated at up to $60 billion.[9]

These needless losses—financial and human—were caused, in large part, by small yet fatal failures of cockpit communication between people and machines. The pilots could tell that something serious was wrong, but the existing controls made it difficult for them to figure out what that was and to work with the system to correct the problem. As a result, in the words of investigative reporter Peter Robison, "the pilots were trying to retake control of the plane, so that the plane was pitching up and down over several minutes." Based on his re-creation of what happened, Robison concludes, "it would have been terrifying for the people on the planes."[10]

When voice becomes a major interface in airliner cockpits, a new tool for preventing such disasters will be available. In traditional aviation, pilots receive commands like "Cleared Direct Casanova VOR" or "Intercept the ILS 3" via radio from dispatchers at air traffic control. After the pilots get this information, they must use their eyes and hands to locate and press a series of buttons to transmit the same commands to the aircraft. In a voice-driven world, that time-wasting, error-prone step will be eliminated. In the first stage of voice adoption, pilots will simply be able to say a few words without moving their eyes from the controls around them, and the plane will respond. According to Geoff Shapiro, a human factors engineer at the former Rockwell Collins Advanced Technology Center, this shift trims the time spent when entering simple navigational commands from half a minute to eight seconds—a huge improvement in circumstances when a few moments can be critical.[11] In the second stage, once veteran pilots have recognized and accepted the power of voice, the plane will automatically follow the spoken instructions from air traffic control, merely asking the pilot to confirm them.

A voice-interface solution integrating the latest capabilities of voice-driven artificial intelligence can improve airline safety in several ways. It gives the system self-awareness and the ability to proactively communicate its state and status to pilots, thereby alerting them to problems even at moments when they might otherwise be distracted or inattentive. Using increasingly powerful voice-technology tools like automatic speech recognition and natural language understanding, it also allows the airplane's control systems to process and act on conversational speech, making the implementation of pilot commands faster and more accurate than ever. It facilitates real-time communications linking the cockpit, air traffic control, the airline carrier, and maintenance engineers to remove inconsistencies in communication due to human indecision or misjudgment. In the near future, it may even be able to use emerging voice-tech tools such as voice biometrics and real-time sentiment analysis to determine stress levels being experienced by pilots—information that could be used to transmit emergency alerts to air traffic controllers and others on the ground.

Voice technology won't eliminate all the traditional activities pilots are trained to perform. But in critical moments when the speed of response to messages from a control tower may spell the difference between survival and disaster, the use of a voice interface will prevent crashes and save lives. This is not a fantasy about the remote future. Today's planes have all the electronics needed to make it possible.

One field of aviation in which safety risks are especially intense is military flying. It's also an arena in which voice-enabled aviation is being avidly pursued. Alabama-based Dynetics has received $12.3 million from DARPA, the Pentagon's storied defense-technology division, to develop the use of AI in "high-intensity air conflicts." The third phase of the current three-phase research/implementation program involves a "realistic, manned-flight environment involving complex human-machine collaboration"—including voice communication.

The US Air Force is not alone in pursuing this technological advantage. The next generation of the MiG-35, the highly advanced Russian fighter jet, will apparently feature a voice assistant to offer advice in high-pressure situations. Test pilot Dmitry Selivanov says, "We call her Rita, the voice communicant. Her voice remains pleasant and calm even if fire hits the engine. She does not talk all the time, she just makes recommendations if the plane approaches some restrictions. Hints are also provided during combat usage."[12]

Voice-controlled flying is also in development for civilian aircraft. Companies like Honeywell and Rockwell are designing voice interfaces for aviation, with an initial focus on reducing pilot workload around tedious tasks involving basic, repetitive commands like "Give me the weather at LAX and any critical weather en route." More extensive and sophisticated use cases for voice tech in aviation are steadily emerging.

Vipul Gupta is general manager of Honeywell Aerospace Avionics. He and his team are deeply focused on perfecting the technology of the voice cockpit, especially its response speed, which is a crucial safety feature. Their engineers have reduced the voice system's average response time to 250 milliseconds, which means, in effect, that the system can react more quickly than a human pilot can.[13]

Over time, voice-controlled aircraft systems will become commonplace in most forms of aviation. But in the short term, the most important use cases will be in general aviation, where single-pilot operators are notoriously overloaded, especially when operating in bad weather or congested areas. Having a "voice copilot" will ease those burdens and make the flying experience safer for pilot and passengers alike.

Voice-controlled aircraft are also likely to dominate the emerging field of *urban air mobility*, which involves the use of small aircraft for purposes ranging from cargo deliveries to sightseeing tours within city and suburban airspaces.[14] New types of aircraft, such as electric vertical takeoff and landing aircraft (eVTOLs) are likely to dominate this domain, with the marketplace for eVTOLs expected to explode from nothing in 2022 to $1.75 billion in 2028.[15] As this new domain of flight expands, experienced pilots will be in short supply, so the industry is now designing simplified cockpit systems, controlled by voice, that trained "operators" will be able to manage.

Vipul Gupta is bullish about the future of the voice-powered cockpit. "Eventually," he says, "we'll have a voice assistant where you will just sit in [the aircraft] and the passenger will say, 'Hey, fly me there, take me there. And then the system does it.'"[16]

Speaking as a licensed pilot with significant personal experience in the cockpit, I suspect he will be right—eventually. As with most innovations, I believe it will take longer than the early adopters and enthusiasts believe. This is especially likely in a critical field like aviation, in which human trust issues and regulatory hurdles can take years to overcome. But the fact is that the challenges of voice-powered flight are actually *simpler* in many ways than those faced by other technologies, such as autonomous automobiles. For example, a plane cruising at 20,000 feet doesn't have to deal with red lights, kids dashing into the street, or other drivers tailgating.

For this reason, I concur with the experts who say that we will have safe, effective voice-controlled planes sooner than autonomous cars. And once the technology is fully developed, the safety advantages of a system that can respond to spoken commands almost instantly in an emergency will be too powerful for the aviation industry to forgo.

BEYOND THE COCKPIT: VOICE-BASED SAFETY FOR OTHER HAZARDOUS OCCUPATIONS

Of course, aircraft pilots aren't the only military professionals who must manage incredible levels of risk in their daily work. A range of voice technologies are under development in numerous branches of the US armed services. Examples include a conversational AI platform being built by the army to allow soldiers to give voice commands to robotic vehicles, and an onboard voice assistant that the navy plans to use to provide real-time help to sonar operators as they search for enemy submarines in nearby waters.[17] These voice-aided systems will augment the effectiveness of American troops and help keep them safe in combat situations—with the caveat that, of course, potential adversaries are also at work on similar projects. As you can imagine, the likelihood that hostile forces we may one day confront on the battlefield will be equipped with voice-controlled weaponry that can respond instantaneously to spoken commands is making the urgency of American efforts to develop the same tools all the greater.

History shows that military needs often drive some of the first uses for new technologies. Aviation, radar, atomic energy, satellite intelligence systems, and the internet are just a few of the technology breakthroughs that were launched or accelerated by military agencies. That's not surprising—the life-or-death pressures of warfare naturally impel governments to make huge investments in money and talent, including in tech innovation. For this reason, I expect military applications of voice technology to be aggressively pursued in the years to come. Some of the early military use cases will likely be closely guarded secrets, but news of some will leak out to analysts and experts who track military technology. For example, there are reports that voice-tech tools by the company Primer are being used by American intelligence experts to tap, transcribe, and interpret Russian communications from the front in Ukraine.[18] It's a harbinger of things to come.

Another field where voice tech is providing risk-reduction tools is law enforcement. Here, the risks involved arise from a combination of factors, especially the human tensions involved when an officer representing the power of the government confronts a citizen who is a possible criminal, whose safety, freedom, and reputation may be at stake. All of these tensions are sharply heightened by the likely presence, especially in the United States, of firearms on both sides of the confrontation, making a miscommunication or error in judgment more likely to result in serious injury or death. No wonder police officers are often exceedingly tense even during routine traffic stops—which can make simple administrative tasks difficult to manage.

Voice technology can play a role in de-escalating these kinds of tensions. One example: IT professionals from the San Diego County sheriff's department have helped to develop Coptivity, a voice-powered AI system connected to a mobile app that lets officers gather background information on a suspect almost instantly. The officer can simply tell his smartphone, "I need data on the following license plate." The app responds with the name of the vehicle's owner and any crucial information—an outstanding arrest warrant, for example. It all happens in critical seconds rather than taking several minutes as traditional live-operator call-in systems do—and the officer never has to take his eyes away from the unfolding, perhaps hazardous situation in front of him. The same motto being applied to work in retail—"Heads Up and Hands Free," as we'll see in Chapter 6—is being applied to law enforcement, with potentially lifesaving implications.

The power of voice technology can also be important in other cases where lethal weaponry is not involved, but where exceedingly complex systems with potentially deadly power need to be managed at high speed and with near-perfect accuracy.

An offshore oil rig is a massive array of equipment, controlled and monitored by hundreds of mechanical and technological components and systems. It's equipped with sensors to monitor degrees of pressure, levels of flow, and minute traces of gas on the rig, with bells and whistles to warn the crew when a shutdown is essential to prevent catastrophic failure.

When these systems fail, as they did on the Deepwater Horizon rig in April 2010, the failure is usually one of communication—among people, and between people and machines.

The ultimate cause of the failure was a series of mistakes by employees of Halliburton (the oil-field-services company that operated the rig) and British Petroleum (the oil company that leased the rig and made many of the major decisions about managing it). The process of drilling the hole in the seabed, lining it with a metal casing, and using cement to ensure a tight, leakproof fit was botched, allowing gas to leak onto the rig.

On April 20, when the failure of the rig kicked in, leading to an explosion that would kill eleven workers, the crew were unable to stop it because of communication and control problems. The information that the Deepwater Horizon's interface provided to its operators proved insufficiently clear for human communication in the moment of crisis, leading to indecision, inaction, and, eventually, disaster. The problems included the inability of scattered crew members to accurately identify the severity of the crisis amid overwhelmed warning and alarm systems, and isolated systems across the rig that created insurmountable information silos. Two days after the explosion, the entire rig collapsed, causing a catastrophic leak that poured more than three million barrels of oil into the Gulf of Mexico over a period of eighty-seven days, devastating both the regional ecosystem and the local economy.[19]

An integrated voice-interface solution might well have helped prevent the Deepwater Horizon disaster. Such a system could have the ability to answer questions regarding the cause or location of alarms, as well as the ability to facilitate communication while people take life-saving measures.

Today, experts in gas and oil production are working on solutions that use AI and voice technology to improve the efficiency as well as the safety of the industry. Field-worker voice assistants are being tested to enable oil-rig workers to keep constantly up to date on equipment status and environmental changes without having to use their eyes and hands to handle keyboards or touch screens. As AI consultant Konrad Konarski, former head of the IBM Watson AI program for Eastern Europe, explains, "Voice-enabled chatbots can assist operators with questions and status reports all with hands-free voice commands."[20]

And bigger systems are being developed that combine multiple functions to help manage all the complex, risk-laden processes that go into well-site management. For example, a team including experts from oil industry giant Schlumberger and Stanford University has built and demonstrated a proof-of-concept system that would provide a complete voice interface for operating a rig like the one that failed so disastrously in 2010. The system they designed "is conscious of process adherence and equipment limitations"—which means that, if an operator asks the rig to carry out a task that is inappropriate or dangerous, the system will point out the problem and ask for an alternative. Noise-shielding technology originally developed for the US military was adapted for the operator headsets; that means the system works effectively even when ambient noise levels exceed 114 decibels, as they often do in emergency situations. And when a simulated fire alarm was triggered in an early test, the system registered the danger and immediately implemented safety procedures to shut down the rig until further human instructions were received.[21]

There's a common thread that connects the power of voice-based tools across fields like aviation, the military, law enforcement, and oil-rig management. In each case, voice tools help solve the problems involved in multitasking—particularly controlling complex technological devices while leaving enough mental bandwidth free for higher-order thinking about the physical, human, intellectual, and emotional challenges involved in handling situations of imminent danger and intense stress. As our technological world keeps getting more complicated, the need for simple, intuitive ways to manage it becomes ever greater. That's where voice will play a critical role.

SAFETY ON THE HIGHWAY

Jet pilots, police officers, oil-rig operators—they all face risks in their work, especially during times of crisis. But, as the story of Gael Salcedo suggests, the most dangerous activity most people engage in every day is driving their cars. Voice technology is now being widely deployed in passenger cars, a new tool that will give drivers the power to use voice commands to respond faster and more accurately to dangerous road conditions. At the same time, voice technology in cars will also make driving mishaps far less likely, simply by eliminating many of the most common causes of distracted driving. Even seemingly harmless activities like glancing at the radio dial or adjusting the knob that controls your car's air-conditioning system increase risk. According to research by the American Automobile Association, removing your eyes from the road for just two seconds doubles your risk of crashing.[22]

One of today's leaders in developing voice technology for cars is Mercedes-Benz.[23] It's not a new concept for them—in fact, as long ago as the 1996 Paris Auto Show, Mercedes demonstrated a concept car with a voice-control system that would soon be introduced to its S-Class cars. This early version simply allowed drivers to use their cell phones hands-free—a limited but useful application.

As Mercedes and other carmakers were developing voice technology through the early years of this century, the emphasis was on communication and entertainment tools as well as safety. Users were enabled to talk on the phone, change the station on their radio, and adjust the air conditioning and heating levels hands-free. This provided them with greater convenience, but not necessarily with a significant increase in safety. In fact, some observers claimed that these early applications of voice technology to the car actually posed a safety threat to drivers. A 2013 study issued by the AAA's Foundation for Traffic Safety found that some voice-based activities—especially the use of speech-to-text tools to compose emails or post updates on Facebook while driving—caused significant distraction and thereby increased the risk of a crash. "The assumption is if you're doing those things with speech-based technology, they'll be safe," said David Strayer, a researcher at the University of Utah. "But they're not."[24]

Thankfully, advances in voice technology have changed the picture. The relatively high level of distraction associated with early speech-based systems was based on their crudeness. Those systems were almost all command-based, forcing users, in effect, to guess the precise word or phrase that would generate the result wanted, then to memorize that word or phrase for future use. Any small mistake would cause a frustrating rejection of the command or, worse, a confusing misinterpretation. Today's voice systems use natural-language-processing tools that can make sense of hundreds of thousands of alternative ways of saying the same thing—which allows drivers to use voice technology much more naturally, easily, and spontaneously than in the past. And because AI enables voice tools to keep learning continuously—expanding their vocabularies, understanding a broader range of contexts, and getting to know more about the needs, interests, and preferences of specific users—the ease and simplicity of using voice will only continue to improve. Now drivers of many makes of cars are enthusiastically adopting voice as an important mode of interaction with their vehicles.

Over the years, Mercedes has taken advantage of these developments to steadily enhance and improve its voice-technology capabilities. The biggest breakthrough came in 2018, when the company made available a voice assistant connected to the cloud. This made the voice tool far more flexible than before, capable of using connections to information sources like Yelp (to find recommendations for local restaurants) and services like Bosch's Smart Home (to transmit commands like "Turn on the lights in my house before I arrive home").

Already, 80 percent of drivers of Mercedes's 2020 MBUX model describe its voice-based command system as "the most important control element" in their cars.[25] Drivers invoke the "Hey, Mercedes!" command an average of forty times per month, most often to make phone calls via Bluetooth connections, to get travel directions to a chosen destination, or to adjust the climate inside the car. The intelligent language assistant learns your voice and even adapts to indirect communications—so when a driver says, "I'm feeling chilly," the car knows it needs to increase the temperature by a couple of degrees, and acts accordingly. Most important, drivers can handle all these tasks without taking their eyes off the road or their hands off the steering wheel, thereby eliminating some of the most common causes of serious accidents.

In addition, automotive voice technology tools are increasingly capable of providing services that directly enhance the safety of the driving experience. Consider, for example, Cerence Co-Pilot, an in-car voice assistant developed by Cerence, a leading developer of technology tools for drivers.[26] Released in December 2021, Co-Pilot uses AI to analyze data derived from the car itself, from cloud-based information sources, and from the driver's activities—voice, gaze, gesture, and touch—to make inferences about safety issues that need to be attended to. Based on these inferences, Co-Pilot will proactively launch conversations with the driver to make suggestions that might sound a bit like this:

"It's time for your annual safety checkup. Would you like me to call your usual service center for an appointment?"

"Your oil pressure is low. I suggest you have it checked right away. There's a service station on your right about half a mile ahead."

Similar tools are also becoming available for riders of two-wheeled vehicles—motorcycles, scooters, and electric bikes. To minimize the problem of overwhelming wind noise, voice-tech companies like Cerence and Jarvish have developed "smart helmets" that include wireless microphones and speakers with integrated connection to a customized voice assistant.[27] These smart helmets allow a biker to simply ask for directions to the nearest restaurant or an update on threatening weather conditions and receive the information in seconds. Linked to the vehicle's own information system, the smart assistant can also proactively alert the rider to a dangerous condition—brakes that need service, for example—before the problem is obvious. Thus, the risks inherent in the joy of the open road exposed to the elements on a two-wheeler can be systematically reduced through information and control systems that are hands-off and distraction-free.

THE OPPORTUNITIES FOR BUSINESSES

As we've seen, a wide range of organizations can benefit from the remarkable ability of voice tools to make life safer. By taking a deep dive into the lives of your employees and customers, you can discover ways that voice technology can offer them the benefit of enhanced safety.

Working with your company's sales, marketing, and customer-experience experts, explore questions like, What sorts of risks do our employees or customers experience? Where could they use help in avoiding or mitigating those risks? How could voice tools be incorporated into our products or services to help our customers live safer lives? The possible answers will depend on the customers you serve and the kinds of products and services you specialize in.

Here are some examples of the ways voice tools may be able to help your business operate more safely.

Voice biometrics is one clear area of focus. The diaspora of remote employees created by the COVID-19 pandemic has created significant security risks for most enterprises, especially those that have hundreds of field reps or work-from-home customer-service employees. Just consider the kinds of company data that a disgruntled worker or a fraudster posing as a remote employee can get access to—sensitive intellectual property, financial data, customer credit-card information, and much more. Voice biometrics is an increasingly important part of the arsenal to ensure that the people using your company's information system are actually your employees and that the data resources they are probing are a legitimate part of their work.

Use cases centered on driving are another important area of focus. Both your employees and your customers should be able to access mobile tools for controlling and communicating with their devices without having to take their hands off the steering wheel or their eyes off the road. In response to this need, more and more companies are launching in-car applications via Apple's and Google's automotive platforms. Whether these are employee-centered (such as tools for handling business emails, accessing company data, or participating in remote meetings) or customer-centered (such as apps for ordering products, tracking deliveries, or obtaining support services), every one of those mobile resources should employ voice as its core medium of communication.

Safety-based voice use cases involving heavy machinery and activities such as manufacturing, distribution, and warehousing are proliferating rapidly. Any tool that allows an operator of machinery to lighten their workload or multitask while keeping their "Heads Up and Hands Free" is going to make the workplace safer. We've seen this dynamic at work in numerous companies, which have shared with us the ways they are quickly implementing voice-based improvements, while requesting anonymity in order to protect what they consider important competitive advantages.

One major utility company recently enhanced their rugged tablets for field maintenance teams with voice technology, allowing technicians hands-free operations on a utility pole while receiving and transmitting critical information. A product-distribution company provided voice-powered apps to its drivers, allowing them to get order updates and changes and to transmit information ("I'm running ten minutes late") without taking their attention off the road. Another distribution company reported a 10 to 20 percent increase in productivity along with a 38 percent decline in accidents after equipping its team with headsets and voice-based tools. Numerous warehouse operators are providing their team members with Bluetooth headsets that are tied into central inventory and order-management systems. Drivers, pickers, and packers are using voice tech for their work orders rather than traditional screens and keyboards. These tools lower distractions and increase safety while making operations more efficient.

Manufacturing facilities are making assembly lines safer and more efficient by using voice tech to enable real-time communication between humans and machines. Voice tech also lets managers implement critical work orders in real time, which is especially important in hazardous circumstances. Emergency shutoff systems are becoming voice-based, which saves valuable seconds in comparison with traditional button-based solutions. Manufacturers of machinery with complex controls are now beginning to completely redesign their interfaces to remove screens, keyboards, levers, and buttons and replace them with voice tools.

Many different industries can benefit from voice-based tools for inspections, maintenance, and repairs. Workers handling complex, sometimes dangerous tasks can follow directions step-by-step through headphones rather than awkwardly referencing printed manuals, a service that's especially valuable for trainees. Safety compliance can be enhanced via the inherent ease of use and real-time information trackability using voice tools rather than cumbersome screen- and paper-based solutions. This is why a major safety inspection firm specializing in restaurants (which often require monthly inspection) has adopted a voice-based system accompanied by the use of smartphones for image capture. As a result, they've been able to reduce site visit times by an average of one-third while increasing compliance with safety regulations.

With examples like these as your guide, take a deep dive into your own operations and look for the many ways you may be able to use voice tech to improve their safety. In the years to come, the spread of voice tech will help make countless everyday activities safer. Your business, your employees, and the customers you serve can all benefit from this change—and the sooner it happens, the better.

3

KNOWLEDGE

Getting Critical Information When and Where You Need It

ONE OF THE MOST AMAZING IMPACTS OF TODAY'S DIGITAL world is having access to a practically limitless store of information—"at your fingertips," as the saying goes. But finding the right information at the right time is one of the great design challenges of our day.

The problem of digital information overload is real. Experts predict that, by 2025, the volume of data created globally each day will be a mind-boggling 463 exabytes. (An exabyte is the number of bytes represented by the digit 1 followed by 18 zeroes, and 463 exabytes of data would be enough to fill more than 212 million DVDs.)[1] Obviously, only a small fraction of that data is relevant to you, your community, or your business. But all of it is flooding the internet each day—which makes the challenge of finding the tiny sliver you need and care about increasingly overwhelming.

Describe the problem of data management on this macro scale and it's virtually impossible to imagine, and tackling this problem has made Google one of the most valuable companies on the planet. The same problem has recently helped boost the valuation of Microsoft and OpenAI given the potential of their AI program ChatGPT to become the search engine of the future. But even on a much smaller scale, the same challenge of finding the accurate information you need when and where you need it—and separating it out from the flood of irrelevant or erroneous data that surrounds us—is often more difficult than we feel it should be. It's a problem faced on both sides of a business—by people trying to find the data and support they need to do their jobs, and by clients and customers who need clear, useful information about the products and services offered by a company.

You may be wondering, in today's world of digital IT management, is information access truly a problem? Here's one simple employee-centered example.

Field technicians at a leading soda company that my company WillowTree works with face a daunting challenge. They are asked to service over 200 different types of machines and devices in the field, deployed over decades from a variety of manufacturers. The roster includes restaurant soda machines, soda dispensers used in corporate and school cafeterias, a wide range of old-fashioned vending machines, and many more. No technician, even the most experienced, can master them all. The company maintenance trucks are literally stuffed with instruction manuals; even though all the information was digitized to their rugged tablets years ago, the technicians say it's often easier to use the paper. But when a technician is deep in the workings of a soda machine and runs into a problem—often in an awkward position under or behind a piece of equipment—it's an annoying, time-consuming, and clumsy task to quit what they are doing, thumb or keypad their way through the printed or online manual, and then get back to work. The same problem arises when ordering parts from the thousands available: doing it using the keypad on a smartphone or the keyboard on a tablet is awkward and error-prone.

Prior to voice, designers had the option of helping users find data either via menus or via search. Both methods have their problems.

Menus take time to scroll through, and it's easy to overlook a particular item. Search requires the user to accurately guess the appropriate term for the item being sought; and when the options are numerous or complex, a lengthy, complicated search term may be needed. In the soda-company example, the technician would have to enter the make and model of the machine being worked on as well as a description of the part needed or the problem being tackled—perhaps eight to twelve words or more. That's a lot to type, especially in a work environment with greasy fingers. Hit the wrong key a few times, and you may have to start all over again.

Voice tools are a powerful game changer for jobs like this, where getting the exact information you need, quickly and conveniently, is critical. They allow users to manage complex searches quickly and effortlessly, getting to the exact information they want instantly.

Similar problems face consumers in a host of situations. U.S. Bank, for example, has one of the most powerful mobile apps for providing services to its customers. The problem is that this app offers access to more than 300 features. Each one is highly useful to certain bank customers at specific times—but imagine trying to find a particular feature from a menu and submenu navigation list of 300 items on the small screen of your smartphone. Creating an effective touch-and-swipe navigation system that provides quick, easy access to all those features is virtually impossible. It's a classic illustration of digital overload on a micro level.

Voice offers a potential solution to the problem of information overload. That's why U.S. Bank has launched a voice assistant that customers can use to navigate the maze of 300 features. Ankit Bhatt, the bank's senior vice president and chief digital officer for consumers, describes it as "a discovery mechanism for our mobile capability"—one that mimics a human bank teller by providing a simple, intuitive way to find a needle in a digital haystack.[2] Suppose you need to order a fresh supply of checks for your U.S. Bank account. Rather than scrolling for minutes through screens listing an array of irrelevant features, you can simply speak the words "I'd like to reorder checks for immediate delivery," and you'll be sent immediately to a confirmation page reflecting the number and style of checks you've purchased in the past.

Consumers face similar problems in dozens of other contexts. For instance, try finding the last set of game statistics for basketball great LeBron James on the Fox Sports app. The numbers are there—but you need to swipe through a series of screens to locate them, and if you haven't been using the app on a daily basis, the quest will take even longer. Users rarely employ the search function, because it takes several seconds or more simply to type the request. The obvious solution: a voice-based tool that lets you simply say, "Show me LeBron James's stats from last night."

This small example illustrates the potential of voice to help solve the crisis of informational architecture that plagues individuals using the small screen of a smartphone or even the larger screens found on a tablet or a laptop. In all these cases, there is only so much screen real estate available, which means the device can only display a fraction of the functionality that is available. In a world where information sources are proliferating so much faster than the human brain can handle them, the idea of using eyes or hands to navigate through screens full of data in search of the specific fact we need is increasingly impractical. Well-crafted voice tools can cut through this dilemma, leading users quickly and accurately to the data points they need. Think of voice as the future "command center" for the navigational systems that allow you to take full advantage of all your apps, websites, and internet resources.

What's more, voice technology as an informational search tool is usable even in circumstances where visual navigation is difficult or impossible. I've already highlighted the dilemma of the soda-machine technician. Consider also the surgeon in the middle of a complicated operation looking for some feedback on a critical step but unable to remove her hands from her tools; the auto mechanic, flat on his back underneath a car and with his hands covered in grease, trying to troubleshoot a complicated glitch in the car's computer-based operating controls; and the warehouse employee toting an unwieldy carton and looking for the shelf where it belongs. All of these people may have the urgent need for one or more vital pieces of data—and none is in a position to drop everything to pick up a cell phone, tablet, or laptop and start swiping, tapping, and pecking away at the keys. At moments like this, having data available "at your fingertips" isn't good enough.

Because voice communication is accessible anytime, anywhere, including in hands-free situations where using a keyboard-equipped device is awkward or impractical, it can make it easy to get instant access to the accurate data that we frequently need, eliminating countless opportunities for error, accident, confusion, or simple embarrassment.

Voice combined with the power of AI has the potential to make the search for information even easier. Instantly finding the specific information a user wants is one of the great promises of ChatGPT and similar solutions. For twenty-five years, we've been accustomed to scanning a list of blue links as the answer to our questions. The future will be a voice-based question with an AI-driven answer delivered via text, graphic, or voice, depending on circumstances.

PROVIDING EASY ACCESS TO MORE ACCURATE INFORMATION IN THE WORKPLACE

Sarah Goldberg has just finished her dinner break and returned to her nursing station. She taps the Call button on her Smartbadge, a compact device weighing only about three ounces, that hangs from a lanyard around her neck. As always, the disembodied "genie" that Sarah thinks of as living inside the gadget responds by prompting, "Say your first and last name."

"Sarah Goldberg," she replies. She is instantly logged in, and the genie goes to work. On the small, brightly lit screen, it provides Sarah with a succinct instant update on the cases currently in her emergency room, highlighting information of special urgency—for example, the fact that Leon Jones in cubicle 4 has requested more pain medication.

Sarah takes in the information with a glance. She quickly decides she'd better check Leon's condition before complying with the request.

"Patient notes," she says. The genie immediately accesses the critical data regarding Leon's vital signs, the last time he received a dose, and other relevant information. Sarah takes in the key info with a glance at the Smartbadge screen. "Okay," she decides. After a quick conversation with Leon, she asks the genie to connect her with Jennifer Lewis, the hospital pharmacist on call. She tells Jennifer about Leon's request, and also asks the genie to send a secure information update to the doctor in charge. In just seconds, the order is on its way, and Sarah can move on to the next challenge of her busy evening shift.[3]

Anyone who has spent time in a hospital will tell you that nurses are among the most vital high-skilled workers in our society—as well as some of the most overworked and time-constrained. Smartbadge is making their lives just a little easier. The timely access it provides to the latest accurate patient data, coupled with rapid, real-time responses and instant communication with colleagues throughout the hospital, reduces the nurses' workload, increases the speed with which they work, reduces the potential for errors, and improves patient care. And because all the controls are hands-free, nurses can concentrate on human interactions with their patients rather than fussing with a keyboard—and without having to scrub up each time they touch a potentially germ-carrying computer or tablet.

Thanks to these and other benefits, the Smartbadge (developed by voice-tech company Vocera Communications) was named one of *Time* magazine's Best Inventions of 2020 based on factors including originality, creativity, effectiveness, ambition, and impact. "Used by more than 100 health care facilities," *Time* noted, "the Smartbadge has proved especially useful during the COVID-19 pandemic because it allows clinicians to make calls without removing personal protective equipment."[4]

Smartbadge is just one of the many ways that organizations are benefiting from the increased access to accurate information that voice technology makes possible.

One of the most widely used tools for improved information access is voice-based search. Introduced by Google in 2011, it was once considered a mere novelty. Today it is rivaling traditional keyboard-based methods of searching for data in popularity, with 41 percent of adults using voice search once a day or more.[5] The primary driver of this trend is that voice makes it much easier than typing for a consumer to conduct a long keyword search. When the user doesn't get the desired results on the first try, refining the search two or three times is much easier orally than via typing.

And while searching the web for information is done by innumerable people for innumerable reasons, voice-based search tools offer specific benefits to companies, nonprofits, and government agencies. They can be used not just for finding the right information, but also for gathering and curating it. Google Duplex, for example, is an automated system for making telephone calls. It speaks in a human-sounding voice and is intended to understand complex sentences and a variety of syntax. Available in fifteen countries (as of mid-2022), Duplex can be used by individual consumers for any number of personal uses, from making a reservation for a haircut or a restaurant meal to holding your place in a phone queue.

However, Google is also working to make Duplex into a useful information tool for businesses. It's currently being rolled out to client companies to handle many kinds of routine information-management tasks, such as booking appointments and checking transaction data. In any business where hundreds of appointments are being booked and confirmed every day—a hospital or clinic, for example—being able to automate this task can be a real godsend, freeing up one or more employees to focus on more complex work.

As Duplex encounters real-world challenges, its capabilities are steadily improving. When Duplex debuted in 2018, only about 64 percent of its calls were completed with zero human interaction. By 2021, the rate was close to 99 percent.[6] That number is impressive, and I don't doubt its accuracy. But it's important to note that "99 percent of calls handled purely automatically" is not equivalent to saying, "99 percent of calls handled without error." Having watched the testing of the system, I can say that, as of 2022, it still has a way to go to achieve the high ambitions Google has set for it. Duplex is excellent at simple interactions and gathering basic information, but I wouldn't expect it to manage complex, unplanned interactions with human interlocutors. As we'll explore in more detail later in this book, it's currently very difficult for a computer to follow the complex shifts in focus and nuances of context that are involved in most human conversations.

Nonetheless, Duplex is already very useful for a variety of simple but massive data-management chores. In fact, Google itself is using Duplex for just such purposes. For example, in fall 2020, Google assigned Duplex to make some 3 million calls to local businesses to confirm their opening hours for posting on apps like Google Search and Google Maps. Duplex was also employed to answer inbound calls from businesses seeking to update their information. That's a trove of information that once would have taken thousands of hours of human labor to gather. Using Duplex in this way relieves thousands of business owners of the task of updating their information on Google apps manually; once Duplex gets the new opening hours from a single call to the company, the listing on every app gets updated automatically.

This use of Duplex by Google illustrates how some big tech innovations arise when a company develops a tool to solve a problem they face themselves—a practice some tech-trend commentators refer to as "eating your own dog food." They then profit by selling the same tool to other companies confronting the same problem. Amazon's massive web-services hosting business originated in much the same way: the company created a powerful system for using the cloud to manage its vast troves of data and software tools, then began selling access to other companies that needed the same kind of help.

Many other organizations—businesses, nonprofits, and government agencies—can use smart voice-based tools like Duplex to handle routine data-gathering tasks. Insurance companies are early pioneers in this regard. They handle millions of claims annually, most of which fall into distinct categories defined by just a few pieces of information. Thus, when an insurance customer suffers damages that trigger coverage—being rear-ended in an auto accident, for example—they can now call the insurance company and submit a claim in just three minutes or so, using a completely automated voice system supplemented with a photo sent via text.

By making the process of asking and answering questions faster and easier than ever, voice, especially when combined with generative AI platforms like ChatGPT, is helping to create a world where having instant access to the correct information can be taken for granted, largely eliminating the outdated or inaccurate information we too often must struggle to work around in our daily lives. It will simplify and streamline a host of time- and energy-consuming administrative and communication tasks that now require human attention, creating new efficiencies in industries ranging from retail, finance, and real estate to travel, entertainment, and media.

MAKING INFORMATION AVAILABLE TO EVERYONE, EVERYWHERE

Workers aren't the only ones who are benefiting from the voice-based availability of more accurate information. All of us in our roles as consumers, patients, travelers, media users, and citizens are also beginning to take advantage of tools that use voice technology powered by AI to manage information in circumstances where it was once difficult or impossible to obtain.

One big advantage of voice tools is that they are usable by millions of people who lack technical skills, computer access, or high levels of literacy. This is critically important when it comes to government services, which must be made available to all people, regardless of their income level, educational background, or other characteristics. For example, many school districts require initial student registrations to be done online, which poses a problem for many families where the necessary skills and equipment may be unavailable. Similarly, basic tasks like applying for a passport, updating a driver's license, or registering to vote are often more difficult for people without Wi-Fi connections or computer literacy. The problem could get worse over time if the concept of "digital government," promoted by some reform-minded gurus in the quest for speed and efficiency, becomes a universal reality.[7]

Voice tech will play a big role in alleviating this problem. So will smartphones. They are relatively affordable devices that are already in the pockets and purses of millions of people who don't own laptops, desktops, or tablets. They can be used whenever and wherever a question arises.

Thanks to voice tech and smartphones, the government apps and websites that manage flows of information from agencies to the general public and vice versa will soon be easily accessible to people who are not computer-savvy or even conventionally literate. A parent with a smartphone will be able to speak with an AI-powered voice tool that represents the local school district. Simply by answering spoken questions, they'll be able to provide the name of their child, their birth date, the location of any previous school attended, and other vital data needed to register them as a student.

Similarly, a driver needing to update her auto registration will be able to connect with the state department of motor vehicles by way of an app or a phone call. Voice and face biometrics using the mic and camera in the driver's cell phone will verify the caller's ID. The driver will then respond to a series of questions, upload a snapshot showing the most recent auto inspection sticker, and provide a credit-card number to pay the state fee. An updated auto registration will soon be on its way.

And because voice is the most natural, intuitive way to communicate, voice tools delivered via smartphone are less intimidating for many people than even the most thoughtfully designed website. Think about tens of millions of older people with questions about Social Security, Medicare, and other vital government services. Many are comfortable with navigating screens and tapping keyboards—but many are not. Voice tech will enable all of them to get access to the information they need.

More and more government agencies are already taking advantage of these features of voice tech to make it easier for citizens to access important information about government. Take election information as an example. The 2020 election was one of the most challenging in US history. It was conducted during a deadly pandemic, in a period of intense partisan division and a time when accusations—mostly fraudulent—of voter fraud, vote suppression, and other irregularities were rampant. Many observers worried that the November balloting would be a fiasco, with potentially disastrous effects on our democracy.

To avoid this, a few forward-looking election officials turned to the use of smart voice tools to provide instant, on-the-spot answers to voter questions like "Where can I drop off my early-voting ballot?" "Has my local polling place been moved?" "What forms of identification are acceptable for voting in my state?" Idaho was among the first states to take advantage of this kind of voter support. In March 2020, the state was forced by rising COVID rates to cancel in-person voting for the primary election scheduled in May. Confused voters flooded state offices with questions.

In response, Idaho government officials turned to IBM's flagship AI product Watson for help. Together they created an election-information tool that was able to respond to almost a million voter questions during the following two months. Recognizing the value of this service, Idaho extended its partnership with Watson through the November election. And IBM decided to offer a similar service for free to other states that requested it.[8] Other jurisdictions, including municipalities from New Haven, Connecticut, to Mesa, Arizona, created Alexa skills (i.e., voice-based apps) that were able to respond to common voter questions throughout the 2020 election cycle.

Voice-tech tools are also rapidly being deployed for an array of other purposes—for example, to help travelers who need or want information while they are on the go. We've seen how the spread of smart voice assistants into automobiles has been making driving safer. Those same tools are also providing drivers and passengers with access to information that is useful, valuable, and enjoyable.

Cerence, a leader in the field of in-car voice services, provides a number of proactive informational tools that make driving easier and more convenient. The built-in voice assistant can alert you when your car needs service, tell you where the nearest service station is, and even make the call to arrange an appointment. Going further afield, Cerence offers a feature called Tour Guide that provides car-based smart assistants with a trove of information about the areas they are passing through. In Planned Tour mode, a driver can prearrange for the voice assistant to offer mini-lectures on local historical sites, suggestions for walking trails, and recommendations for museums. The driver can choose specific topics they want to hear about as well as the frequency of the assistant's presentations. In Explore mode, the voice assistant becomes a "concierge on the go," choosing points of interest to mention as the trip unfolds as well as offering ideas for restaurants and other services that the assistant can contact for reservations. The information is drawn from a number of Cerence partners, including Viator, a subsidiary of Tripadvisor that offers links to some 400,000 activities for easy booking.

Similar shortcuts, powered by AI and accessed by voice, are also becoming available for travelers who are not in their cars. Marsbot is a service created by Foursquare that uses AirPods headphones to play short audio clips of information about the user's current location. It offers historical and cultural facts as well as recommendations for nearby attractions, restaurants, shops, and other services. It also lets users share their own audio responses, such as a tourism suggestion of their own that subsequent visitors can access through the service.

From my perspective as a student of how voice tech works—and how it *should* work—I'm favorably impressed by the design of these voice-based travel tools. A crucial shortfall of many search-tool deployments, especially on stand-alone platforms like Alexa, has been the lack of discoverability or searchability. Users simply don't know what kinds of services are available, nor do they have an easy way to find out. (No one wants to listen to Alexa recite a list of hundreds of available apps, and searching through the same sort of list on a screen is almost equally cumbersome.)

Cerence Tour Guide and Marsbot solve this problem by creating a multimodal experience, based not on the use of a screen or a keyboard but on the link to location. The fact that information is presented only about *nearby* sites and activities eliminates the discoverability problem, making the tool instantly and easily useful.

Before long, voice-based tools for managing a steady stream of information are likely to be available almost literally everywhere—including beyond the confines of planet Earth.

In 2024, NASA has a number of space flights planned that will involve human crews. These include a moon-orbiting mission called Artemis 2 that is scheduled for 2024, and a moon landing planned for 2025 that will be dubbed Artemis 3. As part of the preparation for these missions, NASA is now testing a concept proposed by Lockheed Martin, Amazon, and Cisco in which a specially enhanced version of Amazon's Alexa voice assistant will accompany space travelers on their journeys.

This custom-built assistant—known as Callisto—played a successful role in the Artemis 1 round-the-moon mission that lasted for three weeks from November to December 2022. Artemis 1 was an uncrewed flight, so Callisto wasn't called upon to respond to in-person requests during the trip. But the mission provided an opportunity to test the platform for its ability to withstand the rigors of space flight, including the physical stresses of launch, radiation, vibration, and the often-noisy environment inside a crowded space capsule. Callisto handled a number of basic functions during the flight, such as streaming video, getting readings from the spacecraft's instruments, and controlling the cabin lights.

Among the advantages that systems like Callisto will offer to future astronauts is the fact that their AI capabilities can be housed completely within the capsule, thus eliminating the minutes-long delays involved when a command must be transmitted across the vast distances of space to a controlling system back on Earth.

Wherever they are and whatever they are doing, humans need access to information. Historically, there have always been places and times when that access was simply impossible. Voice tech is gradually eliminating many of those dark spots.

MEANING FROM SOUND: HOW AI IS EXTRACTING VALUABLE INFORMATION FROM THE SOUNDS AROUND US

Voice can do more than simply make information accessible. It can also *generate* information by analyzing and interpreting clues and cues contained in sound, thereby helping people to understand and know things that are currently vague, unclear, or mysterious. By mining information from aural sources that have traditionally been ignored or underused, voice will, ironically, add to the digital overload problem by feeding even more valuable data into the system. Fortunately, voice tech will also power a virtuous cycle in which voice creates much more content, then provides the best way to identify, sort, and navigate that content.

Many environments, especially in the places where we work, are filled with rich troves of sound—ambient noises, spoken presentations, dialogue among individuals, arguments and debates, business interactions, and sales and service calls. Historically, the ideas, factual data, and insights embedded in these fleeting streams of sound have almost always been lost—unless an individual on the scene had the time, energy, and tools needed to take notes, make a recording, or otherwise capture the content in real time.

Today's new voice technologies are changing that. Systems for natural language processing (NLP)—of which ChatGPT is a current example—are increasingly capable of extracting meaning from spontaneous spoken words, thereby capturing information that can be analyzed and used for a wide array of purposes. Thanks to NLP, organizations are now discovering informational assets heretofore hidden and finding ways to make them discoverable and useful. The future will not be one ChatGPT interface for all our questions, but specific versions of NLP technology implemented and optimized for specific use cases by companies operating in those fields.

One example comes from the world of health care. Hillrom—a division of Baxter International that was originally a maker of traditional hospital beds—has been working to help transform the ways hospital personnel share information with one another. Voice technology plays a key role in that effort. Hillrom's Voalte communications platform makes it easy for nurses and doctors to get immediate access to patient data, medication orders, alerts and alarms, and other urgent information. The platform makes use of microphones and speakers that are built into every hospital bed. And in the years to come, the Voalte platform will make increasing use of *ambient listening* techniques to gather and use vital information derived from the sounds present in a hospital room.

Darren S. Hudgins, Hillrom's vice president for R&D, describes some of the possibilities:

> The sound data we can access through the voice communication systems already in place in the hospital can offer important insights into what's happening with the patients. Noises picked up by the system and analyzed using AI could tell us whether there is a situation of stress or conflict in the room, whether a patient is experiencing a fall or a respiratory change, or whether some other kind of emergency may be unfolding. We could use this information to immediately dispatch a security team to assist a nurse who may

be in danger or to make sure a cardiac-arrest team is sent when a patient's voice reveals that a heart attack is in progress.[9]

Warfare is another arena in which voice tech can be used to extract crucially important information from ambient noise. In the arcane world of anti-submarine warfare, sound cues have long played a vital role. During and after World War II, advances in sonar technology enhanced by electronic tools helped warships, airplanes, and later helicopters to detect and attack enemy submarines using weapons like torpedoes, missiles, rockets, and depth charges. Advanced versions of these same tools are still being used, still relying in many cases on sound cues provided by the propellers of submarines. Range recorders and other devices are able to use these cues to locate an enemy vessel and direct an attack against it accurately.

However, reading, interpreting, and using the information provided by sonar systems to launch an effective attack against an enemy submarine while under the intense pressure of combat is extremely difficult, even for highly trained and experienced operators. Varying weather conditions and obstacles such as underwater mountain ranges that shield predatory submarines can make "reading" the sonar data quite complex. Now the US Navy is seeking high-tech partners to help in developing a smart assistant to provide voice-based, AI-powered support for this kind of combat mission. The goal is to have a shipboard system that is capable of analyzing the audio cues provided by traditional sonar and interpreting them more quickly and accurately than a human alone can do. The smart assistant will communicate its findings to the human crew member in charge using a variety of communication modes as appropriate, including both voice and on-screen displays. Such a system will make it possible for navy warships and their supporting aircraft to find and destroy enemy submarines before the submarines are able to attack.[10]

Whether in a hospital room or in the midst of a naval battle, sounds can convey urgent messages to those who know how to interpret them.

UNEARTHING VITAL BUSINESS DATA
BURIED IN EVERYDAY CONVERSATIONS

Other uses for applying voice tools to the delivery of information are less dramatic than combat or saving lives, but do offer fascinating, value-creating opportunities for businesses and organizations.

One is the ability to identify and zero in on key concepts in an unstructured written or spoken communication. In a world that is awash with such communications—in traditional media, in online settings, in social media, and in billions of conversations conducted via telephone, chat, text, and email—there's a critical need for tools that can sort out the meaningful from the merely noisy, and can do so swiftly, accurately, and clearly, without the need for massive, expensive, and time-consuming human participation.

The key insight here is that an incredible amount of sound-based information around us is either going uncaptured or is being poorly captured in ways that are prone to error.

For example, when I order a meal at a restaurant, a server takes that information down, either on paper or on a mobile device. It is then transmitted to the kitchen at least once, creating opportunities for misunderstanding and mistakes. As we saw in Chapter 1, this information should be going to the bar and to the kitchen the second it leaves my lips—which voice tech now makes possible.

New applications for analyzing conversational speech can do much more than just capture ordering information. A variety of voice-tech companies, including Gong, Avoma, and Clari, are using voice tools not just to transcribe language from client meetings and sales calls, but to perform analysis of that language that yields valuable business information.

Here's how it works. At the start of a phone or Zoom call, you'll ask the participants, "Is it okay if we record this call?" Once they give permission—as they almost invariably do—you activate one of the new speech analysis tools. It records the conversation, tracks who is speaking at each point, and parses the contents, using AI to search for key ideas and data points. Later, it enters those critical pieces of information into customer-relationship-management software tools like those offered by Salesforce—items like an impending deadline by which an order must be delivered, or a change in product specifications requested by the client. (Salespeople know and appreciate the value of CRM tools like Salesforce, but they're notoriously inconsistent about entering data into the systems. The new speech analysis tools take care of this for them.)

All of this is enormously helpful to businesses when important conversations are happening. But the latest breakthrough is these tools now do *sentiment analysis*, which means detecting and analyzing the emotional content of the conversation. After the meeting is finished, managers can review the atmosphere and mood of the discussion and use it to help uncover communication techniques that are more or less effective.

Speech analysis tools are becoming steadily more useful and valuable. My favorite insight to date: one company found, through AI-driven analysis of sales calls, that potential buyers were about twice as likely to buy if they (humorously) cursed on the call. They found that playful cursing was an indicator of engagement and comfort that could be correlated to completing a sale.

Arte Merritt has been a pioneering figure in the world of voice tech going back to the mid-1990s, when he worked at creating one of the first consumer-oriented internet sites for the publishing company Random House. He soon launched his career as a serial entrepreneur, founding organizations with such disparate missions as critiquing college application essays (myEssay.com), providing analytic tools for mobile websites and apps (Motally, later sold to Nokia), and offering accelerator services to media companies (Media Camp).

Prior to his leadership role building a conversational AI partnership program at Amazon Web Services, beginning in 2016, Merritt

had founded a conversational AI analytics platform known as Dashbot, which specialized in extracting information and ideas from the
dense, chaotic streams of content that flow through automated customer call centers. Within a few years, Dashbot had attracted some
20,000 business customers and was analyzing *billions* of customer
interactions per month.

"Many company leaders, even specialists in customer service and
the customer experience, don't fully realize how much amazing information is hiding in conversations between customers and their company voice bots or assistants," Arte told us.[11] Dashbot filled that gap.
It used AI tools to tease out common patterns of interaction between
customers and the company, frequent pain points, most-often-asked
questions, and crucial indicators of customer sentiment and attitudes.
These are all vital pieces of information that go so much deeper than
the strictly quantitative data many companies rely on when examining
their customer service experience—statistics like the number of customer calls, average length of calls, and number of buttons pressed.
Using these deeper insights, companies can improve their customer
service in many ways—by reducing the number of calls that fail to
resolve a complaint or problem, by increasing the number of customers
who choose to buy a new product or service, and by identifying new
ways of creating value for customers.

Dashbot, as well as companies like SuccessKPI and Cresta AI, is
offering valuable services for analyzing and using information from
customer-service interactions. What all these companies have in
common—along with IBM and the other organizations that are working to create value from once-untapped flows of information—is their
reliance on the amazing new capabilities of natural language processing (NLP) that are at the heart of the coming age of voice.

Monticello, the mansion in Charlottesville, Virginia, designed and
built by Thomas Jefferson, is both an American icon and a great example of how voice tech can solve real-world problems. Jefferson was an

avid enthusiast for the science and technology of his own day, with interests ranging from botany and geology to paleontology. He would likely revel in the fact that the latest voice technology is now at work in his house, with sentiment analysis as an important part of the mix.

Hundreds of thousands of visitors enjoy the Neoclassical architecture and historic grounds of Monticello every year. In recent times, debate about how Jefferson's historic legacy should be presented has been particularly intense. On the one hand, Jefferson was a brilliant statesman and an eloquent advocate for democracy; at the same time, he owned enslaved people and fathered children with one of them, Sally Hemings. The tour guides at Monticello are thoroughly trained to present the paradox of Jefferson in all its complexity, which, after all, mirrors the complexity of the American story itself. The guides consistently earn praise for their professionalism and sensitivity, but criticism sometimes arises, driven in part by strong political views on both the left and the right.

To deal effectively with this criticism, Monticello has turned to voice technology, with help from WillowTree. Tours of the property are being recorded, including the tour guides' presentations and the questions and comments offered by visitors. Later, these texts are transcribed (anonymously) and analyzed using machine learning. Observations and reactions of all kinds are noted, characterized, and registered, along with the context and the emotional content of the discussion.

This will enable the professional staff at Monticello to evaluate varied opinions—"The tour guide never addressed the issue of racial injustice," "Slavery was overemphasized"—in the light of accurate data: Exactly how many times was slavery discussed? How many visitors expressed discomfort over specific issues? Which questions were most frequently asked? Which topics elicit the greatest interest and the strongest feelings? The program leaders can use the information and insights that emerge from this analysis to help them create improved policies, training materials, and educational tools.

THE OPPORTUNITIES FOR BUSINESSES

Voice technology is not only making it easier to access information whenever and wherever we need it; it is also unearthing and clarifying entirely new sources of information that were once impossible to tap.

One way to zero in on the business opportunities created by voice data is by examining the *long tail* use cases that may exist in your organization: that is, information-driven functions, activities, or questions that are critical to customer satisfaction but occur relatively rarely. Many companies have reasonably efficient systems for handling everyday challenges—but less common ones often create both complex difficulties and unusual opportunities. Voice search will make it easier for your customers and employees to use longer, more complex searches to find the specific information they need. Analyzing website and app usage trends as well as customer-service interactions can enable your organization to identify these trickier, less obvious issues, as well as the kinds of information resources needed to address them. Then you can examine the new AI-enabled voice-tech tools to determine which ones, if any, can provide automated ways to manage those challenges.

The goal is to quickly provide complete, accurate information not just in response to the obvious, everyday questions, but to the countless questions that are just as important but much less commonplace, and therefore much more difficult to answer.

Thus, a company like Home Depot or Target that has thousands of products listed in its database can create a voice-based customer app capable of instantly answering customer questions about any one of those items, even the most obscure. Such an app will free up live sales and service staffers from the drudgery of looking up product specs in a manual or a database, leaving them free to interact more personally and creatively with customers. By making information about those obscure but still-valuable products more readily available, it will likely boost their sales, too.

Similarly, a bank can develop a voice-based tool that can respond accurately not just to the everyday questions ("What's my savings account balance?") but even to questions that may get asked only once a month or once a year ("How can I transfer money to a bank account in Azerbaijan?").

And an HR department can use voice tech, powered by AI, to quickly and easily answer questions about every detail of an employee's benefits package, even ones that might traditionally require time-consuming research by a staff member ("If I decide to retire six months early, how exactly will my monthly pension payment be affected?").

In other cases, examining the arena in which your business operates may reveal a little-recognized gap between information needed and information available—perhaps a gap that can be bridged with the help of voice tech. When this happens, it may even be possible to build an entire new business by adapting voice tools to bridge the gap, thereby creating a new form of value that people will be willing to monetize.

One recent example comes from the world of primary education. Learning to read is, of course, one of the most important challenges any child faces. Helping kids learn to read is also one of the biggest challenges teachers face. A tool used by thousands of teachers with millions of students annually is the Lexile Framework for Oral Reading. Developed more than thirty years ago by two educational researchers and made widely available through a company called MetaMetrics, the Lexile Framework is the world's most popular tool for assessing reading skill. It's used to identify students' strengths and weaknesses, personalize their reading instruction, create vocabulary lists, and select appropriate reading materials.

The Lexile Framework is a very useful, flexible educational tool. But it has some drawbacks. The biggest one is the relative difficulty of calculating a student's "Lexile measure." There's no single test offered by MetaMetrics to test reading ability. Instead, the company partners with over 200 publishers to create "Lexile text measures" for the books and other materials they produce. A student is asked to read aloud from a Lexile text, and a teacher listens while annotating the text on paper, on a laptop, or on a tablet. The result is a grade that reflects the child's mastery of reading skills. But it's a slow, laborious task that can only be done one child at a time and requires the services of a teacher specially trained for the job.

What's more, traditional Lexile measures are not always reliable. Sean Ryan, president of McGraw Hill School Group, which provides educational materials to 90 percent of US schools, says that student assessments created by individual educators can be "wildly inconsistent." Unconscious elements of bias, Ryan says, often enter into the score, based on factors like "the siblings of that student, the clothes they are wearing, or their success in other classrooms."[12]

Thus, there's a gap between the potential of the Lexile Framework and its real-world usefulness. The information about student abilities provided by the frameworks is not as accurate or as readily available as it should be. It's a gap that new voice-tech tools may be able to help bridge.

Attempting to fill the gap is voice-tech start-up SoapBox Labs, which has created a partnership with McGraw Hill to develop an automated system for developing student Lexile scores. The goal is to use modern speech-recognition systems to evaluate a child's reading skill, producing a more consistent score that is free of bias and allows teachers to devise more effective customized learning plans.

This is not an easy task. In recent years, speech-recognition tools have advanced by leaps and bounds—but they are still not perfect. And when it comes to tracking children's speech, the challenge is particularly great. The physical instrument a child uses to speak is different in size and shape from that of an adult; consequently, kids often pronounce words differently from adults, making it harder for an algorithm to convert their speech accurately into text.

Adapting automated speech-recognition software specifically to serve the needs of children accurately has been the core mission of SoapBox Labs. They've been studying thousands of hours of children's speech to develop better analytic models. They've also been collaborating with the Florida Center for Reading Research, based at Florida State University, on developing apps dedicated to this purpose.

MetaMetrics—the creators and guardians of the Lexile Framework—will need to be satisfied with the accuracy of the Soap-Box system before they endorse it as a new tool for educators. They hope that will happen during 2023. If and when it does, it will open a new era in the teaching of reading—one in which the information needed to develop better customized teaching methods will be easily and quickly available to educators for the first time.[13]

The SoapBox story illustrates how a close look at a single field of activity—in this case, reading education—may reveal a giant information gap that the new voice tech can help to bridge.

The competitiveness of any company or organization in the Information Age is largely governed by its ability to generate, access, and intelligently use data. Smart mics will generate petabytes of new data by capturing the words and sounds around us; AI-powered software tools will transform this data into useful information. Think of voice as an effortless search overlay over every piece of information your company owns, giving you the ability to instantly access true business intelligence to benefit both your customers and your employees.

4

INCLUSION

Creating a World Where No One Is Left Behind

INCLUSION—THE CHALLENGE OF MAKING A BUSINESS AND its offerings equally accessible and welcoming for all its employees and customers—is on the agenda of companies around the world. Voice may be the most powerful technology we can use to move the dream of inclusion from an aspiration to an integral part of everyday life.

Today's digital world is one of intense, seemingly ubiquitous connections. Yet as the COVID-19 pandemic has reminded us, it's also a world in which health risks, infirmities, and other circumstances can easily force people into painful forms of separation and isolation. At the same time, age-old social differences such as race, gender, ethnicity, language, and religion continue to separate people and groups from one another. Finding ways to bridge these divisions between individuals and between groups is one of the biggest social, political, and economic challenges humankind faces.

Voice technology can play an important role in the quest for a more inclusive society. As the most basic and universal human communications tool of all, voice can be accessed freely by people with a wide range of physical disabilities, it does not require literacy, and via increasingly powerful voice translation systems, it can make the English-dominated digital world accessible to all the world's people.

Voice technology is already eliminating physical and social barriers that once seemed insurmountable. Future breakthroughs now in development will provide similar benefits to hundreds of millions of people around the world.

OPENING DOORS FOR THE DIFFERENTLY ABLED

As illustrated by the story of Vocable, told in the prologue, voice tools can help the millions of people for whom sensory infirmities make life difficult, and often lonely, to reconnect with society. Incidentally, Vocable is no longer the only phone-based app that can help people suffering from paralysis to speak. In 2022, Google released its Look to Speak app, which uses the camera and speaker built into an Android phone to enable the user to select and pronounce a phrase they'd like to say.[1] Like Vocable, it's great news for the many people who need this kind of support. And those suffering from paralysis are not the only people for whom voice tech tools can play a vital role.

The blind and vision-impaired, for example, stand to benefit in many ways from the growing availability of the voice interface as a way of accessing vital services and information. The World Health Organization estimates that some 2.2 billion people have some form of vision impairment—many of them with limited access to eye care.[2]

One basic voice tool that is already helping millions of people with visual impairment is the screen reader—a tool that can read aloud the contents of text displayed on a smartphone or a computer screen. A number of screen reading apps are currently available, including VoiceOver, which is built into recent models of iPhones, and TalkBack, which provides the same service to users of Android phones. Screen readers are becoming increasingly sophisticated, offering options such as variable speaking rate, adaptability to a braille keyboard, and other useful variants.

Social meda sites like TikTok are among the tech-based organizations that are using voice-based tools to make their services more accessible to people with limited vision. To support people who have difficulty reading the captions that appear in online videos, TikTok makes it simple for them to access a voice-based alternative. It's super-easy to use: just post a video, type a caption, and touch the "Text-to-speech" button; anyone who views the video will hear the caption spoken aloud. Similarly, vision-impaired people can now access Instagram using an alternative text feature that offers rich spoken descriptions of photos as they pop up on screen.

Many other familiar digital tools now provide voice-based forms of support for those with limited vision. Voice tools are making it easier and safer for people with impaired vision to get around. Navigation systems like Google Maps can use voice to communicate the quickest, best route for a pedestrian, including subtle details like the precise location of an entry door. Moovit, a public transportation guide now owned by Intel, not only offers spoken guides to bus, train, and subway routes but also provides help such as the names of stops as they are reached during the journey. And Microsoft Soundscape offers the iPhone user an audible description of their surroundings, describing nearby landmarks and intersections, and allowing the user to create an aural "beacon" to guide movement toward a destination. Another app, called Nearby Explorer, provides similar support for Android users.

One of the most ingenious voice-based mobility tools is the WeWalk cane, launched through a crowdfunding campaign in 2018. At first glance, it resembles the standard white cane long used by the blind to help them travel independently. The big difference: WeWalk includes a touch pad, speaker, and sensory tools that probe for nearby obstacles, as well as a voice-activated smartphone app that responds to the user's questions: "Where am I now? How far is the nearest bus stop? Which way to the supermarket?" For a sightless individual, having a WeWalk cane is almost like having a dedicated assistant available at all times to help you go wherever you want to go—comfortably and safely.

Many other tools are already available or under development to help vision-impaired individuals tackle specific life challenges that are easy for most people but difficult for them.

The Lookout app, created by Google, lets a smartphone user take a snapshot of a food container. The app then reads aloud the nutrition information on the label. Seeing AI is an ambitious app from Microsoft that works with the VoiceOver screen reader on your iPhone to provide a variety of handy services, from reading the text on a printed page held in front of your smartphone camera to describing images captured in photos. Vision-impaired people use Seeing AI every day for such mundane yet important tasks as checking the expiration date on a package of food, distinguishing a twenty-dollar bill from a single, and picking clothes whose colors harmonize rather than clash. The Lookout app offers similar support to users of Android phones.[3]

Perhaps most intriguingly, new voice tools are also being developed that will improve life for those with impaired hearing, or people working or learning in settings where hearing is difficult—a noisy factory floor, for example. Yes, it's counterintuitive—but just as sounds can supplement, augment, and replace words and images, voice tech can also be used in ways that make sounds more useful and understandable.

One basic example is the proliferation of accessible tools for real-time speech-to-text conversion. Ava is an app that's available in several forms—one for smartphones, one (called Ava Web) for use during virtual meetings, and one (called Ava Scribe) that incorporates human judgment for correcting any transcription errors made by Ava's built-in AI. Tools like Ava can improve communication in a host of situations—by transcribing a one-on-one conversation, by live-captioning the speeches and presentations during a giant conference, and even by providing real-time translation from English into Spanish, French, or some other language. A number of companies that provide web-based services for hosting meetings now provide similar automated captioning services, among them Microsoft Teams, Google Meet, Skype, and Zoom.

Today, other voice-driven tools to improve communications are emerging that are even more versatile. For instance, smart earbuds equipped with AI capabilities are being developed that perform like hearing aids, amplifying external sounds for people who are hard of hearing. More impressive, they also use sophisticated recognition techniques powered by machine learning to help them distinguish individual voices in a crowded room—at a party, for example. Voice-activated tools like these can help those with limited hearing engage in social settings with much greater ease and comfort, so they no longer have to shun family gatherings or business meetings for fear of confusion and embarrassment. One such tool is being developed by Google using the project code name Wolverine, named after a character from the comic-book series *X-Men* known for his heightened senses.[4]

DEMOLISHING BARRIERS BUILT BY ILLITERACY

Physical impairments have long created barriers that exclude millions of people from mainstream society. But social barriers such as limited literacy and language differences can create divisions among humans that are just as daunting. Here, too, voice can play a breakthrough role.

In communities where advanced education is commonplace, it's easy to forget that the world still contains billions of people with limited ability to read and write, especially in the developing nations of the global South. And even in countries where literacy rates are high, millions of people still have difficulty with reading. According to a 2019 study by the US Department of Education, some 43 million American adults have "low literacy skills"—that is, they have difficulty in using written texts "to participate in society, to achieve one's goals, and to develop one's knowledge and potential."[5]

When the definition of literacy is modified to set a slightly higher bar, the number of people who fall short balloons. For example, it's estimated that half of American adults have difficulty reading a book written at an eighth-grade level. And on the global stage, illiteracy is a massive problem. Many countries in sub-Saharan Africa and some in Asia and South America have illiteracy rates of 30 to 50 percent. Countries with somewhat better literacy numbers still may have huge numbers of illiterate people. For example, India, with its literacy rate of around 72 percent, has over 370 million people who can't read—a number larger than the entire US population.[6]

In total, the global population of illiterate individuals numbers some 700 million people. Many have access to smartphones and other digital tools—yet, because they can't read, they are unable to take advantage of many of the benefits these tools can offer, such as text messaging.[7]

For these millions of people, avenues to full participation in economic, social, cultural, and political life are partially or completely blocked—because so many of the basic activities require fluency in interpreting the written word. The impact on society, from overall levels of health to civic engagement to economic productivity, is enormous.

Of course, addressing the underlying causes of illiteracy—inadequate schools, economic deprivation, medical and psychological problems—is an important goal to which every society should be committed. But in both the short and long term, voice tech can make breakthroughs in alleviating the social ills to which illiteracy contributes. Incorporating voice technology into the interfaces we use to connect with companies, media, government agencies, health-care providers, and other vital resources can help close the access gap that people with literacy short-falls suffer. Voice-activated apps can open doors for people who have difficulty reading written directions, and text-to-speech tools that trans-late documents into streams of spoken words can communicate ideas and information to people who would struggle to read them.

Voice technology is already helping to integrate the billions with lit-eracy problems into the twenty-first-century economy. One of the orga-nizations involved is software powerhouse Oracle, whose AI-powered digital-assistant division competes with similar offerings from IBM, Amazon, and SAP. Oracle reports that India, with its hundreds of millions of people who lack strong literacy skills, is currently one of the fastest-growing markets for voice bots and voice-based digital assistants. These tools are being deployed to connect millions of people to services and knowledge they need. The Indian Farmers Fertiliser Cooperative, for example, is using an Oracle voice bot to provide information about its products and services to almost 50 million farmers who belong to some 35,000 cooperative societies. Other Indian companies, from Bajaj Electricals to the Indian division of consulting powerhouse PwC are also using Oracle's voice tools to connect more easily with customers.[8]

During the COVID-19 pandemic, the Indian government leaned heavily on a voice-powered WhatsApp voice bot to combat disinformation about the disease and to inform people about the best ways to avoid contracting it. Launched in March 2020 and using India's two most widely known spoken languages—English and Hindi—the voice bot drew information from the national health ministry. Within a year, it took part in more than 45 million conversations with citizens worried about the pandemic.

Voice tech is also being used to combat illiteracy directly. When people—whether children or adults—are working on learning to read, voice technology can play a valuable role in helping them improve their comprehension skills. One expert describes how this works in the context of using audiobooks as a tool for helping people tackle the two distinct skills involved in reading—decoding letter-sound relationships and understanding the overall meaning of the text:

> When decoding, or figuring out letter-sound relationships, is automatic, the mental processes involved in reading and listening are essentially the same, especially when it comes to narrative text. [But f]or those who have not yet mastered phonics or gained sufficient fluency—particularly for students with dyslexia, Attention

Deficit Hyperactivity Disorder (ADHD), etc.—decoding is an additional cognitive load that can prevent them from using their language processing skills to comprehend the text. Audiobooks can take off that additional load so that, while a student works on their other literacy skills, they can practice the higher-level task of understanding what the text means.[9]

There are other advantages to using audiobooks as a tool for literacy training. For example, adults who never had the opportunity to learn to read as children can use audiobooks to skip the embarrassing step of having to struggle through books written for toddlers:

> Students can access books above their reading level on audio, which means they will have exposure to unfamiliar and increasingly difficult vocabulary. . . . This is particularly important for older students who are working on more basic decoding and fluency; by circumventing the stressful and possibly shame-inducing process of decoding, they can access grade-level material, as well as content that is more suited to their interests and intellectual capabilities.[10]

Not every text that might be of interest to a person who is learning to read is currently available in the form of a traditional audiobook, recorded by a human narrator. This is one reason why today's sophisticated speech-to-text software tools are so important. They provide a technological foundation for every voice-tech application discussed in this book without requiring the service of a live human reader. In so doing they create a pathway by which millions of people who are illiterate, or who are struggling to learn to read, can get immediate access to the information, entertainment, and social services they need.

Someone who understands this connection better than most is Cliff Weitzman, founder and CEO of Speechify, which is one of today's leading speech-to-text software companies. Weitzman suffered from dyslexia as a kid and taught himself English in part by listening to the audiobook of *Harry Potter and the Philosopher's Stone*—twenty-two times.

He became interested in software development and used his basic programming skills to begin developing a tool that could read aloud from a printed text. Later, after learning about new developments in AI that could automatically produce more authentic-sounding human speech, he began working on Speechify to help others who, like him, found it easier to absorb information in spoken rather than written form.

Weitzman discovered the huge potential market for Speechify almost by accident: "Somebody told me about a dyslexia conference that was happening in Florida. I snuck into the conference and gave an impromptu presentation about Speechify. At the end, 15 of the schools offered to fly me to their locations, in the US and in Europe and the Middle East, to have me present to their kids about Speechify, and about how to learn by listening."[11]

Working with educators, Weitzman discovered ways to make Speechify even more valuable for people with reading difficulties. For example, he realized that introducing a feature that allows users to adjust the speed with which the software reads aloud lets them take advantage of their ability to absorb information orally more quickly than they can read. Jon Green, head of school at the Hamilton School for Students with Learning Differences, describes the impact this has on students: "Hamilton kids know how many words they can read per minute," he says. "It's quite dramatic when I play [the Speechify narration] slowly and then speed it up." Many students discover they can get through a textbook chapter twice as fast just by increasing the setting on their Speechify software. It makes a major difference in their ability to keep up with classmates and their overall academic self-confidence.[12]

VOICE TECHNOLOGY AND THE BABEL CHALLENGE

I've spoken about how voice technology is being used to bring much-needed services to the millions of illiterate people living in India.

In time, voice will also help Indians overcome another major social barrier—the more than 400 languages spoken by the country's 1.3 billion citizens, many of them in remote villages where government services, educational opportunities, and global markets are difficult to access. When people literally "don't speak the same language," their ability to participate fully in economic and civic life can be drastically limited.

For many Indians, especially those who are lucky enough to speak one of the more widely spoken languages used in the subcontinent, voice is already becoming a powerful connective tool. Real-time voice-activated translation systems from developers like Google and Microsoft have made remarkable strides in speed and accuracy in recent years. Microsoft Translator, for example, now provides real-time voice-based translation services in any of ten Indian languages—Bengali, Hindi, Tamil, Telugu, Urdu, Gujarati, Marathi, Kannada, Malayalam, and Punjabi—which in combination cover 90 percent of the country's population. And in April 2022, the Indian government announced the rollout of a new voice assistant to provide information about government services, developed in conjunction with the conversational AI company Senseforth. Known as the Unified Mobile Application for New-Age Governance, by late 2022 the app had mastered a similar list of twelve of the most common Indian languages.[13]

Unfortunately, Indians who know none of the country's major languages still face the difficulty of making connections with technology. The smaller the number of people who speak a particular language or dialect, the harder it is for a tech company, a government agency, or even a nonprofit organization to justify dedicating time, talent, and money to developing a translation tool purpose-built for that tongue. In addition, speakers of those less used languages are underrepresented among the engineers, programmers, linguists, and scholars working on translation tools. And the substantial data sets needed to facilitate the application of AI and machine learning to these languages—vast, varied files of recorded conversations on many topics by native speakers—are often unavailable. All these barriers contribute to a world in which, at present, a large swath of the population is unable to access some of the most powerful digital communication tools.

Similar challenges exist in much of the world. The African continent is home to some of the world's fastest-growing economies—as well as to an estimated 2,000 different languages and dialects. None of the languages native to Africa is currently "spoken" by Siri, Alexa, or Google Assistant. As a result, hundreds of millions of people—many of whom own smartphones—are unable to make full use of modern technology in their work, their education, and their social lives. This barrier causes a cultural loss as well. Nigerian writer Kọ́lá Túbọ̀sún, who has been working to promote inclusivity for his native language Yoruba, describes the problem this way:

> If a language doesn't exist in the technology space, it is almost as if it doesn't exist at all. That is the way the world is structured today, and in that you spend all your time online every day and the only language you encounter is English, Spanish or Mandarin or whatever else, then it tends to define the way you interact with the world. And over time you tend to lose either the interest in your own language or your competence [in that language].[14]

There are many dedicated people now addressing these problems. Kọ́lá Túbọ̀sún himself is an example. He has created an online Yoruba dictionary as well as a text-to-speech system for translating English into Yoruba for the benefit of people like his grandfather, who knows no English.

Some of the projects are driven by scientists with some of the world's top universities. For example, a team of tech experts from Stanford University, working with an AI researcher from the African nation of Guinea, has founded an organization called GNCode. Its mission is to make voice connections to digital technology possible for speakers of some lesser-used African languages. They gathered and organized radio broadcasting archives that captured hundreds of hours of

West African speech to serve as a data set for their work. Based on this raw material, they've developed the first speech recognition models for three African languages spoken by 10 million people in seven countries with low literacy rates—Maninka, Pular, and Susu. They've also prototyped a multilingual intelligent virtual assistant for speakers of these languages. And they've made their language data, code, and models available to other researchers in order to stimulate further work along the same lines.[15]

Other projects for expanding the reach of voice tools to less used languages are being supported by major tech organizations. For example, in April 2022, Amazon released a giant set of voice AI data in fifty-one languages. Dubbed MASSIVE, the data set is intended to encourage and support efforts to create multi-language, AI-driven voice tools for Alexa and other systems. Simultaneously, Amazon launched its Massively Multilingual NLU 2022 competition to select, honor, and publicize the best new tools created.[16]

Still other innovations are driven by grassroots efforts using open-source tools. Kathleen Siminyu is a data-science expert who grew up in Kenya, where millions of people use the language Kiswahili. But popular tech tools for speech recognition, natural language processing, and translation have not yet embraced Kiswahili. This leaves many Africans excluded from the use of such tools—or forced to restrict their online activities to English, a serious linguistic and cultural barrier for many.

Siminyu is working to overcome this problem. As a Kiswahili machine-learning fellow with the software company Mozilla, she is using Common Voice, a platform created by Mozilla, to assemble a vast corpus of speech and text files in her mother tongue. This data set will be a major resource for teams developing speech-to-text, natural language processing, and translation tools that can handle Kiswahili. The project has attracted a large number of willing volunteers among young Africans, for whom preserving and extending the life of Kiswahili is a matter of cultural pride as well as practical importance. And Siminyu is making a special effort to encourage contributions from women, whose voices are often underrepresented in the data sets used to train voice-tech tools—a subtle but important aspect of the inclusion challenge that voice technology is rising to meet.[17]

THE OPPORTUNITIES FOR BUSINESSES

As the stories and examples in this chapter show, AI-driven, voice-based tools, incorporated into technology systems used for purposes of education, government service, health care, and business, are increasingly opening doors for hundreds of millions of people who have long been excluded from many areas of mainstream life. These tools are having an enormously powerful impact on many organizations and people. Many stand to benefit:

- The tens of millions of Americans—and the billions of individuals around the world—who are functionally illiterate, and therefore find it difficult or impossible to use digital tools that require reading, including traditional web pages and mobile apps
- The hundreds of millions of people with a wide range of physical and functional disabilities, from those who have trouble using keyboards (such as people who are paralyzed or suffer from severe arthritis) to people with limited eyesight or hearing
- Marketers who need to sell goods and services to diverse customer groups in large, multiethnic markets who may not speak English or another of the currently dominant digital languages
- Doctors, nurses, and other health-care providers serving people of varied backgrounds and abilities in clinics and hospitals or via remote services

- Government agency workers who need to serve diverse populations with a wide range of native languages, varying literacy skills, and differing physical capabilities
- Employees of global companies who have to interact with colleagues, supervisors, and human resource specialists whose native language may be different from theirs

The impact of voice technology on employment opportunities around the world is likely to be particularly significant. Given the current progress in making voice tools available to users of practically all languages, it's foreseeable that, within a decade, language constraints on global employment will be largely eliminated. Companies doing business around the world will be able to employ staff members from almost anywhere to handle digital, clerical, and service work that currently demands literacy and, in many cases, knowledge of English or another major "mainstream" language.

One simple example: tagging data to images, for use cases such as the compilation of massive online product catalogs, is still a manual task. Today, this is largely gig work done in countries like India. A voice-first future will open these roles to workers who may be illiterate or semiliterate, allowing them to speak descriptions in whatever language they know, which would then be instantly translated and attached to the appropriate image. Access to jobs like these has the potential to help lift millions of people out of poverty.

In addition, many of the millions of people who are commonly thought of as "unemployable" due to physical or behavioral limitations can be integrated into mainstream jobs with the support of voice-based tools. I am thinking, for example, of an older member of my family whose work opportunities were limited by an undiagnosed learning disability. He got a job as a financial clerk but ended up losing it when the work was increasingly computerized. His problem was not a lack of intelligence, but rather an inability to absorb the written instructions used in teaching the new computer-based skills. If he were a student today, he could likely master the same information as his colleagues simply by using flexible tools like Speechify that would facilitate learning through a communication mode more appropriate for him—voice.

There are countless people who face challenges similar to the one that limited work options for my relative. In our research for this book, we've met many individuals and business leaders whose lives and careers have been transformed by voice tech.

Danielle Ralston is a business operations manager and career coach working out of Birmingham, Alabama. For years, she struggled to handle communications methods that came naturally to most of her colleagues. Taking notes while remaining engaged during a group meeting seemed very difficult, and she had trouble absorbing information from online instructional videos.

Eventually, Danielle discovered an expert who diagnosed her problem as ADHD—a common condition that affects millions of children and adults.[18] She also discovered that voice tools could help. She experimented with several popular speech-to-text tools, including the market leader, Dragon, and found that, for her purposes, they weren't quite right. Eventually she tried Otter, a speech-to-text and translation tool created by a California-based software company, which turned out to be her ideal business partner. Danielle now uses Otter to transcribe spoken notes and comments during live meetings and to capture takeaways during webinars and online classes. The written notes created by Otter are then sent to Danielle's assistant, who can edit them and, when needed, share them with colleagues and clients.

Danielle has since developed a successful coaching program designed especially for business leaders with ADHD. She has helped many executives and entrepreneurs overcome the same barriers that once thwarted her by teaching them to use voice tools to manage information. (Danielle notes that her daughter-in-law also uses Otter to capture notes and information from her college classes—and finds the software very helpful, although she does *not* have ADHD.)[19]

Lauren Becker is regional manager with the nonprofit Braille Institute of America in Laguna Hills, California, which provides a range of support services to people who are visually impaired. She must communicate regularly with some 500 clients as well as a team of seven staff members—one of whom is himself visually impaired. She makes use of a range of voice tools, including Dragon, Google, Cortana (which conducts voice-based data searches), and Amazon Lex (which uses AI to help people and organizations create conversational voice bots). These tools make it easy for her to make voice-based versions of memos, reports, brochures, meeting notes, and other documents available and usable by people with widely varying abilities.

She also found these tools to be a godsend when she suffered a wrist injury that made it difficult and painful for her to use a keyboard—a reminder that practically anyone can find themselves "disabled" at some point in their lives, even if only temporarily.[20]

As all the new tools described in this chapter illustrate, voice tech can play a major role in liberating and empowering individuals who have too long been excluded from mainstream society and its economic, educational, and cultural life. Whatever kind of organization you may help to lead, and no matter what kind of products or services you provide, you can probably use voice tech to make breakthroughs on behalf of a broader population of customers, as well as to cast a wider net when seeking candidates for employment. Integrating these hundreds of millions of people into the world economy will create tremendous opportunities for businesses eager to serve them.

5

ENGAGEMENT

Making Life More Creative, Entertaining, and Enjoyable

INCREASED PRODUCTIVITY IN THE FORM OF GREATER SPEED and convenience can fuel the adoption of a new technology. Yet it's often the entertainment value of a new technology that drives it into the consumer mainstream. Steve Jobs deeply understood this when he made music the centerpiece of his iPod/iPhone strategy. Today, voice is positioned not only to create new paradigms of entertainment, but to be the cornerstone of an entirely new type of media—*generative AI*—which, in turn, is likely to be the primary building block for the emerging digital arena known as the *metaverse*.

Generative AI tools like ChatGPT (which is text-based) and DALL-E (which is image-based), both developed by OpenAI, took the world by storm in late 2022. But the story of generative AI goes back much farther. Like most "instant hits," it's been many years in the making, and will take many more years to achieve its full potential.

Let's begin with a simple example that illustrates how generative AI works.

Actor Val Kilmer was just fifty-six years old in 2015 when the voice that had helped power him to stardom was stolen by throat cancer. It seemed likely that he would never be able to use that familiar voice again. In the past, this would have been a career-ending event. But in 2020, the UK-based AI company Sonantic (since purchased by Spotify) worked with Kilmer to recreate his voice. Using just thirty minutes of audio clips from old Kilmer movies—the amount limited by legal licensing restraints—Sonantic's algorithm was able to produce an artificial version of Kilmer's youthful voice that can read lines of dramatic dialogue and even convey the impression of a character's powerful emotions as needed.

For the movie sequel *Top Gun: Maverick* (which was released and became an instant megahit in 2022), Kilmer was able to reprise his role from the original 1986 film thanks to Sonantic's AI-based voice technology. The actor's cancer survival saga, voice loss, and recovery were even written into the sequel's script as part of his character's history.[1]

In the years to come, Kilmer will be able to use the custom-built voice-synthesis software to take on other new acting assignments, unhampered by the physical limitations his cancer produced. The software uses recordings of his youthful voice to "speak" the new dialogue that is then spliced into a movie or video, while Kilmer acts the role. "It's exclusively his model," Sonantic's CEO Zeena Qureshi says of the underlying algorithm. "He could use it for personal use or professional use if he wants to."[2]

It's easy to imagine a host of practical benefits that this new voice-synthesis technology can provide, especially for the entertainment industry in which Kilmer has built his career. An actor whose vocal cords have been scorched by many takes of a demanding movie scene—an angry quarrel involving lots of screaming, for example—can use the software to speak for her until her natural voice recovers. The same technology can also enable a filmmaker to record additional dialogue demanded by a last-minute script revision even if the actors involved are busy on a different project, thereby avoiding costly production delays that could derail the planned release of a picture. These show-business applications of voice synthesis will produce concrete, dollars-and-cents advantages for movie and TV studios, radio and podcast producers, and similar companies in the decades to come.

But at its core, voice-synthesis technology is an amazing artistic accomplishment with powerful human implications. As Kilmer says in an audio clip for Sonantic, narrated by his new synthetic voice,

> When we think of the most talented creative people, they speak to us in a unique way. A phrase we often hear is "Having a creative voice." But I was struck by throat cancer. After getting treated, my voice as I knew it was taken away from me. People around me struggle to understand me when I'm talking. But despite all that, I still feel I'm the exact same person. Still the same creative soul. A soul that dreams ideas and stories constantly. But now I can express myself again. I can bring these dreams to you and show you this part of myself once more. A part that was never truly gone. Just hiding away.[3]

The previous chapters in this book have spelled out many of the practical benefits that voice technology is beginning to produce. Some, like the voice-based safety tools now being created for auto dashboards and jet cockpits, are literally matters of life and death. Others are making business activities like customer service, marketing and selling, and the supply of accurate information more convenient and accessible than ever. Still others, like the voice-driven productivity tools winning adoption in offices and factories around the world, are helping to make internal organizational processes more efficient and profitable.

But human beings don't spend all their time grappling with practical challenges. Just as important are the ways that voice will make all our lives more creative, productive, entertaining, exciting, surprising— in a word, more fun.

WHY FUN IS A CRUCIAL INGREDIENT IN
A NEW TECHNOLOGY BREAKTHROUGH

History shows us that the human drive for sheer enjoyment—what Freud called "the pleasure principle"—has always been a prime mover behind the adoption of new technologies.

Radio originated as a tool used by oceangoing sailors, military commanders, and weather-forecasting services. But it exploded in popularity when innovative uses driven purely by their entertainment value were launched, beginning with the first broadcasts of prizefights and baseball games by KDKA in Pittsburgh in 1921 and reaching an early peak with the invention of the soap opera in the 1930s.

Television was transformed from a curiosity in a few thousand homes to a mainstream staple after slapstick-laden shows like *Howdy Doody* and Milton Berle's *Texaco Star Theater* were embraced by millions of fans.

The PC revolution of the 1980s was sparked, in part, by practical applications like VisiCalc, the first widely used digital-spreadsheet program—but an outsize role in popularizing home computers was played by games like Microsoft's *Flight Simulator* and *Adventure*.[4]

The smartphone is a superior tool for convenient communication, but it made its way into billions of pockets and purses because it also provides the world's favorite camera, music player, gaming device, and more.

In all these cases, tech innovations were originally designed with practical benefits in mind. But they swept the world largely because millions of people discovered how much *fun* they provided.

In a similar way, voice interaction and generative AI have the potential to create a significant number of applications that are purely fun. Because voice-activated tools and apps don't require carrying around a keyboard or the distraction of staring at a screen, they can become an integral, natural part of many of our most enjoyable pastimes.

We'll explore some of the innovative ways that voice technology will bring greater personal enjoyment to our daily lives, as well as the huge new business opportunities it will create for companies in media, entertainment, gaming, travel, consumer product marketing, and advertising. Which means that, in the long run, the distinction between "pure fun" and "practical benefits" isn't quite as rigid as one might assume. Fun can also be enormously profitable.

FROM PASSIVE TO ACTIVE: ENTERTAINMENT THAT'S YOURS FOR THE ASKING

Music and video streaming are among today's most widespread uses of digital technology, and the voice interface has already become one of the most popular ways of searching for and controlling online entertainment choices. Siri and Alexa are used millions of times daily to call up favorite tunes, radio programs, podcasts, and other forms of audio entertainment. TV remote-control systems like those produced for Roku and Amazon Fire TV now routinely include voice-control functions that eliminate the need to type out the name of a show or to scroll by hand through lists of hundreds of available movies. And smart TVs, with built-in voice-control systems, have become the most popular "smart home" devices on the market, having penetrated almost 40 percent of American households as of 2021.[5]

Now Spotify, the world's most popular music streaming service, is among those creating new ways to use the voice connection to make entertainment even more ubiquitous and enjoyable. In 2020, Spotify patented a tool that augments its existing speech-recognition technology to analyze additional information about the user before making a song or playlist recommendation—information that includes the user's "emotional state, gender, age, or accent," as well as "environmental metadata" about their location. (To address privacy concerns, this kind of analysis will need to be triggered by a specific user request and permission.)

Result: soon, at times and in places when you want it to happen, a simple voice command will empower Spotify to automatically provide you with the perfect music to fit your mood—or to transform it.

Other fun-oriented voice innovations that enhance our entertainment options are steadily appearing. Many are focused on transforming the entertainment experience from passive enjoyment to active engagement. Clubhouse, for example, is a wildly popular "social audio app" that lets fans use their voices to connect directly with celebrity performers they admire, from musicians and actors to athletes. Performers like Oprah Winfrey, Drake, Ashton Kutcher, Kevin Hart, and Chris Rock were among the first to appear in Clubhouse "rooms," answering fans' questions and responding to their comments. The celebrity visits helped to drive the app's membership from some 10,000 in October 2020 to more than 10 million just four months later. The later appearances of business celebrities—including controversial figures like Elon Musk and Mark Zuckerberg—attracted additional attention to the site.[6]

Clubhouse's success has spurred a host of competitors to challenge its leadership of the social audio space. Spotify Live, for example, which the music service company purchased under its original name of Locker Room, allows popular figures to participate in group audio conversations with up to 1,000 fans at a time. Rapper Waka Flocka Flame, *Call Her Daddy* host Alex Cooper, and comedian Hasan Minhaj were among the celebrities who appeared in 2022.[7] In a similar vein, digital-radio streaming site Gimme Radio has created a social audio site dedicated to fans of two wildly disparate music genres—heavy metal and country. Those who visit the Gimme Metal and Gimme Country sites are able to connect with their favorite artists as well as other fans, choose the music played by the DJs, buy concert tickets and merchandise, and even donate online payments—"tips"—to musicians who many believe have been shortchanged by the corporations that dominate the traditional record companies.[8]

Technology has always impacted the way we enjoy entertainment. But the connections of twentieth-century media were one-way-only transmissions that left audiences unable to talk back. In the new era of voice, that is changing. Not only are audiences able to curate their own playlists with greater ease and flexibility than ever before—now they are even able to communicate directly with the artists they love thanks to Clubhouse, Spotify Live, and other voice tools accessible by the phones in everyone's pocket.

DRIVING THE NEW WORLD OF GENERATIVE AI

The story of Val Kilmer's post-cancer voice re-creation vividly illustrates how, as natural-language-generation methods continue to improve, software designers are increasingly able to deploy digitally created voices that sound convincingly human and individually distinctive. Thanks to algorithmic tools that can understand what other people say and that use AI to formulate logical, appropriate responses, these artificial voices are also increasingly able to engage in realistic, spontaneous conversations while expressing appropriate emotions through variations in timbre, volume, tone, pacing, and pitch.

There's a limitless range of applications for these lifelike digital voices—and many of the most remarkable will be in the world of entertainment. In particular, these digital voices will be at the heart of the new technology of generative AI, which combines video, other forms of visual content, and audio content into a seamless whole, designed with the help of artificial intelligence and featuring an unprecedented degree of realism and immersiveness.[9]

One simple form of generative AI is the use of voice-synthesis technology to recreate familiar voices from the real world with a convincing authenticity no human impressionist could match. Filmmakers are already producing mainstream movies that take advantage of this new capability, and in some cases the process has stirred controversy. In 2021, director Morgan Neville used speech-generating AI software to replicate the voice of legendary chef, author, and TV host Anthony Bourdain in a documentary film, *Roadrunner*, produced after Bourdain's death. In the film, only a handful of lines from Bourdain's writings, involving about forty-five seconds' worth of synthesized speech, were generated using AI; most of the movie's voice-overs were drawn from thousands of hours of video and audio recordings left behind after his death. But in part because the filmmaker chose not to disclose the use of AI-driven voice technology to moviegoers—and in part because of disagreement over whether Bourdain's widow Ottavia Busia-Bourdain had authorized its use—many fans reacted negatively, calling the sound of Bourdain's synthesized voice in the movie "awful" and "ghoulish."

New Yorker writer Helen Rosner considered some of the ethical issues around the Bourdain voice simulation in a July 2021 article. Among those she quoted was Sam Gregory, a director who heads a nonprofit organization that examines ethical questions related to documentary filmmaking. Gregory told Rosner that the controversy in the Bourdain case might be related largely to the newness of voice tech:

> "I'm not sure that it's even all that much about what the director did in this film—it's because it's triggering us to think how this will play out, in terms of our norms of what's acceptable, our expectations of media," he said. "It may well be that in a couple of years we are comfortable with this, in the same way we're comfortable with a narrator reading a poem, or a letter from the Civil War."[10]

By contrast, no backlash greeted the use of similar technology in *The Andy Warhol Diaries*, a documentary series released by Netflix in 2022. In this case, voice synthesis software produced by the company Resemble AI created a digital voice that mimicked Warhol's own voice, with its accent drawn from his boyhood home of Pittsburgh. The digital voice was then blended with that of actor Bill Irwin reading excerpts from letters by Warhol, drawn from a book with the same title as the film. Thus, the documentary was able to feature the pop artist's reflections on his life in spoken tones practically the same as his own—thirty-five years after his death in 1987.[11]

It seems likely that the Warhol film escaped the pushback experienced by *Roadrunner* for at least three reasons. First, the use of voice tech to simulate Warhol's voice was openly acknowledged on screen. Second, director Andrew Rossi sought, and received, advance permission to use the technology from the Andy Warhol Foundation, which was also acknowledged in the film. Third, and perhaps most important, a year had passed since the Bourdain controversy, giving the public more time to become accustomed to the idea of "fake" voices being used for entertainment purposes.

In Part Two, we'll return to the ethical issues surrounding generative AI technologies—including their potential misuse for deceptive or propagandistic purposes. It will be important for filmmakers and others who use AI voice synthesis to create entertainment products to adhere to basic standards to avoid misleading and alienating audiences. But in the years to come, voice-synthesis tools will be used more and more widely by filmmakers, audio producers, podcasters, and other creative artists for a wide range of applications. As this happens, the public in general will become more and more accustomed to such uses—just as few people today are surprised by the idea that a photo might be retouched or altered for use in a magazine. And these new voice tools will open up many creative new avenues for artistic expression, in movies and elsewhere.

One simple yet valuable use of voice synthesis in entertainment is as a substitute for live actors in the dubbing of foreign translations for movie dialogue. Deepdub, an Israeli-based AI company, has begun using this technology to create artificial voices for entire movie casts, based on sample recordings of the original actors speaking in their native tongues. Thus, in early 2022, the American horror movie *Every Time I Die* was released across South America with a Deepdub-generated soundtrack in which the on-screen characters speak believable Spanish or Portuguese—all without the investment of time and money required to assemble a live cast of actors and record the complete movie soundtrack all over again.

In an even more creative vein, AI is also being used to generate variations on movie actors' voices to fit specific artistic needs. When the character of Luke Skywalker appeared in the 2020 series *The Mandalorian*—looking and sounding much as he did in the original *Star Wars* movie in 1977—computer-generated special effects were used to produce a youthful visual avatar for seventy-year-old actor Mark Hamill. But advanced voice tools also played a crucial role. The voice of young Luke was simulated by software from the AI company Respeecher, which built a voice-generating algorithm based on snippets of Hamill's dialogue from the 1977 movie, as well as excerpts from an audiobook recorded by Hamill around the same time.[12]

There are many other creative uses of generative AI technology that entertainment companies will eventually explore. Theme-park visitors touring a movie-based attraction might be able to interact with avatars that can engage in spontaneous conversations using the voices of familiar performers—Daniel Radcliffe in his role as Harry Potter, Gal Gadot as Wonder Woman, the late Mel Blanc as a wisecracking Bugs Bunny. Filmmakers depicting historic events might recreate dramatic moments using synthetic voices that replicate those of the real participants—Eisenhower addressing the troops on D-Day, Rosa Parks refusing to sit in the back of the bus in Montgomery.

In recent years, audiobooks have been the fastest-growing segment of the publishing industry. But recording the full text of a 300-page book is a laborious task that requires days in the studio—as well as elocutionary skills most authors don't possess. Voice-synthesis technology has the potential to transform the process.

In fact, the incursion of generative AI into the audiobook realm has already begun—and, again, it has sparked some controversy. Popular film and TV actor Edward Herrmann, who died in 2014, also served as narrator for audiobooks by authors like Stephen King and Walter Isaacson. Now his synthesized voice has been made available by London-based start-up DeepZen through an arrangement with Herrmann's estate.[13]

New books narrated by the synthetic Herrmann contain a disclosure notice. But as of 2022, they are *not* available on Amazon's Audible platform, which is the most popular distribution service for audiobooks. The reason is an Audible policy requiring live human narrators on every audiobook it offers. The policy dates back to 2014, a time when voice-synthesis technology was much cruder than it is today; it was put in place as part of an effort to maintain high quality standards for Audible products. Customers who want to buy a new audiobook narrated by the digitized Herrmann must visit another online store, such as those run by Google or Apple.

(In fact, as we were writing this chapter, in January 2023, Apple announced the launch of its own service to provide AI-powered narration for audiobooks using a suite of synthetic voices designed to complement various writing styles. The service is designed to cater to self-published authors and small independent publishers, both of whom have often shied away from entering the audiobook market because of the expense of hiring a live narrator. A small selection of sample audiobooks is already available for purchase.)[14]

Now that the improved quality of synthetic voices has made them generally indistinguishable from live human performances, it's only a matter of time before Audible's policy against them is lifted. Some professional narrators worry that voice synthesis will eventually displace them. For some audiobook projects, that will probably happen. Among other reasons, the use of synthetic voices in audiobooks often makes economic sense. Many books have limited or niche audiences whose size may not justify the significant investment required to hire a live narrator to create an audiobook. The more affordable cost of a synthesized narrator offers a solution. Similarly, synthetic audio can provide an economical way to produce audio versions of books in languages that are less widely spoken than English.

On the other hand, the most talented and sought-after human voices may become *more* valuable when their availability can be expanded through voice synthesis. Next year's best-selling thriller could be presented in audiobook form using the synthesized voice—and the dramatic skills—of, say, an Anthony Hopkins or a Keanu Reeves. The next pop singing megastar turned author could produce the audiobook version of her published memoir using a synthesized version of her voice—and without having to cancel a single lucrative concert gig.

And as the Edward Herrmann example illustrates, the earning potential of a much-loved performer can be extended even beyond death through the power of generative AI. It's easy to imagine that we will soon be able to send personalized audio messages using the voices of favorite personalities, past and present—Marilyn Monroe singing "Happy Birthday" especially for your dad, or John Lennon inviting callers to "Imagine" an inspirational message to leave on your answering machine.

Eventually, generative AI may enable studios to release brand-new movies and TV shows featuring history's most iconic stars. John Wayne, Ingrid Bergman, Fred Astaire, and Judy Garland may all be returning to the silver screen before long—provided that appropriate legal arrangements can be made with their heirs and representatives, of course.

PLAYING GAMES IN A METAVERSE OF VOICES

Voice technology is also poised to create revolutionary new forms of fun in the vastly popular world of digital gaming. It's a world in which voice technology is already playing a significant role.

Voice-based quiz games played through popular devices like Siri and Alexa, such as *Question of the Day*, *Song Quiz*, and *Popcorn Tycoon*, skyrocketed in popularity during the lockdown period of COVID-19 in 2020–2021. The fad seems to have legs beyond the pandemic; experts say that as many as 7 million individuals play such games every day. In addition to creating new voice games, the game development company Volley (which has been buying up other developers in the field) is also forging licensing deals with preexisting game-show brands like

The Price Is Right, Are You Smarter Than a 5th Grader?, and *Who Wants to Be a Millionaire?*[15]

It makes intuitive sense that generations of quiz-show fans who have vicariously participated in voice-based gaming through TV shows like *Jeopardy!* (another of the shows for which Volley has purchased the gaming rights) would gravitate naturally to voice-based games they can play at home, at work, in their car, or wherever they may be. What's more, tech-assisted voice games don't require you to assemble a group of live competitors to have fun, as demanded by traditional board games like Trivial Pursuit—you can compete one-on-one, anytime, against your AI-driven opponent.

However, the most dramatic voice-based innovations in gaming will likely be connected with role-playing fantasy games. Voice-company executives foresee customized voices individually designed by gamers bringing imaginary characters to life more vividly than ever before. When you create your personalized avatar to compete in a fantasy world—a swashbuckling pirate, a scepter-carrying queen, a wand-waving wizard—you will also be able to develop a unique voice to accompany the character, whose spoken commands will shape the action on the digital playing field.

Competition to convert this alluring possibility into a practical reality became especially fierce during 2020–2021 with the development of the *metaverse*—a network of virtual worlds in which people will interact with one another and with their environments in one or more imaginary 3D spaces. The buzzword entered the popular lexicon in 2021 when the corporation behind Facebook renamed itself Meta—and reportedly invested more than $10 billion to develop its own slice of the metaverse.[16] Many other companies have since jumped on the metaverse bandwagon, and leaders in industries from entertainment, travel, and retail to finance and marketing are scrambling to figure out whether the metaverse is really going to live up to its apparent potential—and, if so, how they can grab their piece of the action.

According to metaverse enthusiasts, it will be a vast, complex creation, facilitating activities that include social engagement, commercial transactions, educational forums, and artistic projects. However, in the short run, the most popular use of the metaverse will likely be to provide staging areas for role-playing games. Already, popular video games like *Habbo*, *World of Warcraft*, *Minecraft*, and *Fortnite* have found a home in the metaverse, and purpose-built metaverse games such as *Axie Infinity* and *Decentraland* are attracting legions of followers.

A range of technologies are being adopted to help make the metaverse a reality. If the metaverse is going to succeed, several technologies will have to be further developed and made truly seamless for the end user. These include virtual reality (VR) headsets like Oculus Quest, which provide immersive, 3D-like experiences, and blockchain currency, which can be used to buy and sell goods and services in the virtual marketplace.

But generative AI will also be crucial to creating the sense of reality and immediacy that will be essential to the success of the metaverse—and that includes great voice-tech tools. While many aspects of the future of the metaverse remain unclear, one fact that practically all observers agree on is that voice will be its dominant communication method. For this reason, companies seeking a foothold in this new technological frontier are pushing hard to improve their voice-tech capabilities on many fronts. One example is the massive effort being undertaken by Meta to build a next-generation voice assistant, one that has advanced "beyond the current state of the art for smart assistants" to "support true world creation and exploration," in the words of Mark Zuckerberg.[17]

Is this a practical or realistic approach? The jury is still out. As we've shown through several examples, users tend to shy away from human-like, all-encompassing assistants, which all too often fall into the alienating "uncanny valley." The challenge is further complicated by the sheer complexity of making human avatars that can simulate most of the human experience. It's much easier to create a voice experience that just answers your banking questions!

To attempt to make Zuckerberg's vision of the future happen, Meta has been pursuing a project known as CAIRaoke (the first four letters of the name stand for *conversational AI research*). Its goal is to build a self-learning AI model capable of training itself rather than relying on training through curated data sets, which is the traditional way in which AI models have been developed. For example, a software development team trying to build an AI tool capable of telling jokes might load up thousands of examples of real-world jokes into the system. By studying the characteristics of these jokes and learning to mimic them, the AI tool would gradually learn how to respond when a user makes a request like "Tell me a joke about golf."

By contrast, self-learning models, like the one CAIRaoke hopes to build, are capable of finding and analyzing relevant training cases themselves. The engineers at Meta hope that CAIRaoke will make it much easier for organizations that want to participate in the metaverse to create avatars that can simulate human-style interactions.

Meta's goals for the metaverse include the ability for a user to simply *speak* what she wants to see in virtual reality and have it immediately appear—a tool Meta calls a "BuilderBot."[18] Imagine being a virtual traveler navigating through a medieval-style fantasy world and encountering an impassable canyon separating you from the enchanted castle that represents the end of your quest. You'll be able to say to the BuilderBot, "I need a rope bridge across that canyon," and have one materialize within a few seconds. Then, if a fire-breathing dragon jumps out from a nearby cave, you can tell the BuilderBot, "Give me a sword and a fireproof shield," and your avatar will instantly have a fighting chance to survive the fearful encounter.

Making the metaverse feel like a real world in which true-to-life experiences can happen requires powerful voice tools. In pursuit of this goal, companies that build VR hardware are investing heavily in *spatial audio* technology, which creates an authentic-sounding "sense of presence" that reinforces the visual cues that produce the illusion of real life—the distant sound of the rushing river at the bottom of the canyon, the roar of the flames as they belch from the throat of the dragon. (Of course, spatial audio doesn't enhance only the game-playing experience; it's also extremely helpful when conducting meetings for business or other purposes in the metaverse, making it easier to identify which member of a group is speaking.)[19]

At the same time, technology companies are working hard to enhance the other side of the voice experience in the metaverse—to give users the ability to communicate with any kind of voice they like, whether gaming or engaging in other activities. Spanish-based Voicemod, for example, has long used digital signal processing (DSP) tools to tweak voices, letting an individual sound like a robot or the *Star Wars* character Darth Vader, for example. Now it is expanding its capabilities, learning both to create all-new synthetic voices and to help people sound better while interacting in the metaverse. They've begun licensing their technology to makers of headphones and VR headsets, so that voice-altering software will be built into the hardware itself. "We want to be the voice of the metaverse," Voicemod CEO Jaime Bosch declares.[20] And if you like, your voice will be able to replicate that of your favorite personality, whether you fancy yourself sounding like a comical Gilbert Gottfried, a sultry Lauren Bacall, or a dignified Morgan Freeman.

It remains to be seen whether the metaverse will, in fact, become the primary arena for technological innovation and discovery in the decades to come. But if it does, voice tech will be one of the most crucial tool sets that make it possible.

CATERING TO THE VOICE-NATIVE GENERATION

JetBlue was an early pioneer of bringing live television onto airplanes. Today they are still one of the few airlines to offer a complete live-TV experience similar to one you might have via satellite or cable in your home.

I've always found it delightful to be able to watch live news and sports while in the air. But a recent flight with my school-age kids made the future power of voice very clear to me. As we deplaned, I asked them how they liked the live TV. The kids responded with eye-opening dismissiveness, contrasting the experience with the voice-based streaming commands they have at home: "Why couldn't we just *tell* the TV what we wanted to watch? Instead, we had to click around these annoying 'channels'!"

My kids instinctively understand what business leaders are now discovering—that voice is the mode of communication that comes most naturally to humans. Therefore, any task that can be converted into a voice interaction will instantly feel easier and more natural. As time passes, the next generation—including my own kids—are growing up as *voice natives*, intuitively comfortable with using voice technologies and insisting on the ease and simplicity that voice communication makes possible.

In response to this social change, one of the biggest explosions of fun-oriented voice applications will be centered on the needs and interests of children. In the years to come, kids will enjoy a profusion of smart toys, apps, web services, books, and other interactive devices that are voice-based. Many of the emerging voice-driven products for kids will combine entertainment with education, providing these voice natives with countless new ways to play, create, learn, and grow, even before they've become proficient at the traditional skills of reading and writing.

One example that hit the market during 2022 is Snorble, an "intelligent buddy" designed to connect with small kids during the often-troublesome hour when they are getting ready for bed. Snorble serves as a bedtime companion for toddlers, talking them through rituals like bathing, toothbrushing, and donning pajamas; when it's time for lights out, Snorble can tell them a story and even help them perform breathing exercises accompanied by calming music and a light show.[21] The hope is that kids will find it entertaining, while parents will find it a helpful tool for easing the transition from day to night.

So far, the business buzz about Snorble has been positive: *Toy Insider*, an industry publication, named Snorble one of its Top Holiday Toys for 2022. But kids and parents themselves will decide whether or not it emerges as a popular favorite. Some may consider it an example of "voice gone too far," one that asks a digital device to take over tasks that parents themselves have traditionally handled.

Yet Snorble is entering a market for voice-based toys that is already large and growing. More and more families are becoming fans of voice-based games for kids, which could be considered a positive change of pace from screen time spent passively staring at a tablet or a TV. To serve this market, Volley, the voice-game company behind quiz games like *Question of the Day*, offers an array of games designed for kids and families. One is *Yes Sire*, in which players imagine themselves as rulers of a medieval-style kingdom. Some parents say they like the fact that kids are challenged to use their imaginations to envision the world of the game—to picture the kind of castle they'd like to inhabit and then to modify it in their mind's eye, for example.[22]

Other games, like those from Pretzel Labs, use voice tech to help kids practice real-life skills. In *Kids Court*, children who are having an argument get to make their case before a voice assistant who helps them resolve their differences. (This game won the grand prize in a competition for kid-centered skills conducted by Amazon.)[23] *Garbage Hero* challenges kids to help the people of Stinkytown learn to recycle their trash and save their challenged environment.

As you can imagine, the looming metaverse and the explosion of generative AI are playing a big role in the future planning of companies that cater to kids. In February 2022, Disney appointed Mike White, a veteran company executive, to the role of "senior vice president of next-generation storytelling and consumer experiences," and charged him with developing a strategy for all of Disney's activities related to the metaverse. The first Disney flag planted in the metaverse: a new

AI-driven theme park assistant named Genie, which will be added to the My Disney Experience and Disneyland apps.[24]

Other companies are joining the land rush. Lego Group, one of the world's biggest creators of toys and games, has teamed up to build a kid-friendly metaverse with Epic Games, developer of *Fortnite* and proprietors of a platform known as MetaHuman Creator, which produces unusually realistic virtual people for use in games and other activities.[25] And smaller companies are jockeying for position as well—for example, Snorble, maker of the bedtime buddy, is also developing a "digital experience" platform called Lullaboo that it plans to make an entry point to its own corner of the metaverse.

Like the adult version of the metaverse, the kids' version will be heavily dependent on voice technology. If the vision of tech impresarios like Mark Zuckerberg comes true, we may see millions of people of all ages roaming the virtual worlds of cyberspace, using voice tech in combination with other digital tools to play, explore, and create—and having fun in innovative ways we can only imagine today.

THE OPPORTUNITIES FOR BUSINESSES

As we've seen, in today's world, the line between entertainment and commerce—between pure fun and business-driven applications—is blurry at best. And the companies that can derive serious economic benefits from the use of voice technology won't be limited to movie studios and game developers.

Advertisers will use the new generative AI tools for solid economic purposes that are also fun—for example, to create customized product spokespeople who can flexibly and persuasively interact with consumers. It's easy to imagine an animated Mr. Clean answering consumer questions about tough stain-removal challenges, or a digital Betty Crocker providing customized recipe advice for home bakers. Equipped with appropriate, synthesized voices and AI-powered stores of useful information for consumers, brand avatars like these could become celebrities in their own right with large, avid fan bases.

The metaverse is likely to be one of the main arenas in which these new developments will play out. In fact, as it grows and develops, the metaverse will have the potential to transform many of the ways we shop for goods and services. Gaea Vilage of voice-tech company Read-Speaker describes three kinds of commerce we can expect to experience in the metaverse:

- *Buying virtual goods for use in the metaverse.* You'll be able to use real money to buy virtual items—clothes, tools, vehicles, houses, and much more—for your avatar to use as you play games, interact with friends, and otherwise explore the metaverse.

- *Shopping for real-world goods in a virtual store.* Your avatar will be able to walk into a virtual shop, talk with a sales associate, try on an item of clothing or some other product, and then make a purchase—which will arrive on your real-world doorstep in a day or two.

- *Taking part in a virtual brand experience.* Love the outdoors? You'll be able to go kayaking on a river in the metaverse using a craft from L.L. Bean—available for purchase later if you like the way it handles.[26]

Some of these developments are speculative—but they are rapidly becoming realities. In March 2022, some sixty brands, including Tommy Hilfiger, Fred Segal, and Estée Lauder participated in the first-ever Metaverse Fashion Week. The event included virtual shopping in digital stores, concerts, branded parties, and other activities.[27] Other companies are experimenting with their own metaverse-based shopping options. Amazon is inviting customers for its furniture and home-decor products to visit their Room Decorator space in the metaverse, where they can see what items they're considering for purchase will look like in their own homes. Eyewear giant Warby Parker can let you try on any pair of frames from its product catalog in the metaverse.[28] CVS Health is planning a digital pharmacy where users can get nutritional coaching, receive health advice, and stock up on health and beauty products, including prescription drugs. And Victoria's Secret is reportedly considering reviving its once-popular, now-defunct fashion show as a regular event in the metaverse.[29]

For all of these creative new ways of experiencing brands and products in the metaverse, voice-tech tools will be crucial. As Gaea Vilage of ReadSpeaker points out, "Think about the ways we interact with the digital world: keyboards, mouses, taps, and swipes. None of those are currently available in the metaverse. . . . [F]or now, voice is the simplest way to interact with metaverse systems."[30]

To make this work, tech companies are working with social media giants like Meta and branded-commerce companies to perfect the digital tools needed to make voice as flexible, reliable, and easy to use in the metaverse as it is in the real world. Voice biometrics, which we've seen at use in real-world banking applications, will play an important role in validating your identity before you make purchases in the metaverse. Shopping assistants and other company representatives in the metaverse will need to be equipped with high-level skills for conversational AI so they can respond in spontaneous, natural ways to encounters with avatars.

What's more, not every business has a preexisting human symbol like Mr. Clean or Betty Crocker. Companies doing business in the virtual space of the metaverse will need to devote time and energy to designing their own generative AI avatars that embody their brands effectively and consistently—in terms of voice, physical appearance, perceived personality, behavioral characteristics, and deep knowledge and understanding of consumer needs and interests. When done poorly, this could have the potential for producing embarrassing and damaging online experiences. But when done well, it will offer an amazing new way to combine fun with commerce to create profitable, lasting bonds between companies and their customers.

6

TRANSFORMATION

Voice-Enabled Business Models That Will
Change Industry Landscapes

RECALL MY KIDS' COMPLAINTS ABOUT THE NEED TO USE OLD-fashioned menus and buttons to select TV programs on an airline flight. They're not alone. The next generation of consumers—those who will come to dominate marketplaces and entire economies over the next twenty to forty years—will be voice natives, for whom using speech to communicate with devices will be natural and taken for granted, and for whom anything less convenient will simply be unacceptable.

The impact of this change can't be overstated. In response to this new demand, service and product providers of all kinds—for-profit businesses, nonprofit organizations, and government agencies—will be required to make voice connections a routine option whenever they serve the public. The resulting ease of access will make products, tools, and services available more freely, frequently, and widely than ever. We've already seen a number of examples, from the travel information Cerence makes instantly accessible in your car to the patient data a busy nurse can retrieve, immediately and hands-free, just by asking the Smartbadge "genie" to deliver it.

Even more important, *the shift to multimodal voice will also empower and accelerate fundamental changes to business models.* Because voice will eliminate existing constraints and friction points in many industries and across numerous forms of user interaction, we will not simply do what we do today faster. We will also find completely new ways of doing things.

The TV viewing habits of my kids and millions of their peers represent one obvious example. As the emergence of voice portends the death of the TV channel, it heralds a basic reorganization of the media industry, in which the delivery model shifts from whatever TV executives program on a channel to what individual consumers choose to demand.

As of this writing in 2023, we are in the midst of this transformation. The so-called *linear programming* delivered via channels remains a feature of broadcast and cable television. But users are no longer passively accepting this mode of content delivery. Instead, they are becoming accustomed to navigating straight to the content they want, and they are increasingly demanding this option. Until recently, they have been constrained to using either visual navigation or search tools that force them to type letters on remote controls, which is awkward and error-prone. Voice search finally allows users to navigate directly to the content they want.

Media companies are still adjusting to this new model. They are discovering that the game of cross-promoting content (for example, by slotting in a new show right after an established hit, by running ads for one show during another, or by picking off users looking for one streaming movie and proposing an alternate title to them) is getting harder and less effective. As more and more viewers use voice to navigate straight to the shows they want, the old media adage "Content is king, but distribution is King Kong" is losing its force. New ways to attract and keep viewer interest will need to be developed by marketers for networks, cable channels, and streaming services if they hope to remain relevant.

As we'll see, the media business is just one example of the growing impact of voice. In both a literal and a figurative sense, the voice of the consumer is now being heard more clearly and loudly than ever. As a result, disruptive changes are in store for one industry after another.

MANAGING DAILY ACTIVITIES THE EASIEST WAY—VIA VOICE

The convenience of voice is so compelling that it is already making its way into many of our daily activities. Voice-based tools are rapidly becoming the mode of choice for controlling such home devices as thermostats, lights, doorbells, security systems, lawn sprinklers, and more. Paying for basic purchases of goods and services, from gasoline at the pump to parking time at the garage, is increasingly being facilitated by voice tools accessed through your cell phone.

Then there are other tasks that we perform so frequently and automatically that we tend to think of them as part of the natural order of things—even though they are often irksome and irritating. Voice can change all that.

Consider the task of establishing your identity whenever you visit a website or open an app. As we saw in Chapter 2, this can be an important matter of security. But it's also a significant time drain—a chore many of us must perform many times each day. For most people, it generally involves remembering and laboriously typing in a unique password, which is not only time-consuming but error-prone. According to one 2017 study, the average internet user is registered to ninety online accounts—each requiring a unique password, again as a matter of security—and 25 percent of users forget at least one password per day. As a result, forgotten passwords are the underlying cause for one-third of all online sales abandoned at checkout.[1] The frustration for users—and the huge economic loss for businesses—is self-evident. (To the great amusement of our family, my wife gave her seventy-eight-year-old mother a birthday card this year that said "Hooray! I remembered my password!")

The good news is that this irritating routine is rapidly becoming outmoded. You'll soon find yourself making regular use of voice-recognition software that identifies you simply by hearing your voice—an identification method that is even more secure when combined with other biometric factors like facial or thumbprint recognition. This multimodal approach to online security is both difficult to hack and largely passive, allowing the user to seamlessly engage with technology rather than having to work at it.

At WillowTree, we've been testing these passive, voice-based identification systems for years, and we've seen them steadily improving in reliability and ease of use. As a result, more companies are adopting them, and more individual users are opting to use them. My personal experience confirms that they are a delight to use; I can't imagine ever wanting to go back to the old system of having to type in a password, PIN, email address, or Social Security number, or especially two-factor, password-based authentication.

Voice recognition is now secure enough so that other financial firms, including Chase Bank and Wells Fargo, have joined Schwab in relying on voice recognition as a tool for signing in to your bank account. Because of these trends, Grand View Research, one of the leading market research firms, has looked closely at the market for voice-recognition software and is forecasting significant increases in demand. Grand View estimates that the global market for voice-recognition systems—that is, the money invested by companies to deploy voice recognition and processing systems across early adopting industries such as automotive, health care, B2B, financial services, retail, military, education, and government—will grow from about $14 billion in 2022 to more than $53 billion by 2030.[2] These investments are happening because voice recognition is rapidly becoming the new standard that will eventually make today's inconvenient log-in methods appear ludicrous.

Another daily activity that is ripe for transformation is calling a business for personal service, whether it's to get help with a product problem, to make a travel or dining reservation, to manage an online account, or for any other purpose. In most cases, before you can connect with human support—or, for that matter, an automated voice assistant—you may have to spend a few minutes or more on hold, waiting to reach the front of a queue. It's boring, frustrating, and time-wasting. And if anything, the problem has gotten worse in recent years. As one journalist points out, "The problem is that hold times are not just endless Muzak anymore. Now, most toll-free call wait times are actually an endless collection of prompts and pleads from an automated announcement, urging you to let the system call you back when company representatives are not busy. So it's really hard to stay focused on something else and ignore the hold because the phone systems won't let you alone."[3]

Some companies have begun offering a "call me back" feature that reduces the frustration somewhat, especially when an estimate of the wait time is provided. But in too many cases, the promised call back never arrives or takes far longer than promised, forcing the user to start the process all over again. Visit any website that collects customer comments about service systems and you'll encounter a host of complaints about this:

> "I've tried using the callback feature a number of times, and I get a call back on the same day maybe 30 percent of the time. Sometimes I get a call back a day or two later, or other times not at all."

> "[My internet provider] did call back at a rather unusual time, sometime after 6 pm, and I was not able to get to the phone then. . . . That kinda failed the callback idea for me then."

"I get a callback maybe 50 percent of the time. Due to that, I
    dread the callback. I'm less likely to deal with a company in
    the future if they use the callback method."[4]

Voice technology now offers better solutions for the problem. For
example, in 2021, the latest Google phone, dubbed the Pixel 5, was
equipped with a new feature called Hold for Me. When a business
number puts you on hold, Google Assistant can wait on the line for
you. The call will be muted, allowing you to get back to work or whatever you were doing. Real-time captions appear on your screen so, if
you wish, you can check up on the call from time to time. As soon as
someone is on the line and ready to talk, Hold for Me will notify you
with sound, vibration, and a prompt on your screen.

The service is made possible by Google's Duplex technology, which
we mentioned in Chapter 3. Its AI-powered combination of natural
language processing and speech-synthesis capability has been trained
through analysis of thousands of hours of real-life telephone conversations.[5] (We'll explain more about how such training programs are
designed and carried out in Part Two.) Using these tools, Hold for Me
recognizes hold music and also understands the difference between
a recorded message (like "Your call is important to us . . .") and a live
representative on the line.

The freedom from having to wait through an interminable telephone hold is a big deal. It matters to individuals because, when you
multiply the minutes you spend on each such experience by the number of times you might encounter them in a typical year, the cumulative inconvenience is far from insignificant. It matters to businesses
because the fear of getting put into a hold queue is a major reason
customers give up on imperfect products and services, often abandoning brands altogether. The arrival of voice tools that eliminate such
aggravations offers a big improvement in the daily lives of millions of
people—and a valuable way for companies to build better relationships
with their customers.

TRANSFORMING FINANCIAL SERVICES

Many pundits have argued that the industry that will be most disrupted by generative AI like ChatGPT will be customer experience centers, where humans today answer millions of chats and voice calls. The first line in the coming years will be handled by generative AI voice platforms, allowing human beings to take on the more challenging, uncommon requests.

Financial services is one of the industries that is using voice to lead the world into a more convenient future. For decades, technological breakthroughs have been gradually reshaping the business model of the financial-services industry. The process began with the invention and spread of the modern credit-card network in the 1960s and accelerated with the deployment of ATMs in the 1970s and 1980s, which rendered the traditional bank-branch model largely obsolete. Now companies in banking, insurance, and investment management are investing heavily in the AI and machine-learning systems needed to convert large parts of their operations to voice, including services that go way beyond the ability to sign in to your account quickly and easily.

Since its founding, Capital One has viewed itself as a company that uses technology to improve customer experiences. It got its start by using advanced data analytics to create personalized credit offers, then evolved to become one of the world's preeminent financial institutions, spanning credit cards, banking, auto loans, and business lending. Capital One understands the concept of *360-degree customer engagement*, which means that every customer touch point is critical, needing to be captured and managed appropriately. For example, a call-center rep should be able to see that the customer, or someone posing as the customer, has tried three failed log-ins in the last five minutes, which could mean either a frustrating technical snafu or an attempt at fraud; a conversation with the customer will quickly determine which.

Voice has played a meaningful role in Capital One's recent service improvements. Ken Dodelin, the company's vice president for product management, explained to us how, when Amazon introduced the Alexa skills kit, Capital One was the first bank to build a skill that enabled customers to check their balance, pay bills, and handle other basic tasks through their Alexa-enabled devices. They soon discovered that customers communicating with voice tools can use an almost infinite variety of natural-language expressions—for example, more than 2,000 ways to ask about their account balance. (We'll explore the techniques companies can use to teach voice tools to understand the varied ways their customers communicate in Chapter 9.)

Thanks to complexities like this, Capital One understands that improvements to the user experience are rarely step functions (i.e., single rapid changes); instead, they are mostly incremental changes implemented gradually and relentlessly over time. To continue pursuing such improvements, in June 2022 they launched a B2B software development unit called Slingshot. The goal is to take some of the developer tools Capital One has created in-house and bring them to the open market, in much the same way Amazon has made its cloud hosting service available to other businesses.

As in any highly competitive field, other financial services companies are working hard to rival Capital One's voice-based offerings. Bank of America's voice-activated app, known as Erica, can provide users with weekly updates on their spending, including alerts when a regular expense seems to be running noticeably higher than usual (a possible symptom of fraud), and let you know when a significant change in your credit rating occurs. It can also coordinate with your investment account through Merrill, letting you track the performance of your investments, place trades, and connect you with your advisor as needed. As of 2022, Erica offers these and other personalized financial insights to more than 19 million users. In fact, during 2020, as COVID-19 raged in the United States, Erica added a million users *per month*, reflecting another of the unique advantages of voice in an era when pandemics may be a normal rather than a rare occurrence.[6] After all, when simply touching the surface of a keyboard or screen has the potential to spread a deadly virus, people prefer using the hands-free interface of voice.

Other financial institutions are building their own voice tools, each with its unique set of capabilities. TD Ameritrade has created a voice-based "ticker tape" app, accessible through Amazon's Alexa, that lets investors ask for market updates and price quotes for more than 75,000 securities, including stocks, mutual funds, exchange-traded funds, and 3,800 indices, covering all the major US exchanges.[7] Customers of Turkish bank Garanti BBVA can use Ugi, the bank's smart voice assistant, to perform more than 200 kinds of financial transactions, including buying and selling foreign currencies, tracking the latest exchange rates, and getting answers to such arcane questions as "What is the dollar equivalent of one gram of gold?"[8]

All these changes mean that voice tech is fueling a new round of transformation in the financial-services industry. AI-powered smart voice tools are providing customers with sophisticated, customized information, advice, and services at a level comparable to what human agents can offer—but at times and places chosen by customers rather than limited by bankers' hours, and at a fraction of the cost to the organization.

By making digital service channels far more convenient, versatile, and responsive, voice tech is encouraging more financial-services companies to adopt direct-to-consumer sales and marketing approaches, enabling customers to design their own products. Voice also creates new opportunities for financial firms to create tech-driven partnerships with companies in related industries, from insurance to real estate, as well as to partner with nontraditional "neobanks" like Chime, One, Current, and Bella, which provide financial services mainly through mobile apps.[9]

The changes coming to banking illustrate how, when the customer convenience curve reaches a tipping point, the shift can help trigger industry changes that go beyond the merely incremental, making radically new business models not just thinkable but practically inevitable. Voice can play a key role in making this happen.

HEADS UP AND HANDS FREE—A NEW MODEL FOR RETAIL

As we've seen in earlier chapters, many retail businesses are moving fast to launch and enhance their own voice-based systems. Like the restaurant industry, retail has been beset by employee attrition in recent years, causing deteriorating levels of consumer experience. Voice technology is a key component of many retailers' strategy to fight back by delivering incredible in-store experiences even with an inexperienced workforce.

For example, a variety of systems have begun to emerge that allow employees equipped with Bluetooth-connected headsets to transmit and receive vital data while continuing to work with customers. Retailers like the Container Store, Walgreens, Cabelas, and Tractor Supply all use an all-in-one voice platform developed by Theatro, which supports a range of use cases. When workers pick up their headsets and log in at the start of a shift, they may hear a recorded "message of the day" from their manager. When struggling with a problem, they can use the system to ask another team member for help. They can also access automated voice tools that let them do tasks like checking inventory in real time (without having to go to a computer or run into the back room) or getting detailed product specs.

One of the fastest growing segments of retail is Buy Online, Pickup in Store (BOPIS). Managing curbside pickup is one of the most challenging aspects of today's new retail environment. It involves matching inventory control, picking and packing, and delivering the goods at a prearranged time to the waiting vehicle. It can really only be managed by an effective voice strategy that lets the team members communicate with each other to coordinate information from the back-end system (such as inventory status) with the status of the consumer ("the customer is four minutes away")—all while continuing to work actively with their hands. New voice-tech tools are making it possible to manage the flow of information throughout the system, making it faster and easier than ever to meet customers' ever-changing needs.

Yes, it takes time for companies to adopt, learn, and master these new voice tools. (We'll discuss the ups and downs of the process in Part Two of this book.) But the investment in time and energy is usually more than worthwhile. John Thrailkill at the Container Store, which is using new voice-tech tools to manage its Buy Online, Pickup in Store process, says it takes days, not weeks, for a store to get up to speed with the new technology. He adds, "We've gotten raves from customers about it," and "I truly think in the next few years every retailer is going to have this tool. The potential for the future is huge."[10]

It seems increasingly clear that the future of retail will be "Heads Up and Hands Free"—and the underpinning technology to make this happen is voice.

VOICE CONVENIENCE TRANSFORMS THE MEDIA BUSINESS

Another industry that is already being transformed by the new convenience of voice is the media business. Millions of people today—including my kids—have access in their homes to voice-activated remote controls and smart speakers that let them simply ask for whatever song, movie, or game they want rather than having to scroll through menus or awkwardly type a title. Encouraged by this new convenience, the marketplace shift from traditional media sources like cable TV to streaming sources with voice controls, already well underway, will only accelerate in the years to come.

The emergence of voice as the most convenient channel for accessing media is having an impact beyond Hollywood. Companies involved in publishing, journalism, and news broadcasting are also taking advantage of voice. Already in 2017, Britain's BBC radio produced a twenty-episode interactive science-fiction story for voice-assistant devices, which encouraged listeners to interact vocally. More recently, Reuters, the *New York Times*, the *Washington Post*, and CNN have all developed new-format audio briefings specifically for delivery via Siri, Alexa, and other voice assistants; local news outlets like the *Tennessean* and the *Texas Tribune* have followed suit.[11]

As you can imagine, the companies pioneering the use of voice tech to deliver media content are also exploring how voice can enhance the power of advertising, the traditional way of monetizing media content that has been upended by the internet. One of the pioneers in this area is Pandora, the music streaming service. In June 2020, Pandora launched a beta test of a new series of voice-based ads. Created in partnership with such big brands as KFC, Unilever, Doritos, Home Depot, and Acura, these ads allow listeners to request additional information when they find a particular pitch engaging.

To measure the effectiveness of the voice ads, Pandora used a new metric—*say-through rate* (STR), the voice equivalent of click-through rate (CTR). They found that the most effective voice ads educated listeners by using a tagline such as "This is an ad you can talk to." And the results were encouraging: engagement rates soared, with voice ads earning STRs up to ten times higher than CTRs, and with listeners reporting purchase intent averaging 27 percent higher than with traditional audio ads.[12]

These are early outcomes, but as any experienced marketer will tell you, numbers like these are highly impressive—in fact, virtually unheard of. They suggest that voice ads offer a new marketing channel with the potential to break through media clutter in a powerful way.

Like Pandora, most media companies rely on advertising revenue to keep their bottom lines healthy. But demonstrating a direct link between advertising dollars spent and sales enjoyed by the companies buying the ads has always been difficult. Voice offers a way to bridge the gap. Interactive voice tools that allow customers to respond directly to ads can make possible a clear, immediate payoff for advertising expenditures—a huge potential boon to media organizations.

Now many media industries are exploring the transformational potential of voice. For example, a major movie-theater chain I work with at WillowTree is using voice to dramatically streamline and enhance the moviegoing experience. As you might expect, they've created and deployed an app that uses voice tools to allow customers to easily order tickets with reserved seats for a particular showing of a specific movie. But this is just the beginning. The theater chain is now adapting other, more complex services to voice—for instance, the ability to let customers preorder their favorite snacks and beverages while on their way to the theater. Their distance from the theater is automatically detected by the mobile app, which then schedules the perfect time to deliver the snacks to their seats upon arrival. A big deal? Yes, because a theater's largest margins by far are driven by snack and soda sales—so even a small increase in these sales drives a much larger percentage increase in profits.

The ability for moviegoers to preselect seats is also more important to a theater's business model than one might assume. As the theater chain's chief marketing officer explained to me, a tool like this is an effective way to alleviate "seat anxiety" (that is, the stress moviegoers feel when they worry about not getting a good seat), which discourages many moviegoers from waiting in line at the refreshment stand before the film begins.

Through such subtle but powerful enhancements of the moviegoing business model, voice tech is making the experience more fun for countless fans—and more profitable for theater chains.

MAKING IT EASY TO SAY YES: MULTIMODAL VOICE MAKES SHOPPING MORE CONVENIENT

These examples of how voice tech is making the customer experience more convenient illustrate that removing friction leads customers to purchase more. It also reduces costs for all parties to a transaction, creating greater value for consumers and businesses alike.

Restaurant ordering, online banking, and moviegoing are all examples of this evolutionary step. Another is Exxon Mobil pay by Alexa, which was activated in 2021 at 11,500 gas stations in North America. Reached via your smartphone mic, the system knows you are at an Exxon station and allows you to approve payment by simply saying "Alexa, pay for gas" before pumping. A modest innovation, except for one thing—the most consistent complaint consumers have about filling up their gas tanks is that it takes too long. (By contrast, cost complaints tend to rise and fall along with prices at the pump.) For safety reasons, the slow speed of the pump is regulated, so the only available way left to make the user experience faster is by accelerating the financial transaction, which is what voice tech does. The service is also a boon to solo female travelers and others who might feel uncomfortable with a prolonged period of standing outside at an unfamiliar location, especially at night.[13]

The convenience of voice tech is also being harnessed to make it easy for customers to make the initial decision to order a product or service. A powerful use of multimodal design for this purpose can be found in tools that connect queries spoken by the user, a source of information, and the sounds and images flowing through your TV screen.

One example is Disruptel, a St. Louis–based company launched in 2017, which has created a connected platform, now available through TV manufacturer TCL, that uses voice tech to make TVs ultra-smart. Because the platform "sees" and "hears" the same things as the viewer, its built-in AI capability is able to answer questions that a viewer speaks aloud: "Who's the actor on the right-hand side of the screen?" The tool will also be able to carry out transactions—product purchases, for example—that the viewer might choose to initiate based on TV content, such as an advertisement: "I'd like to order those customized floor mats for my car. It's a 2019 Subaru Legacy." Amazon, Google, and Netflix are reportedly at work on similar systems for incorporating voice-assistant services into the TV viewing experience.[14]

Using voice tech as a key link in this kind of multimodal experience is a great way for companies to enable users to act on periods of unusually high motivation to engage in a particular activity. For example, I am a very big fan of the Baltimore Orioles baseball team, but I live three hours away from Camden Yards, their stadium in Baltimore. I normally manage to get to just a handful of games each season. That means motivating me to buy tickets is usually pretty hard—but if the timing is right and it's super easy, I just might pull the trigger.

Voice tech can help the Orioles take advantage of those moments when my feelings of fandom are at their strongest. When I've just watched the last inning of a dramatic Orioles victory on my TV, my receptivity to an ad for tickets will be at a high point. If my TV is equipped with an AI-powered smart mic, I may respond to the ad by saying, "Yes, I'll take four tickets for next Saturday's game!" Voice and face biometrics will authenticate my identity, and a confirmation message will pop up on my smartphone screen offering me seating options. In just one tap, my ticket purchase will be completed.

Jon Stine is the executive director of the Open Voice Network, a consortium of voice-tech leaders working to advance the industry. He brings to the task a deep understanding of the power of voice technology. "Voice makes it easy for the user to say yes," Jon often says. As you can imagine, that's a benefit that shoppers appreciate—and it's one that companies with products and services to sell find even more alluring.

Voice will become a bridge between motivation and action in a variety of consumer scenarios. I'm watching TV with my kids, and an ad pops up for the latest action thriller in the *Top Gun* series. We're all pretty excited by it, so I simply say, to either my voice-enabled TV, my smartphone, or my stand-alone voice assistant, "What are the local show times on Friday night?" The answer appears on my smartphone. I confirm with "Four tickets at 8:00 p.m. at the Regal Cinema," and I'm done.

Elaine is watching the news on TV, waiting for a weather update, when an ad comes up showing the new VW Jetta. She's been looking for a new car and she's impressed with this one's style. She also likes the financing options being offered. She asks her TV, "Where can I test-drive the new VW Jetta?" The information appears on her smartphone. After a glance at the times, she says, "Great, set up a test-drive at 2 p.m. Sunday at the Main Street dealership." It all happens within seconds, and without interfering with Elaine's viewing of today's weather report.

Alex has his buddies over for the big game, and, right before kick-off, a Domino's ad runs offering three large pizzas for the price of two. Alex speaks to his Apple watch: "Use Domino's coupon Game Day Trio and get three large pizzas—one cheese, one pepperoni and sausage, and one supreme." After the order is confirmed, Alex adds, "Ask John and Leon to send me twelve dollars each by Venmo."

It's easy to underestimate how important this frictionless shopping will be for consumer-marketing companies. The quest to tie advertising and promotions to action has been the holy grail of marketers for 150 years. John Wanamaker (1838–1922), one of the pioneers of the department store industry, famously said, "Half the money I spend on advertising is wasted; the trouble is I don't know which half." Voice will play an important role in finally linking advertising to response.

There will be issues and challenges involved in making this vision a reality. There's a potential for data privacy and ethics violations, which the voice-tech industry will need to address. Rules will be needed to ensure that kids can't access their parents' credit accounts without permission, people uninterested in "Buy now" pitches will need to be enabled to turn off the voice connections at will, and everyone will need to be persuaded that permitting access to their personal data will not unleash a flood of irrelevant and unwelcome solicitations.

But all the relevant issues are manageable. (In Chapter 7, we'll delve into the details of how responsible voice-tech leaders are already starting to tackle them.) Not everyone will embrace the new world in which voice tech makes consumption even easier and faster. But millions will. History has shown that, when users discover that a new technology makes activities they enjoy—such as shopping—more convenient, they will be happy to take advantage of it.

BRINGING LIFESAVING TRANSFORMATION TO HEALTH CARE

My wife, Lynn, has one of the most responsible and stressful jobs imaginable. She is a surgeon, a job that requires the highest order of mental *and* physical dexterity—the ability to juggle numerous tasks and responsibilities simultaneously, all while knowing that a careless mistake could have life-and-death consequences.

I've long admired Lynn's skill, developed over many years of study and practice. But I didn't really understand just how much dexterity she'd developed until recently, when she shared this story with me:

> When I'm in the middle of an operation, I often need to access the functions provided by a special system that uses a probe to measure the level of radiation in a particular part of the patient's body. Those functions are controlled by buttons on a touch screen that sits on a tray table close to where I'm operating. But the screen isn't sterile, which means it would be dangerous for me to touch it myself. So instead, when a particular button needs to be pushed— say, the "Take Time Count" button—I usually ask one of my colleagues, known as the circulator nurse, to handle that task for me.
>
> But occasionally, the circulator nurse is busy elsewhere—and that button needs to be pushed right now! Luckily, I've found a way to solve the problem without breaking sterility. I slip one of my feet out of the clogs I always wear in the operating room . . . balance ever-so-carefully on the opposite foot . . . and reach up with my foot to touch the button with the tip of my big toe!
>
> It works. But it's ridiculous! I can't help thinking that a voice control option could really be helpful at times like this.

When we're talking about health care, it's hard to overstate the importance of natural, intuitive, easy-to-access modes of communication between humans and machines. While Lynn's experience may seem small in itself, the potential power of voice innovation in an environment like the operating room is enormous. Voice-powered systems can provide surgeons and technicians with the tools they need when they need them and will allow team members to record crucial notes and comments, including follow-up items or concerns, all hands-free and in real time.

In fact, as voice becomes an integral part of surgical practice, it creates the potential for a redesign of the physical operating room, a reimagining of surgery workflow, and a rethinking of the personnel required to support the process.

Dr. Yaa Kumah-Crystal is a practicing physician and an assistant professor of pediatric endocrinology at Vanderbilt University Medical Center in Nashville. She is also a leading innovator in the use of voice to streamline and improve the delivery of medical care. As the project lead for the Vanderbilt Electronic Health Record (EHR) Voice Assistant initiative, she heads a team that is working to incorporate voice interfaces into the hospital workflow.

Kumah-Crystal knows from personal experience how hectic and harried the daily work of health-care providers can be. Many of her colleagues at Vanderbilt have already become accustomed to some uses of voice technology to make routine tasks easier—for example, the use of voice dictation tools like Dragon so that doctors can record clinical notes accurately without laborious typing. Now they are beginning to get used to new voice-based tools that can make other chores easier— ordering lab tests, placing medication orders, and requesting updates on a patient's condition. Being able to perform these tasks hands-free, while on the run between one hospital unit and another, can be a godsend for a super-busy physician.

Kumah-Crystal and her team have been working with Epic Systems, a software company specializing in electronic-health-record management that handles over 50 percent of the patient information files in the United States. They're involved in designing and testing an array of voice-based health-care applications, continually getting feedback from the professionals they serve so each iteration of the technology can be easier to use and more efficient than the previous one. And Vanderbilt's medical center is just one of several hundred facilities across the country where Epic's new tools are being tested and steadily improved.

Kumah-Crystal is excited by the potential for voice-based tools in health care:

Right now, our voice assistants are like medical students— beginning to learn what it takes to be a health-care professional, but still needing a lot of specific guidance to understand what they are supposed to do. In the future, they're going to become much more sophisticated.

For example, they'll be empowered to listen to ambient sounds, including ongoing conversations among health-care providers and patients, and to begin drawing conclusions about the kinds of support services the professionals need. Then, the voice assistant can take proactive steps in response.

So, suppose I'm talking with a patient and I say, "It looks like your lab results have been trending off. I think we'd better increase the dosage on your prescription. In about two weeks, we should check your thyroid levels again to see how they're trending, and we'll decide then whether to keep you on the higher dose." The voice assistant will be able to hear what I'm saying, understand what it means, and take appropriate actions—writing out a prescription for the new, higher dosage of medicine and ordering a lab test for two weeks in the future.

Over time, I see our voice assistants becoming more proficient and experienced, and finally "graduating" from being like medical students to being like resident physicians or expert nurses. Eventually, the voice assistant will be a ridiculously smart and talented colleague in the room with you—a great doctor or nurse who intuits what is needed and moves quickly to provide it, with a minimum of fuss.[15]

That level of ability on the part of medical voice tools is still a few years away. But already, voice-based tools are providing a range of important and useful services that are making the work of medical professionals more convenient and productive, and expanding health-care access to many people who might otherwise go unserved. Some examples:

Creating new voice-powered diagnostic tools. We learned in 2020 that we now live in a world where quickly spreading diseases can impact tens of millions of people across the planet within days, leading to deaths for hundreds of thousands and needless suffering for many more. When millions of people are potential vectors of illness, how can doctors and nurses be deployed in sufficient numbers to rapidly identify, track, and treat all those who pose a public-health risk?

Voice technology is beginning to help solve this dilemma. Computer scientists have begun developing AI tools that can identify voice-carried symptoms—*vocal biomarkers*—for a wide range of medical conditions. Working with physicians, they are creating apps that can listen to an individual speak and quickly recognize biomarkers that reflect physical ailments—not yet with sufficient accuracy to make a final diagnosis, but accurately enough to provide triage services to today's overstressed medical systems, saving valuable time and resources early in a patient's journey.

One company, Vocalis, quickly developed a smartphone app that uses vocal biomarkers of COVID-19 to identify people who likely need testing, quarantine, or an in-person examination: speak for a few seconds into your phone (describing an image and counting from fifty to seventy) and the app can determine with 80 percent accuracy whether you are infected with COVID—even if you are otherwise asymptomatic.[16] By 2022, as the pandemic began to subside, other teams of researchers from Carnegie Mellon, Cambridge, and the University of Augsburg in Germany started gathering thousands of additional voice samples to refine the technology. They hope to make it available as COVID-19 evolves from a global pandemic into a long-term, endemic health threat.[17]

Similar tools are being developed to identify signs of other medical conditions ranging from dementia and depression to autism. Winter-Light Labs, for example, uses short samples of speech to identify those at risk of dementia. In research with Genentech published in 2022, they showed that people with higher accumulated levels of a cerebral protein known as tau—a core characteristic of Alzheimer's disease—had differences in speech that were identifiable by voice markers, including higher use of filled pauses (like "um" and "ah") and simpler vocabularies. In addition, researchers found that the speech markers increased in line with accumulation of tau. The research claims 93 percent accuracy for its voice-based diagnoses of Alzheimer's disease.[18]

Max Little, a machine learning researcher at the University of Birmingham (UK), is one of many experts who have studied vocal cues for the presence of Parkinson's disease, for which there is no definitive diagnostic test. When these and other voice-based diagnostic tools are perfected, they'll save countless hours of work for medical professionals and allow people desperately in need of help to get it far faster than today. "This kind of technology," Little says, "can allow a high-speed snapshot, an almost continuous snapshot of how someone's symptoms are changing."[19]

Empowering the boom in telemedicine. The COVID-19 pandemic generated almost unprecedented stresses for health-care systems across the US and around the world. Voice tools helped alleviate the pressure. Telehealth systems that connected patients with care providers remotely—saving time and replacing face-to-face meetings that carry a risk of infection—morphed from a little-used sideshow to a mainstream form of care. One report found that Medicare visits conducted via telehealth increased sixty-three-fold, from approximately 840,000 in 2019 to 52.7 million in 2020.[20]

At the same time, hospital and clinic phone banks were flooded with calls from anxious, homebound patients seeking answers to basic questions: "How do I access the new telehealth services?" "What should I do if I may be experiencing COVID symptoms?" "How can

I find out whether I'm eligible for the vaccine?" To manage this over-whelming demand, voice bots and voice assistants built by companies like Hyro and Orbita—or customized from templates built by companies like Microsoft—were pressed into service. These new tools were developed and deployed rapidly, relieving the burden on live service providers and helping patients determine for themselves how to have their health-care needs met most easily and efficiently.

The speed with which this trend developed—even in the normally conservative world of health-care administration—illustrates the power of an emergency to drive change. In the words of Bret Kinsella, a former strategist at Accenture and Sapient, and the creator and chief editor of Voicebot.ai, the primary news site dedicated to covering the emerging voice industry, organizations that "typically prefer resisting new technology implementations reversed course and started deploying the conversational technologies in a matter of weeks."[21] As of this writing, even as the acute threat posed by the pandemic begins to recede, the enhanced capabilities of telehealth remain in place, creating a higher level of convenience for patients and freeing up care providers to devote more time and energy to those with the most unusual or serious problems.

Monitoring patients to improve care plan compliance and speed recovery. Health-care experts have found that one of the biggest dangers to patients recovering from serious health problems or living with chronic conditions like diabetes, asthma, or heart disease is simple noncompliance with the prescribed care plan. Studies show that up to 50 percent of such patients fail to stay on their medicine, don't stick to the right diet, or otherwise backslide, often leading to avoidable consequences such as hospitalization.

Voice-based technologies can help reduce this problem. The Israel-based company Healthymize, for example, is developing a voice tool that can monitor patients for conditions such as asthma and chronic obstructive pulmonary disease (COPD). It analyzes patient voice patterns for clues that indicate a flare-up in one of these respiratory conditions. An alert can then be sent to the relevant medical professional, who can intervene quickly and often make a costly, disruptive hospital stay unnecessary.[22]

Similar tools for other conditions are on the way. For example, a recent study conducted at the MedStar Heart and Vascular Institute, Washington, DC, found that a voice-activated system could effectively monitor patients suffering from heart failure, alerting medical caregivers when symptoms worsen and professional intervention is needed.[23]

Providing basic levels of mental health support. One form of health care that leaves far too many people underserved is mental health. Inadequate government funding, inconsistent coverage by private health-insurance plans, the lack of care providers in remote, rural areas, and the social stigma still associated with mental illness are all factors. By one estimate, almost 60 percent of Americans in need of mental health care currently go without treatment.[24]

Voice tech is beginning to help remedy the problem by making access to basic mental health care more convenient for many people. The most complex, deep-seated psychological problems still require the intervention of a live caregiver. But when such care is difficult to get, therapeutic voice bots programmed to provide human-like support can provide short-term care that can sometimes be literally lifesaving. In the words of Dr. Alison Darcy, the psychologist founder of Woebot Health, "I think people have probably underestimated the power of being able to engage in a therapeutic technique in the moment that you need to"— for example, in the middle of the night, when a patient might suffer a serious bout of anxiety or depression at a time when their human therapist is unavailable. Woebot, the therapeutic voice bot developed by Dr. Darcy's company, uses AI to engage in natural-language conversations that use the techniques of cognitive behavioral therapy, encouraging patients to think through the issues that plague them and develop behavior changes that can improve how they feel.

Other voice-driven tools provide additional forms of mental-health support. Some help to monitor patients who may be at risk of suicide;

others teach patients how to track and manage their moods; still others provide help with guided meditation. All in all, the American Psychiatric Association reports there are more than 10,000 apps currently available that offer varying types of digitized mental-health support for those in need.[25] Are these always adequate substitutes for human care? Surely not—but in a world where the need for convenient, accessible mental-health support exceeds the supply, voice tools can play a critical role in closing the persistent gap.

THE OPPORTUNITIES FOR BUSINESSES

To discover the ways voice tech can create greater value for both customers and employees, start by researching all of the pain and friction points that currently exist in your interactions with these individuals. In-depth research using surveys or focus groups may be one way to uncover them. So is analysis of the kinds of complaints and questions that flow through your existing customer-service pipelines.

It can also be helpful to create a detailed timeline that tracks the complete cycle of any common interaction between a company's systems and the life of a customer or employee. We call this kind of timeline a *journey map*. (The details of how to create and use one will be covered in Chapter 9.) For example, you could produce a journey map listing all of the actions a customer must undertake when using one of your products, from researching and making the purchase to receiving the product, unpacking and assembling it, using it through its entire lifespan, and ultimately discarding or recycling it. The process will uncover a number of specific spots at which customers typically encounter difficulties, questions, or problems. For each one, ask yourself whether a new voice tool can provide a simple, convenient solution. In many cases, the answer will be yes.

A major financial institution recently completed this type of journey map covering the top twenty reasons their customers call into the call center. They mapped not simply the business reason behind a customer's call but, more important, the likely emotional state associated with the call. Details like these bring the journey map to life and make it easier for app designers to create tools that respond to the nuances of a user's situation.

Suppose Charlie and Nadia are two customers of the same bank. Charlie is a service worker whose average checking account balance is less than $1,000, while Nadia is a high-earning attorney with an average balance over $20,000. Charlie is calling to check his balance and to check the status of a check he has deposited. The service team for the bank can infer that Charlie is likely to be in a state of stress—he may be low on cash and worried that the checks he has just written to pay his phone and electric bills are going to bounce. In response, it would be great for the bank to be able to handle his call as quickly as possible via automatic voice technology.

By contrast, Nadia is calling to arrange a cash transfer to her daughter, a freshman at a prestigious East Coast university. She is not in a high state of anxiety, but she needs to talk to someone who can walk her through the complexities of setting up the transfer. She is also very time-constrained and has set aside a few minutes on her drive home to deal with this transaction.

In both these scenarios, shortening the time to get to resolution is critical for customer-service satisfaction and will reduce the bank's costs in the long run. But the differing nature of the two challenges calls for a voice system that is flexible and adaptable. The financial institution selected, modified, and tested a voice authentication process designed to meet these demands, while making it easy for both Charlie and Nadia to get the kind of convenient service they need.

The benefits to the company are significant. This financial institution handles about 16 million customer-service calls a year, each lasting on average slightly over five minutes and costing seven dollars per call to handle. Voice authentication is now reducing call handling times by 22 percent, resulting in happier customers and saving the bank $1.54 per call. What's more, each 1 percent increase in voice-authentication enrollment is projected to save the bank about a million dollars in fraud-prevention costs. It's hard to find win/wins in business where you can cut costs and improve customer satisfaction at the same time, but this voice case is one such example.

As one industry after another discovers the incomparable convenience provided by voice, the ultimate interface will become more and more familiar to people around the world—who will soon find themselves wondering how they ever got along without it. It will also enable businesses in many industries to consider and develop new models for serving customers, managing their operations, improving their efficiencies, and out-competing rivals—as we already see happening in financial services, media, health care, and other arenas.

That's the very definition of a game-changing technology—and a portal to a wide array of opportunities for any business you help to run.

VOICE TECHNOLOGY HAS THE POTENTIAL TO BENEFIT HUMAN BEINGS in countless ways. If smartly conceived and artfully executed, it can make our lives safer, more efficient, more convenient, better informed, more inclusive, and simply more fun.

In the process, voice tech also creates huge business opportunities for companies that recognize its benefits and move quickly to take advantage of them. How can you get started? We'll explore that question in detail in Part Two.

PART TWO

RISING TO THE CHALLENGE

7

FALLING BARRIERS

Overcoming the Technical, Organizational,
and Social Challenges to Voice Technology

ADAM CHEYER IS ONE OF THE LEADING PIONEERS OF VOICE technology. As much as any single individual, he is largely responsible for putting voice technology on the map. A lot of the history of voice tech, the challenges it has overcome, and the barriers it still faces on its march to becoming the dominant tool for human-to-machine interaction are best illustrated by looking at Adam's career.[1]

One of Cheyer's first jobs was back in the 1990s at SRI International, where he served as chief architect of CALO, the largest-ever government-funded artificial-intelligence project. Its purpose was to create an intelligent assistant that learned and self-improved "in the wild" (e.g., with no code changes). Later, as cofounder and vice president of engineering at Siri, Cheyer helped to create the pioneering voice assistant that was acquired by Apple in 2010. (As of 2022, Siri has been distributed on more than 1.5 billion devices—a number that is still growing steadily.) Cheyer served Apple as director of engineering in the iPhone/iOS group, leading all AI and server-side aspects of the Siri assistant. He later went on to cofound Viv Labs, an artificial intelligence (AI) company acquired by Samsung in 2016.

Cheyer has played one of the leading roles in putting voice technology into the pockets and purses of billions of people around the world. Yet Cheyer's thinking about how voice tech ought to work has never been fully realized, a fact that has left him both bemused and frustrated.

It was way back in 1993—the earliest years of the internet—when Adam Cheyer first began dreaming of the potential for a voice assistant equipped with AI. But what he imagined is quite different than today's Siri or Alexa. In those days before the creation of search engines like Safari, Explorer, or even the pioneering Mosaic, there was no convenient way to scan the nascent World Wide Web for interesting and relevant content. Cheyer imagined a voice assistant that could serve as what we now call a web browser, intelligently accessing information from linked computers all over the world. In his work at SRI International, he set about building dozens of voice assistants, all of which could be considered early prototypes of Siri.

Cheyer envisioned a voice assistant that would operate freely within an open ecosystem. Its built-in AI system would be capable of understanding virtually any kind of queries, and it could, in effect, build new programs and applications as needed to respond to these limitless requests. Using these purpose-built tools, the voice assistant would visit any website in the world, gathering information wherever it was stored and connecting to any service a user might find helpful. Cheyer also assumed that a voice assistant would operate in multimodal fashion, using voice, screens, and keyboards interchangeably depending on what mode of communication is most appropriate for a given purpose.

Together with two partners, Dag Kittlaus and Tom Gruber, Cheyer set out to build a voice assistant that would embody this vision. In February 2010, they launched Siri as a free app available in Apple's App

Store, which had been created two years earlier to provide software applications for the then-new iPhone.

Amid the explosion of interest in the iPhone and its amazing capabilities, Siri didn't appear to make an immediate impact. Exaggerating more than slightly, Cheyer says, "We were one of 202 million apps available then." But three weeks later, Apple's Steve Jobs surprised the partners with a personal phone call.

"Hey, it's Steve," he said. "How about coming over to my place to talk about Siri?"

Of course, Cheyer and his partners were happy to meet with the legendary tech innovator. Jobs explained that he was excited by Siri's potential—so much so that he wanted to buy Siri and reposition it as an Apple product.

Cheyer's team members were flattered by Jobs's interest. However, they'd just completed a successful round of investment funding and developed ambitious plans for marketing and promoting their product. So they weren't interested in entertaining acquisition offers.

But Jobs persisted. He called Cheyer and his partners frequently in the weeks to come, and the sums he suggested as a possible purchase price kept increasing. Finally, in April 2010, the offer became irresistible. They agreed to sell Siri to Apple for a reported $200 million.

But the question of how Siri would connect with users and with the ecosystem of the World Wide Web was still to be decided. Cheyer wasn't shy about sharing his own vision with Jobs:

> I said to Steve, "Many people think voice is going to replace the keyboard. But that's not how it's going to work at all. If the information or the action you need is already on the screen, then the best way to access it is through clicking a mouse or tapping an icon. (The iPhone had already reinvented the touch interface with multi-touch pinch and zoom.) But if what you need isn't on the screen, the easiest way to access it is to ask for it. That's where

voice will come in. The perfect interface will be when you can mix direct manipulation with conversational interaction so seamlessly that you don't even think about it. After all, that's what humans do in other contexts every day."

Steve Jobs fully grasped Cheyer's vision of what Siri could become—and Cheyer believes that he shared it. But Jobs's plan for launching Siri as the voice of Apple didn't embody that vision. Initially, he preferred to have Siri operate within a narrower sphere, accessing a limited set of applications approved by Apple rather than serving as a portal to every site on the World Wide Web. Cheyer paraphrases Jobs's attitude as "Web services are great. But Apple also has an app ecosystem. So we'll start with the ten apps that Apple ships with every iPhone—calling, messaging, news, weather, stocks, and so on. Later, we'll open Siri up to developers—and by then, Siri will control access to every app on the phone and every service on the web."

Jobs also wanted Siri to interact using voice only, reasoning that this unique new connection to technology would intrigue and delight users. "I think Steve saw it from a marketing point of view—the novelty of voice," Cheyer says. "I believe that was the main incentive, and on that point he was absolutely right."

Jobs's alternative vision defined how Siri would initially be implemented by Apple. Following his lead, for more than a year after the deal was reached, Cheyer and his team, now part of Apple, worked to perfect Siri for its relaunch in the fall of 2011.

Through this period, Steve Jobs's health was an evolving story in the background of everything Apple did. Back in 2004, he'd publicly revealed the fact that he was battling against a rare form of pancreatic cancer. For years, he remained thoroughly engaged in running the company he'd founded, and his cancer appeared to be largely under control. But then matters became more serious. In June 2009, it became known that Jobs had received a liver transplant two months earlier. And in January 2011, Jobs took a medical leave of absence,

while announcing that he planned to remain CEO of Apple and participate in every major company decision.

There are many stories of people near death who struggle to remain
alive in order to experience one more event of deep personal importance to them. History buffs know how both Thomas Jefferson and
John Adams managed to remain alive until finally expiring on the same
day—July 4, 1826, the fiftieth anniversary to the day of the signing of
the Declaration of Independence.

For Steve Jobs, a dream that kept him going in the final months of
his life, even as his health failed, was his wish to see Siri launched into
the world. Jobs did live to see that launch on October 4, 2011—before
dying the very next day.

The continuing growth of the smartphone era was not slowed by
the passing of Apple's inspirational founder. Driven by iPhone sales,
Apple's stock price doubled over the next six months. The company
was on its way to becoming the most valuable corporation in the world.

It should be noted that Steve Jobs's belief in the power of the voice
interface wasn't of recent vintage. As far back as 1987, a video shown at
an Apple shareholders' meeting demonstrated a then-futuristic product
concept called the Knowledge Navigator. The video depicted a college
professor accessing research, connecting with colleagues, analyzing
data, and planning presentations—all using a device that looked a
lot like today's iPad and a voice assistant clearly powered by artificial
intelligence. At the time, the iPad, the iPhone, and Siri were all purely
figments of Jobs's imagination. But before he died, twenty-four years
later, all three would become realities. What's more, as Adam Cheyer
points out, the imaginary scenario depicted in the Knowledge Navigator video is shown as taking place in 2011—the very year when the real
Siri would debut. Prescience or coincidence? Maybe a bit of both.[2]

Today, of course, Siri is in hundreds of millions of homes, and other
so-called smart speakers, like Amazon's Alexa, have also achieved enormous popularity. Cheyer's brainchild, as adopted by Jobs and marketed
by Apple, has transformed the way vast numbers of people interact

with the world of technology. Siri's success illustrates the widespread desire people have to be freed from the tyranny of the keyboard.

Yet the uses to which voice tools like Siri and Alexa are put remain very limited. Surveys show that the overwhelming majority of people who engage with these tools use them for a handful of specific, basically simple purposes: to conduct a Google-style search for information from a website, to play a selected piece of music, to turn on a media link such as a radio station, or to access a weather report. According to a 2018 survey by PwC, "For now, the bulk of consumers have yet to graduate to more advanced activities like shopping or controlling other smart devices in the home."[3] More recent surveys, such as a 2021 study by Vixen Labs, a voice strategy consultancy, show only small, incremental changes in this pattern.[4]

Conversely, almost no one thinks of the voice in their smartphone or desktop speaker as a "personal assistant" or "all-purpose valet." Yet this is the role that these tools were once supposed to perform—if only Siri had been developed along the lines that Adam Cheyer had dreamed about.

To this day, Cheyer is convinced that the story of Siri would have been different had Steve Jobs not succumbed to illness. "Since he died immediately after the first vision of Siri launched," Cheyer says, "the open ecosystem part of the vision got lost and de-prioritized by the people who followed. I believe if Steve had remained alive, I would still be at Apple, and we would have pursued the full vision I imagined."[5]

Instead, Cheyer eventually left Apple and launched Viv Labs to build what was, in effect, his open-ecosystem version of Siri. Viv created an AI platform capable of understanding complex requests spoken in informal, conversational language and responding to them with appropriate information and actions using links to far-flung locations throughout the internet. The company was purchased by Samsung, which launched this new voice-based assistant for the Android operating system under the name of Bixby. If you've never heard of it, that's not surprising. Unfortunately, Samsung marketed Bixby with just a fraction of the investment, energy, and creativity that Apple expended on Siri. And Bixby itself has not been developed as fully as Cheyer had hoped.

Cheyer remains convinced that his vision of voice tech as a tool for freely and easily navigating a world of online services is attainable. And a growing number of people and companies around the world are finally recognizing its powerful appeal.

I contend that Cheyer's open-ended, multimodal voice vision is much closer to what people really want than the more constrained vision embodied in stand-alone, voice-only assistants like Siri and Alexa. In the near future, we will see the emergence of more and more multimodal tools capable of handling a growing array of interactions across the entire web-based universe. As that happens, one of the major barriers that has limited the appeal of voice will finally collapse.

In this chapter, we'll consider some of the other barriers that have prevented voice from achieving the widespread adoption the world needs—as well as the changes now happening that are helping to finally remove those barriers.

WHY TECHNOLOGY BREAKTHROUGHS HAPPEN: THE ROLE OF CRISES

Experts have long tried to model exactly how, when, and why innovations evolve from novelties or niche interests into powerful shapers of everyday life. While the models are theoretically elegant, sometimes a technological and economic change is powered by unpredictable world events whose transformative power exceeds what any model might portend.

That's what happened with the use of voice tools in health care when the COVID-19 pandemic exploded. Medical providers have long sought to use technology tools to deliver services remotely using the latest tools for digital communication. After all, this can be an economical way to provide remote or underserved populations with health-care services that normally remain out of their reach. But adoption of the technology proved to be very slow. There were a number of reasons. One was a lack of economic incentives, and even some positive disincentives that discouraged the use of telemedicine. Physicians had nothing to gain financially from speaking with patients remotely rather than in person, and some health-insurance companies erected barriers that actually made it harder for doctors to get paid for virtual visits. Cultural factors also played a role. Physicians and other providers were so accustomed to face-to-face meetings that they were reluctant to alter their behavior. For their part, patients worried that remote consultations might make their relationship with their doctors less intimate and more impersonal. All these concerns kept telemedicine from gaining a significant foothold.

Then COVID arrived, bringing with it the enormous need for new information, processes, and training to deal with the challenges of the pandemic. Combine that spike with travel restrictions, quarantines, and overwhelmed doctors and nurses—and suddenly the demand for remote health-care services skyrocketed. In April 2020, the overall volume of health-insurance claims for telehealth services was seventy-eight times what it had been just two months earlier. In response, major funders of health insurance altered their policies to be more supportive of telehealth services. For example, the Centers for Medicare & Medicaid Services made more than eighty new forms of service temporarily eligible for telehealth reimbursement.[6]

Still, many health-care providers struggled to meet the surge in demand for remote medical consultations. The new voice technologies played a huge role in filling the gap. Voice systems took the place of thousands of support workers who were now stuck at home without access to their data banks. New chatbots and voice assistants, rapidly designed and implemented, were able to respond to the flood of questions from staff and patients. Companies specializing in voice, like Hyro and Orbita, rushed to produce COVID-centered apps that hospitals and clinics could offer to their clients. Other voice tools led the huge cadre of new patients through the intricacies of the tele-health system. In 2022, as the pandemic moved into a new phase, new chatbots emerged to help patients swiftly determine whether they were eligible for the vaccine and find out where the nearest pro-vider was located.

Partners HealthCare (subsequently renamed Mass General Brigham) was the parent organization behind two of the nation's most prestigious medical institutions, Brigham and Women's Hospital and Massachusetts General Hospital in Boston. Their story illustrates how the advent of COVID-19 helped to jumpstart the application of voice tech to medicine.

The leadership team of Partners HealthCare recognized the seri-ousness of the COVID-19 challenge on March 9, 2020, shortly after they launched a telephone hotline to address questions about the new virus. Staffed by expert nurses, the purpose of the hotline was to tell patients, clinicians, and members of the general public how to identify the symptoms of COVID-19, where to find testing sites, and how to determine whether or not a person might need emergency care. The plan for the hotline was carefully developed—but within hours it was overwhelmed by a level of demand the hospital administrators hadn't anticipated. Thousands of frantic callers drove average wait times above thirty minutes, and many people hung up in frustration. The Partners HealthCare team realized a better solution was desperately needed.

Searching for ideas, they learned that the Providence St. Joseph Health system in Seattle—which had treated some of the first Ameri-can COVID patients in early March—had collaborated with Microsoft to build an online tool to screen potential victims of the virus. The chatbot they developed had succeeded beyond expectations, serving more than 40,000 patients in the first week alone.

The Partners HealthCare team set about to adopt a similar model. Using screening questions developed by the US Centers for Disease Control and Prevention, they developed an interface that patients could use to determine their level of COVID-19 risk. Without needing to speak with a live nurse or doctor, callers could run through the key questions and receive a preliminary evaluation of their health care status, including a referral to the appropriate medical facility, whether that was an urgent-care center, a primary-care physician, or the emergency room at a hospital. Thanks to this chatbot, the flood of calls to the Partners HealthCare hotline was reduced to a manageable level, and patients were able to get the reassurance and the expert guidance they needed.

Soon after this turnaround, the leaders at Partners HealthCare reflected on what had happened:

> Our economy and health care systems are geared to handle linear, incremental demand, while the virus grows at an exponential rate. . . . This is because traditional processes—those that rely on people to function in the critical path of signal processing—are constrained by the rate at which we can train, organize, and deploy human labor.
>
> Moreover, traditional processes deliver decreasing returns as they scale. On the other hand, digital systems can be scaled up without such constraints, at virtually infinite rates. . . . We hope and anticipate that after Covid-19 settles, we will have transformed the way we deliver health care in the future.[7]

As the story of the role of voice tools in combatting COVID-19 illustrates, the impact of dramatic world events can be a catalyst for a new technology to move overnight from fringe to mainstream. Of course, this can only happen if the underpinnings of the new technology are present and available to take advantage of such an event. Thankfully for the world, by 2020, voice tech had developed to the point where it was ready to take on a significant supporting role in health care—as well as in a growing number of other industries.

FLIPPING THE SWITCH: MOTIVATION, DIFFICULTY, AND THE FOGG MODEL OF BEHAVIOR

Driven in part by the COVID-19 emergency, health care is one of the realms in which voice is rapidly gaining acceptance. As we've seen in Part One, similar changes are emerging in other industries, including personal finance, automotive, aviation, retail, education, media, and customer service. Taken together, they begin to provide the evidence of the move of voice from the fringe to the mainstream. Some of these changes, like the exploding popularity of telehealth, have garnered headlines. Others have flown under the radar, going almost unnoticed even by industry experts. Why is this happening now? Why didn't it happen in, say, 2005? And why isn't it being further delayed, until, say, 2030?

If we want to understand the emergence and shape of adoption trends, the model created by B. J. Fogg, founder and director of Stanford's Behavior Design Lab, offers a useful tool. It expresses in quantitative terms an insight that may seem intuitively obvious once it's articulated: *A specific technology will be widely adopted when and only when the motivation to use it is greater than the difficulty.*

But less obvious is one of the crucial corollaries to this insight: *It's typically more difficult to impact the level of motivation that users have to perform an activity; it's often much more achievable to make it easier to perform an activity.*

Ken Dodelin, vice president for product management for Capital One bank, speaks to the phenomenon of the way a technology application moves from the fringe to the mainstream when he analyzes Eno, the bank's AI-driven assistant. For a variety of reasons, Capital One is very interested in having its customers use Eno as well as—or in place of—the traditional modes of customer service: website tools, smartphone apps, and people working in a call center. Dodelin explains that Eno is potentially faster, more efficient, and less expensive than any of these other service providers—which means that, when Capital One customers use Eno, the bank will save money even as it serves customer needs more effectively.

But persuading customers who are used to traditional service tools to switch to Eno is not always easy. "Do people wake up in the morning thinking 'I can't wait to start banking today?'" Dodelin asks. The answer, he says, is obviously no. "It's more that they are banking to enable other things they want to do in their life, and having a voice assistant working on their behalf in the background can help them spend less time banking and more time living." Here is where the Fogg model kicks in. As Dodelin observes, once people try Eno, "They love the notifications—the positive feedback has exceeded our expectations. People just love the convenience of saying a command and then receiving a quick text to get information and then get back to living."[8]

In other words, the motivation to bank online is at a fixed (and relatively low) level. But if you make online banking *incredibly* easy— as Eno does—even a digital banking app can become widely popular. Voice makes this kind of transformation possible.

The Fogg model helps to explain the barriers that have prevented voice from becoming a ubiquitous technology in the past as well as the changes that need to happen if voice is to become the dominant mode of interaction between humans and machines. As the Fogg model suggests, one key to flipping the adoption switch is changing the relative strength of the barriers that discourage use of voice and the benefits that encourage it—either by lessening the barriers, enhancing the benefits, or both.

BUSTING BARRIERS: TECHNOLOGICAL BREAKTHROUGHS THAT ARE MAKING VOICE EASIER AND BETTER

One major reason for the growing potential of voice as a strategic business tool has been a series of technological breakthroughs that are making voice tools more powerful, accessible, and convenient.

For simplicity's sake, we often refer to "voice technology" as though it is a single discipline. In reality, it is a set of technologies that are increasingly working together to pave the way for potential breakthroughs. Unless you're a software engineer, you don't need to be an expert in these various technologies. But if you're a business leader who will be working with tech experts on developing voice tools to benefit your company and its customers, you need some familiarity with the basic terminology so you can understand what needs to be worked on, as well as how and why. What follows is an overview of the key technologies that are now making the power of voice increasingly useful and accessible.

Automatic speech recognition (ASR) is the technology that enables a machine (like a computer, smartphone, or tablet) to recognize spoken language. In effect, ASR is about the ability to transcribe words and sentences, turning them from oral form into written form.

For many years, programmers labored to develop computer applications capable of performing this task with a high degree of reliability and accuracy. The use of computerized tools to replace human typists when performing tasks such as transcribing speeches or notes from business meetings was long held back by the fact that these tools had relatively high error rates. Yes, they produced rough drafts much faster than human typists—but the task of reading those rough drafts and correcting the many errors they contained often made the entire process into a net loss. To improve accuracy, the men and women dictating letters or reports were sometimes forced to speak unnaturally slowly and carefully so as to avoid confusing their easily confused software assistants. The early transcription apps also required lengthy periods of training when called upon to capture the speech of people with unusual accents or other "difficult" voice patterns. All of these weaknesses were enormous sources of frustration for people seeking fast and accurate support.

These problems with ASR have now been largely solved. Today's off-the-shelf ASR tools are able to recognize and transcribe informal speech with a remarkable degree of accuracy. The best ASR services—such as Nuance, Google Cloud Speech-to-Text, Azure Speech to Text, and Amazon Transcribe—incorporate language models to improve the accuracy with which sounds are translated into words. This is no easy challenge. Casual human speech includes a stream of sounds in which units of meaning—words, phrases, and sentences—are often blurred together in ways that make them ambiguous and easy to mis-understand. When we're talking to other people, we can usually avoid such misunderstandings because we're deeply embedded in the social context of the conversation. Until recently, grasping this context and applying it to help with interpreting the flow of uttered sounds was very difficult for computers.

Today's ASR systems have gotten remarkably good at this task. This enables them to avoid the misunderstandings to which they were once prone. For example, based on a second or two from a spoken sentence, an ASR system might generate two different possible verbal interpretations:

- "recognize speech"
- "wreck a nice beach"

Say these two phrases aloud, and you can see that they sound almost identical, especially when spoken fast and casually. Thus, the two sets of words are both possible interpretations of the same stream of sounds that a person might utter in a conversation. The question is, which would be the correct interpretation in a given situation?

Modern ASR systems handle this challenge by examining the broader context of the utterance. They've gained skill at doing this through training that used thousands of hours of real-world human speech. The process involved, often called *machine learning*, is anal-ogous to the way all of us learned to listen, understand, and speak when we were children—by paying attention to the way speech was used by the people around us, and gradually getting better at grasping the intended meanings. The software uses the computer's almost limitless capacity for remembering, comparing, and connecting billions of items to master the same interpretative skills that a toddler develops over time.

In the example above, the language model embodied in the ASR system will use skills derived from its study of real-world human speech to examine and interpret the social context of this utterance. When the system looks at the surrounding sentences in the conversation, do they deal with issues surrounding the development of voice tools (just as this chapter does)? If so, then the interpretation "recognize speech" is more likely to be correct. Or do the surrounding sentences deal with environmental issues like the damage done to shoreline properties by pollution? In that case, the interpretation "wreck a nice beach" is more likely to be correct.

When dealing with ambiguous utterances like this one, modern ASR systems are able to use such context clues to rank the possible interpretations from most likely to least likely, and select the most likely one for use in the written transcript. This process greatly increases the chances of delivering an accurate transcription to the user—and it is behind most of the recent improvements in speech-to-text software.[9]

What's more, most companies developing a voice tool will supplement the off-the-shelf ASR system with a custom-built language model that is tailored to the specific business domain in which the company operates. The ASR system incorporated in a personal-banking service system will be trained to easily recognize terms like "account," "balance," "funds," "transfer," and so on, rather than confusing them with unrelated terms that might sound similar. On the other hand, the same off-the-shelf ASR system being used in an airline's customer-service system will learn to recognize terms like "ticket," "arrival," "baggage," and "destination." The ability of software systems to hone their speech interpretation skills to fit a specific business context enables an even higher level of accuracy.

Today's ASR systems are also much better than older tools at coping with a wide variety of speaking styles—tones, accents, rhythms, speeds, and so on. As a result, transcription tools have become increasingly popular and are even replacing human typists in a range of professional applications. These include software development and the preparation of notes by health-care professionals (as discussed in Chapter 1) as well as the transcribing of legal documents, the production of written notes from in-person or online meetings, and the generation of emails, memos, letters, and reports for business and other uses.

Equally significant, however, is a second breakthrough that is less widely appreciated but that is helping to make ASR even more useful and accessible. Prior to 2020, ASR software programs were so large and complex that they generally needed to be housed in the cloud—that vast universe of interlinked computer memory banks where giant stores of digital content are maintained. Users seeking access to ASR systems to perform specific tasks needed high-speed internet access to tap into the software, which meant ASR was basically out of reach in countless circumstances—when technicians are working on jobs in remote locations like out at sea or in the desert, or employees are deep in a warehouse with limited Wi-Fi, for example. Adding to the inconvenience, the need to access ASR tools in the cloud meant a built-in delay of up to a few seconds in every process managed by these tools. Computer users, as we all know from personal experience, are incredibly impatient. Having to wait for a few seconds, repeatedly, for the software to "catch up" while you try to communicate with a device simply made ASR too frustrating for many users.

That has now changed. Starting in 2020, technology leaders like Microsoft, Google, and Apple, working with hardware manufacturers, began deploying ways to embed the same level of processing power right into a phone, tablet, or laptop. Now mobile and other devices are capable of doing real-time voice processing without resorting to cloud-based tools. This new trend toward decentralizing computational power, often referred to as *edge computing*, reduces the time lag in human-machine conversations to almost zero. And in those instances when remote, cloud-based processing is still required, 5G networks and other innovative technologies are pushing the time lag lower and lower. Thus, your smartphone, laptop, or tablet is likely now equipped with simple yet powerful tools that are able to accurately transcribe spoken words with ease and speed.

These improvements are fundamentally changing the user experience of voice. This makes voice tech much easier for users, of course. It also greatly lessens one huge hurdle for companies and organizations interested in developing voice tools for their internal or external use. Teams charged with creating voice apps no longer have to devote a lot of time, energy, money, and effort into creating a usable ASR system. Instead, they can simply choose one of a number of proven plug-and-play ASR systems and focus their work on more advanced challenges related to customizing the system to meet the specific needs of their employees and customers.

For all these reasons, the transformation of ASR from a complicated, imperfect technology into a commonplace, affordable, and highly accurate commodity service is a critical breakthrough in cost and convenience that is a key factor in making the coming voice revolution possible.

Natural language processing (NLP) comes next. Once the software knows the words you've said, the next task is understanding what they mean and responding to them correctly. This is the process captured by NLP, and, like ASR, it's extraordinarily complex. Imagine a driver using her car-insurance company's voice-based customer-service system to make a claim after a driving mishap. She might start the exchange by saying, "I've been in a collision," "I got hit by another driver," "I'm calling to report a crash," "I've been in a fender-bender," "I was just rear-ended," "My car got sideswiped," or any of many other near-synonymous phrases, in this example literally hundreds or even thousands of possible iterations. Google has identified several thousand ways in which users do something as simple as ask for an alarm to be set. The NLP tools embedded in the system need to be able to make sense of all these locutions just to begin the conversation.

The challenge of NLP has not yet, as of this writing, been met with the high degree of accuracy that ASR has now attained. OpenAI's GPT framework has come the farthest. While it has achieved startling results in use cases where pattern recognition is bounded—like taking an SAT exam or composing a thank-you note—there is still a lot of work to do in unbounded business use cases where 95 percent accuracy is nowhere near good enough. Among other difficulties, the requirements for an effective NLP system vary enormously from one use case to another. The vocabulary, syntax, command and query forms, and other language characteristics of a neurosurgeon, an elementary-school teacher, a submarine commander, an archaeologist, and an auto mechanic will all be dramatically different—which means that the voice tools serving such varied users will need to be able to understand and respond intelligently to a wide array of language styles. It's a difficult task even for intelligent human employees; no wonder it's a tough challenge for an AI system.

Companies all over the world are working hard to develop the software capabilities needed to make NLP both truly effective and widely accessible. The work includes subfields of NLP whose names you may also encounter, such as *natural language understanding (NLU)*, which refers to the ability of a machine to understand human speech, and *natural language generation (NLG)*, which is the computer's ability to talk back to people in a way that sounds convincingly human. NLP has made huge strides in recent years—and recent developments in the field promise even greater progress in the years to come.

One of the big challenges in developing NLP tools has been the need to use vast troves of real-world voice interactions when training AI systems to understand language. If you want to build software that can participate easily in conversations about banking, it helps to have millions of hours of recorded conversations about banking for the software to analyze. The same goes for ordering food, handling travel reservations, dealing with health-care questions, or any other topic. Getting access to big, varied databases with real-world voice data is much easier for large, established companies, which means that such businesses have had a big edge over smaller ones when it comes to creating powerful voice tools. Tech giants like Amazon, Apple, and Google have also had an advantage in the voice sphere for much the same reason. This is one reason many of the pioneering leaders in the use of voice tech have been large companies—such as Capital One and Schwab in financial services, McDonald's and Domino's in fast food, Walmart in retail, and Disney in entertainment.

However, the challenge of accessing data troves is now beginning to be overcome thanks to recent technological breakthroughs. Software platforms like Genie and Open Virtual Assistant 2.0 have been developed that can generate synthetic voice data from relatively small real-world samples. Dr. Monica Lam, a professor in the computer science department at Stanford University, is the faculty director of the Stanford Open Virtual Assistant Laboratory. She and a team of researchers have been working to build and train a crowdsourced voice assistant called Almond, and they've been using Genie as a key tool in the training process. Dr. Lam reports that Genie has enabled them to conduct NLP training with significant efficiency gains, using a much smaller trove of real-world data and spending only about 1 percent of the traditional investment required to fund this kind of software development project.[10]

Conversational AI refers to the ability of software to use AI tools to both understand and generate language with a high degree of sophistication and flexibility, thereby simulating the kind of spontaneous, free-flowing conversations that people find natural and easy. Rather than requiring a human interlocutor to use set words or phrases contained in a pre-developed database, a voice system capable of conversational AI can interpret informal language, understand the speaker's underlying intention, and respond in kind. This level of linguistic prowess represents the highest development of both speech-understanding (NLU) and speech-generating (NLG) ability.

As you can imagine, natural language generation—the ability of a machine to talk in a quasi-human style—is particularly complex. But one fact you may find surprising is that NLG is *not* one of the most important goals for powerful voice interfaces to achieve. Studies have shown that most people *really don't care* whether the device they are talking to sounds like a real person—in fact, they often find it disturbing when it does. As we've noted, humanoid voice-activated assistants often end up occupying the "uncanny valley" (which we first discussed in our introduction), which makes simulations of human conversation feel more creepy than satisfying. Research shows that people trying to accomplish something with their computing tools want a fast, accurate response— not one that devotes time and energy to simulating human speech.

Furthermore, until recently, computers were unsuited to holding extended conversations. One of the core problems is that to hold an extended conversation—one that includes more than three exchanges between the two participants—significant understanding of the social context is required. This is something that software systems have long struggled with.

Here's an example—a conversation I held with Siri in August 2022:

> TOBIAS: "What's the weather in Miami today?"
>
> SIRI: "It's eighty-five and sunny today."
>
> TOBIAS: "What about tomorrow?"
>
> SIRI: "It's ninety-two and sunny tomorrow."
>
> TOBIAS: "Can you get me a flight?"

Disappointingly, Siri responded not with a suggested airline flight from my hometown to Miami, or even with a list of flight options, but rather with a link to Kayak, the travel service website.

In this example, the good news is that Siri was able to hold the conversation for two turns, "remembering" that we were talking about Miami when my query moved from today's weather to tomorrow's. That's an advance from a few years ago, where that type of context was often lost between the first turn and the second. But when we took a bigger context turn on the third interaction, Siri's conversational abilities broke down. Unlike a human assistant, Siri didn't make the obvious inference that the flight I was asking about would be Miami-bound.

Limitations like this mean that open-ended, or *unbounded*, conversations with devices have long been difficult to achieve. ChatGPT 3.5, which was released by its developers at OpenAI in November 2022, appears to have achieved new levels of competency for such unbounded conversations. Users have been impressed by this chatbot's ability to "remember" the topic of a conversation from one exchange to the next. Over time, this capability will find its way into a growing number of voice applications.

However, the key insight is that the multimodal approach to interface design makes the challenge of unbounded conversations less problematic than it might otherwise be. In most use cases, people don't necessarily want to engage in human-like conversation with their devices. They just want a fast, easy, efficient way to communicate in both directions. Taking advantage of *all* the communication modes available—including voice, text, sounds, images, and "haptics" (touch or vibration)—is generally more effective than relying on voice alone. As a result, voice adoption via multimodal interfaces can move forward rapidly, even as natural language generation continues to evolve.

Voice biometrics and *sentiment analysis* are two categories of voice tools that go one or more steps beyond natural language processing. Voice biometrics use voice data to identify individuals; sentiment analysis enables a computer not merely to understand the *meaning and intent* of the words a person says but also to recognize the *underlying emotions* that accompany those words. Like natural language understanding, these are tasks that most of us find natural and easy, but ones that are quite difficult to train a software tool to perform accurately, especially when cultural and age differences need to be taken into account. For example, our baseline analysis of sentiment when analyzing German and US customer-service calls is quite different.

Voice biometrics are fairly widely used today. However, as of 2022, sentiment analysis is still in its infancy, and current applications to real-world tasks are generally quite simple: for example, if the customer-service software senses that a customer's voice is expressing a rising level of frustration or irritation, it may signal a human customer-service specialist to enter the conversation. Sentiment analysis is likely to grow in effectiveness and importance—but significant technological refinements that may be a decade or more out will be required for it to become a reliable, multipurpose tool.

LOWERING ANOTHER BARRIER:
SMART, MULTIMODAL INTERFACE DESIGN

The key barrier to the mainstreaming of voice technology has been the failure to design interfaces that take the best advantage of the strengths of voice while minimizing its weaknesses.

Voice user interfaces (VUIs) vary from poor to good, better, and best. A well-designed VUI uses voice technology to create a user experience that is as efficient, frictionless, and pleasant as possible. And as every encounter with a poorly conceived app or web page reminds us, the art of interface design is a subtle and complex one. For voice to be an effective strategic tool and a source of competitive advantage, the leaders of a business have to devote the time, thought, research, and experimentation to ensuring that their company's voice user interfaces serve customer needs effectively.

Reinventing a business model to incorporate voice requires a deep dive into customer needs, expectations, assumptions, and preferences so that the interfaces they design can accurately reflect what customers find easy and efficient to use. Up to now, too many companies have failed to do this.

Here's an example. A restaurant menu is a relatively fixed list of choices from which a customer can select. This means that designing a voice app that can understand spoken menu orders and translate them into actions to be taken by the business—preparing a hamburger, for instance—is fairly straightforward. But our burgeoning experience in voice technology shows that, as the number of variations and the level of customization around menu items increases, the complexity of designing a practical voice interface grows rapidly. When a user can ask for the hamburger "rare," "medium," or "well-done," and with a choice of a dozen different condiments and garnishes, individually or in combination, then teaching the app to understand the instructions gets much, much tougher. As a result, the number of possible "error states" that the process may fall into can easily become unmanageably high.

It has taken a lot of deep research into customer behavior to find good solutions to this dilemma. A key approach is to limit the number of choices a user can select at any given time. Say a hungry smartphone user visits the app of her favorite fast-food store and declares, "I want a hamburger." The screen then morphs to show a picture of a hamburger along with the choice, "Rare, medium, or well-done?" Only after she answers this question will she be given a chance to choose add-ons like pickles, tomato, or avocado. This system is called *decision bounding*. It makes offering a voice option relatively quick and easy, without the complexity involved in having to create a system that is capable of understanding a much more extensive array of spontaneous utterances.

As of this writing in 2023, decision bounding is the most common design structure used in voice tech. It underlies the kinds of simple, voice-based customer-service systems most people are familiar with. For example, many businesses have adopted *interactive voice response* (IVR) systems that interact with callers and gather information by giving them choices via a menu. The IVR system then performs actions based on the answers of the caller through the telephone keypad or her voice response. When you call a business and get answers to basic questions like "What hours are you open?" or "What's your address?" through a series of prerecorded messages, you're interacting with an IVR system.

One step up in sophistication are voice systems that use artificial intelligence to recognize and respond to requests that are somewhat more varied and complex. However, most of these systems still retain the decision-bounding approach rather than attempting to engage in free-wheeling, open-ended conversations.

As you can see, using a decision-bounding system limits the flexibility of the voice interface by requiring users to proceed through the menu of options one choice at a time. However, if your user interface is well designed, most users will happily accept this kind of conversational structure. Here are some important tips for creating an interface design that users will find easy and convenient to use.

Explicitly guide the user through the steps of the interaction. From the start of the conversation, your voice interface should let users know what they can do at each step, including the kind of information the interface is prepared to accept. For example, suppose a visitor to an airline app begins the interaction by saying, "I need to fly from Boston to Indianapolis on Wednesday, March third." In response, the interface should guide the user to the next piece of information needed— for example, by displaying on the screen or saying, "What time of day would you like to travel?" If the options for a particular step in the interaction are limited, the interface should guide the user by providing those options: "We have three flights from Boston to Indianapolis on that day—one at 10:30 a.m., one at 2:25 p.m., and one at 5:15 p.m. Which flight would you prefer?" Walking the user through the process with clear, step-by-step instructions avoids needless confusion and frustration.

Provide examples to facilitate clear communication. If a user response needs to be framed in a specific way, the user interface should give an example to illustrate what's needed. For example, if the interface needs the user to provide a birth date, it could guide the user to the preferred format by displaying a date selection field, including specific options and formats for the day, month, and year.

Use visual or other cues to confirm the accuracy of communication. Human communication is largely nonverbal. According to UCLA psychology professor Albert Mehrabian, 55 percent of the meaning in conversation is conveyed through body language, 38 percent through tone, and just 7 percent through the words we use.[11] Designers need to bring this insight and way of thinking into the ways they design voice and multimodal experiences. Out-of-the-box ChatGPT does not solve this problem.

In a live person-to-person conversation, various kinds of cues are used to show that information is being transmitted and received accurately. A voice-based interface needs to provide the same kind of confirmation using visual or other signals. For example, while the user speaks, the microphone icon or other symbol appearing on the mobile screen might blink or flash, which sends the signal "I'm listening." And as each piece of necessary information is delivered, the screen can record it in visual form. Thus, when the request for an airline ticket between two specified cities has been received, the words "Boston to Indianapolis" can appear on the screen. The same "information received" message can be reinforced using sound cues or haptics—for example, a pleasantly chiming bell accompanied by a gentle vibration. These kinds of confirming signals provide the user with a small dose of emotional gratification, encouraging her to continue the interaction with a sense of confidence.

When communication fails, explain the cause of failure clearly. When the system is unable to understand or respond appropriately to the user's words, it's important for the interface to explain the problem as clearly and explicitly as possible, so the user can easily remedy it. Consider, for example, a user who asks a voice-based assistant, "What's the weather in Springfield?" The words in this question are easy for any speech-recognition system to interpret. But the communication lacks some vital information, since there are no fewer than thirty-four towns named Springfield in the United States! A well-designed voice interface will explain specifically what's needed to clarify the request—for example, by saying, "Springfield in what state?"

Interestingly, a researcher (based in California) who used this challenge to test the performance of several popular voice assistants found that some failed to take this simple step. Instead, they made an assumption about which Springfield was intended, providing the weather for towns in Oregon, Illinois, Missouri—and even Australia. The result would likely be confusion and perhaps annoyance on the part of users.[12]

As you can see, smart interface design is crucial to taking full advantage of the potential benefits of voice tech. I'll offer more insights and guidance about interface design in Chapter 9. For now, please note the power of a multimodal approach, the most flexible way of thinking about communication between people and devices.

One of the fundamental reasons that freestanding, voice-only assistants like Alexa often fail to meet our needs is because they can't engage in many of the activities that we like to perform with our devices. They can't

- Use visual or haptic cues to guide and confirm the accuracy of our communication with them
- Display text to communicate information that is easier to absorb through reading than listening
- Provide visual images to inform or engage us
- Show video clips to entertain us
- Link us to online communities where we can connect with other people
- Usher us into new spaces, enable us to participate in games, or empower us to be creative

For the most part, all they can do is speak to us—which is usually not enough to meet our ever-changing array of personal needs, and in some cases, it's exactly the opposite of the response we want or need.

The multimodal approach to interface design overcomes this problem. When used with devices such as smartphones, laptops, and tablets—all of which can communicate via screen, sound, and haptics as well as voice—the multimodal approach offers the most convenient and easiest way to connect with our devices:

- It lets users *read* information when that is the fastest way to absorb it.
- It lets users *type* information when that is the easiest and clearest way to transmit it to a device.
- It lets users *absorb* information through other, nonverbal means when that is the most efficient and effective mode of communication.

Think, for example, about the times and circumstances when the most powerful message you can receive from a device comes in the form of a melodious "ding" or a discreet vibration in a pocket. The multimodal approach to communication is a crucial breakthrough in the effort to lower the barriers that have discouraged more people from using voice technology.

To take advantage of this breakthrough, subtle but important shifts in our thinking are essential. For example, we need to change the terminology we use to describe our voice-driven devices from "smart speakers" to "smart listeners" or "smart mics." After all, what makes most voice-driven applications powerful and useful is their ability to hear and understand what we are saying, and then to respond appropriately— sometimes in spoken words, but most often through other modes of communication.

Thus, the "smartness" of Alexa and Siri should lie in their listening skill, not their speaking skill.

It also requires a rethinking of some of the assumptions of voice enthusiasts. For example, app designers excited by the growing capabilities of voice tools sometimes assume that voice is always the best choice for a user interface. In some cases, however, when designing responses to human voice requests, we should use voice only as a *last* resort. For instance, suppose the device's answer to a request from a human must be in the negative. In that case, a gentle buzz might be faster and more effective—and less obnoxious—than a "No" spoken by a computer, especially in certain cultures. When we get used to multimodal thinking, this reality is obvious—and the creative possibilities for effective interface design are multiplied.

The multimodal way of thinking is rapidly spreading. For example, in May 2022, Google announced a new way of interacting with its Google Nest Hub Max, a so-called smart display that provides tools for managing your home and the technology it contains. Called "Look and Talk," it lets you activate Google Assistant simply by *looking* at the device and talking to it, rather than having to use a wake-up phrase like "Hello, Google." Using AI tools for voice and face recognition, the Look and Talk system can distinguish a passing glance from a focused look, and it can offer a response tailored to the specific individual user.[13]

The combination of communication modes employed by this smart display illustrates how multimodal design can work. It offers great flexibility to interface designers who are seeking ways to make their systems easier and more convenient for users.

ONE MORE BARRIER: BRIDGING THE TRUST GAP

One additional barrier to voice adoption that leaders need to address is the *trust gap*. As with any new technology, customers and employees must be convinced that voice tech is being used to advance their best interests and never to manipulate, exploit, or mislead them.

Tech giants including Microsoft, Amazon, Google, and Apple were all implicated in voice technology's first major scandal in the summer of 2019, when third-party contractors revealed they had been paid to listen to and analyze users' recorded speech. In the process, they'd overheard conversations they were not meant to hear, including some that were embarrassingly intimate.[14] Precisely because voice is such a natural mode of human interaction, people feel doubly betrayed when their spoken words are misused.

Research and experience suggest that this is a potentially solvable problem—provided companies are willing to devote the time, energy, and resources to addressing it seriously. Research has shown that users are willing to make reasonable trade-offs between privacy and convenience, so long as the choices they face are presented with transparency and in good faith. Following this principle scrupulously and thoughtfully is especially important for non-tech companies. While the Amazons, OpenAIs, Googles, and Apples of the world may be able to rebound from minor breaches of trust, the businesses and brands that play on these platforms, such as banks, health-care providers, and retailers, may not be able to. Voice-technology users should always be able to ask their devices or applications, "What data do you collect, and what do you do with it?" Clear, accurate answers to these questions that users can judge for themselves should be readily accessible on company websites. Corporate spokespeople should be thoroughly informed about the details of privacy policies and empowered to respond to questions and challenges honestly and openly. And users should be able to easily opt out of data-sharing options before or after making use of a voice-powered application.

These basic principles are easy to articulate, but not so easy to apply. Bridging the trust gap is a serious challenge for practically every institution in today's high-tech world, and companies that use voice tools are no exception.

Many leaders in the voice-technology space are deeply engaged in working on ways to bridge the trust gap. One of the most important efforts has been launched by the Open Voice Network, a nonprofit community of the Linux Foundation. It has enlisted the help of tech designers and practitioners, entrepreneurs, academic experts, social and community organizers, and users of voice tech to begin developing a set of ethical guidelines that can help ensure that uses of voice technology are trustworthy, inclusive, and socially beneficial—while also, of course, providing economic and practical benefits to everyone involved. The network is in the early stages of its work, but some of the steps it has taken are useful pointers to the kinds of issues the entire voice-tech industry must address in the years to come.

The Open Voice Network's Ethical Use Task Force issued its first set of working guidelines in April 2022. This document grapples with a number of the core issues that companies using voice technology need to take seriously. Here are two of the most crucial:

- *What guidelines should be employed to limit the uses of voice technology to identify, analyze, and deduce sensitive personal information about a user?* As we've seen, new tools are making it possible to diagnose health conditions, emotional states, and other personal characteristics simply by analyzing their voice. This raises challenges related to privacy and bias, among other issues. Who "owns" the data generated by analysis of a user's voice? How should that data be verified, stored, used, and shared? Abuse of the information generated in this way could seriously damage the willingness of customers to use voice tools—and understandably so. It's important that we develop clear, consistent regulations and principles to guard users' privacy and respect the rights of users to understand fully how their voice-related data is being used—and it's essential for companies to follow those regulations and principles throughout the entire process of designing and implementing voice-tech tools.

- *How can we ensure that voice-tech tools are designed to maximize diversity, inclusion, and fairness?* One of the enormous potential benefits of voice technology is its ability to make a wide range of activities accessible to people from many backgrounds, including those with physical impairments, those with varying levels of literacy, those who speak less widely used languages, and many others. Yet these benefits will not happen automatically. The leaders of organizations need to assemble diverse teams to develop voice tools, to test those tools with widely varying user groups, and to take concrete, proactive steps to avoid building any forms of bias into those tools or into the AI systems that drive them.

Users' early experience with the ChatGPT chatbot illustrates another aspect of the trust challenge. ChatGPT is extremely skilled at generating text that sounds persuasive and "human"—intelligent, thoughtful, articulate, and relevant to whatever question or prompt the user provides. The problem is that some of the information that ChatGPT packages so attractively turns out to be simply false. An example: when a technology blogger tried to test ChatGPT by asking it to name "the largest country in Central America that isn't Mexico," it responded with Guatemala—but the correct answer is Nicaragua.[15]

It goes without saying that a voice tool that gives false information to users will instantly forfeit their trust—and rightly so. Thankfully, there's a relatively easy fix for the vast majority of organizations using AI-driven voice tools to serve customers or employees. In almost every case, your voice system will be addressing a tightly limited set of topics and tasks. It's very possible to train an AI system on a set of specific data points—the complete inventory of all the products your company sells, for example—and instruct it *not* to contrive or offer information that goes beyond the limits of that data. The problem with ChatGPT— at least as of early 2023—was that it purported to serve a virtually endless array of purposes. This led to users quickly discovering, and exceeding, the very real limits of its capabilities.

To earn and keep users' trust, design your voice system to provide a limited number of useful, important services—and then deploy AI tools as needed to provide those services correctly, every time.

Jon Stine is the executive director of the Open Voice Network. He brings a deep understanding of the power of voice technology to the challenge of user trust. "Voice makes it easy for the user to say yes," as Jon says. That's the great strength of voice—its convenience, speed, and ease of use. But industry leaders have a responsibility to make sure that these qualities do not come to be seen as seductive ways of luring users into choices they will later come to regret. Stine and his team have set a goal of helping the emerging voice-tech industry to develop tools that are worthy of user trust—because, as Stine says, this is the only way that voice tech can create *sustainable*, long-term value for the enterprises that use it.[16]

THREE WAVES OF VOICE-TECH ADOPTION

As we've seen in this chapter, the spread of voice technology has been held back by a number of barriers—technical, organizational, social. These barriers have begun to fall—first slowly, now with increasing speed.

As a result, we're now witnessing the first of three waves of change that the spread of voice will bring to the economy. With each successive wave, the impact of voice will be more powerful, pervasive, and transformative. In the years to come, every industry will be impacted by the coming three waves. Here is a brief description of each, along with some examples of how they will work in three model industries— banking, restaurants, and hospitals. I've chosen these three because they are arenas in which voice tech is already making significant inroads, enabling us to forecast with some clarity what the coming stages of adoption may look like.

Wave One: Productivity Gains Through Automation

In Wave One of voice adoption, the automation via voice technology of processes formerly handled through live human conversations, keyboarding, or other relatively slow and expensive communication modes will produce significant productivity gains and cost savings—all while leaving the underlying process largely unchanged. Here's how Wave One may play out in our three model industries.

Banking: The current basic interactive voice response systems for customer service will be replaced with smart in-app voice interactions, saving banks an estimated 90 to 95 percent of their costs per call while significantly improving customer satisfaction. Service personnel freed from handling basic inquiries will be able to focus on more challenging services, such as offering investment options or handling complex transactions.

Restaurants: Voice-based smartphone and computer apps, drive-through terminals, and delivery services will increasingly receive orders and payments using voice technology. This will reduce the need for personnel to handle routine, noncreative tasks, freeing them up to focus on more challenging work that requires the human touch—for example, greeting customers, handling special requests, and developing innovative menu options. It should also significantly improve user satisfaction—for example, by enabling a customer to order a meal in less than ten seconds rather than requiring several minutes with a live waiter or a minute or more using a typical graphic interface.

Hospitals: Health-care facilities will expand the use of voice-tech tools to manage tasks such as dictation and real-time data/order entry. This will result in cost savings of some 60 to 80 percent as compared with traditional techniques for dictation and data entry. The real-time capture of data within hospitals—for example, from nurses, therapists, and technicians—will also help to make the data in the system more accurate and timely, improving the overall quality of care.

Wave Two: Business Process Redesign

In Wave Two, the spread of voice technology to additional processes within the organization will enable the redesign of some traditional business operations. As a result, some familiar elements of the organizational structure may change their nature, shrink in importance, or disappear altogether. As tech tools automate activities, employees will be able to shift their time and energy to more complex, creative, and challenging tasks, making the organization as a whole more innovative and competitive. Here's how Wave Two may play out in our three model industries.

Banking: Voice-based interfaces will help to make banking accessible to all demographics, including less affluent individuals and those who live in poorer communities, many of whom are currently among the "unbanked." As the need for branches to handle routine transactions plummets, the long-sought vision of the "branchless bank" will finally become a reality. Human employees will move to taking seamless handoffs from the voice system to manage complex or novel problems and to provide customized financial advice to customers. As service options multiply, consumers will increasingly flock to banks that can offer both the lowest fees and the best user experience, both driven by voice technology.

Restaurants: Service at fast-food and casual-dining restaurants will be reimagined as ordering and payment both become automated through voice interfaces. With routine communication tasks handled by voice tools, service employees will be able to focus on delivery of food to homes, pickup areas, and dining tables. As a result, we can expect significant cost savings, increased service speed, redeployment of personnel from routine tasks to more challenging services that demand "people skills," and eventually the redesign of restaurant spaces to reflect the diminished importance of administrative activities.

Hospitals: Health-care processes and patient handoffs will be redesigned, as data-entry tasks that now require unwieldy activities (such as wheeling computers and keyboards around wards) are replaced by efficient, voice-based data-capture processes, often using smartphones. As a result, hospital workloads, equipment costs, and error rates will be reduced. In time, the physical layout of hospitals will be significantly changed to take advantage of these new efficiencies.

Wave Three: Business Model Transformation

In Wave Three, as voice technology becomes even more widely and deeply embedded in organizations, some industries will find their business models radically altered. New ways of delivering value, new forms of competition, and new strategic challenges will emerge in many business arenas. Here's how our three model industries might be affected by the changes occurring in Wave Three.

Banking: Traditional banks as a concept may begin to disappear as the ease of use of multimodal interfaces makes old paradigms largely obsolete. Voice-powered platforms focused on delivering the best possible user experience—like today's Venmo and PayPal, but more versatile, efficient, and powerful—will begin offering a wider array of services, from accepting direct employer deposits and paying interest on account balances to delivering voice-driven payment capabilities and even customized advice on investments. Over time, consumers will increasingly question the value of traditional banks, and teenagers will start asking their parents questions like "What is a savings account?" and "What is a check?"

Restaurants: The entire concept of a restaurant begins to morph into unfamiliar new forms. With ordering and payment automated, central kitchens located in low-cost areas will be established to prepare food for delivery to homes, pickup locations, or communal dining areas serviced by multiple restaurants. (Uber founder Travis Kalanick is already working on this concept as his "next big thing"—and flirting with controversy in the process.)[17] This business-model transformation, with massive implications for the restaurant and real-estate businesses, will be driven by voice technology and the improvements in efficiency and consumer satisfaction it makes possible.

Hospitals: The traditional way in which health care is delivered will be reimagined. Voice-analysis tools will be used to diagnose a range of common illnesses. With the entry of patient data automated and accelerated, the real-time analysis of patient/caregiver interactions will be used to generate care plans, monitor progress, and issue alerts. Some hospital functions will be replaced by services offered at home or in convalescent centers, with voice tools making telemedicine increasingly accessible, efficient, and powerful.

As you can imagine, the rate of progress toward widespread voice adoption varies widely from one industry to another. Our work with companies from many arenas at WillowTree gives us a good vantage point on these variations. As of this writing, we see voice tech already making major inroads in industries such as financial services (banking, credit cards, insurance, investing); media (the internet, streaming entertainment, movies, news); restaurants, especially fast food; hospitality (hotels, airlines, travel agencies); retail (especially product discovery and ordering); and in customer service (across multiple industries).

By contrast, the industries where voice is beginning to make inroads but where only a fraction of its full potential has so far been realized include health care (hospitals, clinics, primary care providers); office and business administration; manufacturing; resource extraction (mining, forestry, oil and gas, sustainable energy); and supply chain management (warehousing, fulfillment, shipping).

The growth of voice tech is continuing to accelerate across all these fields. As it does, the opportunities for smart business leaders will continue to expand. So will the competitive pressures, as some companies change the way their customers and employees interact with computers, while other companies are left behind.

8

MAKING VOICE AN INTEGRAL PART OF YOUR EXISTING BUSINESS SYSTEMS

THERE ARE THREE CRUCIAL STEPS COMPANY LEADERS SHOULD be working on *right now* in order to address the challenges and seize the opportunities offered by voice technology, and to position themselves to take full competitive advantage of the voice revolution unfolding over the next five to ten years. The next three chapters will explain these three steps.

Finding ways to integrate voice tech into your existing business systems is your first step. This process starts with breaking free of the misleading vision of voice technology as a kind of freestanding connection between people and machines, operating in its own sphere through an array of specialized devices. Historical accidents have made this vision widespread—specifically, the fact that stand-alone "smart speaker" devices housing voice avatars like Alexa have helped to launch the battle to dominate the age of voice. But though such devices have helped to make many people more comfortable with the idea of talking to their machines, they do *not* represent the next phase of the voice revolution.

Some technology gurus—including the brilliant Adam Cheyer, whom we profiled in Chapter 7—have promoted the idea of a "robotic valet" that responds to voice commands and, at least in theory, is capable of handling all our needs and wants—ordering groceries, balancing our checkbook, buying theater tickets, making a doctor appointment, planning a vacation. According to some, voice assistants like Alexa and Siri are supposed to represent the early versions of such an all-purpose robotic helper.

There's just one problem with this vision. Customer experience backs up what market research shows: very few people are attracted to the concept of the voice-driven, robotic valet. A stand-alone device that specializes in listening and responding to voice commands is *not* what most people want for at least three major reasons.

The first is the discoverability problem. Most users have no easy way to figure out what a voice assistant can do or cannot do. They may realize that it can easily handle a Google search or a simple question like "Will it rain in Chicago today?" But they don't intuitively know, for example, whether the assistant can find and suggest a great spot for a picnic in the Chicago area, choose a nearby deli that can pack a delicious lunch, and order it for pickup at the perfect time. Without knowing what the voice assistant can do and precisely how to access that support, the user is left to experiment blindly, often with frustrating results.

Second, a true robotic valet would be required to understand and interact effectively with a broad swath of the human experience. As we saw in Chapter 7, the ability of AI-powered algorithms to comprehend the social context of conversations is currently quite limited, even with the latest GPT models from OpenAI. As a result, at this point in their evolution, digital assistants remain highly unreliable when asked to apply the kind of sophisticated insight needed to rapidly grasp and act upon the instructions provided in an unbounded interaction. Narrow and highly bounded application assistants, like Capital One's Eno, are easier to develop and much more reliable.

Finally, as we've discussed, the more human-like an assistant becomes in its appearance and behavior, the less people are likely to trust it. This problem of the uncanny valley, which I explained in the introduction, continues to pose a barrier to the acceptability of a robotic valet as a companion for our everyday lives.

Instead, at least for now, what people really want is to continue to use all the many separate interfaces they know, trust, and like, including the various apps and websites they use on their smartphones, laptops, and tablets, each dedicated to a particular range of activities—only with the added convenience of voice. Thus, in the world of the near future, the average person will want to use voice technology to talk directly to the grocery store, the bank, the movie theater, the doctor's office, and the airline rather than using a robotic valet to do it for them.

As this alternative future vision becomes reality, you won't spend your day with Alexa or Siri listening in to your activities and serving as a voice intermediary to handle a range of chores on your behalf. Voice tech will indeed play a valuable role in your life, but not through a robotic valet. Instead, when you want to make a reservation at your favorite hotel chain, you'll speak directly with the company's AI-powered representative, who will recognize your voice, remember your past visits, know your special preferences, and quickly confirm your upcoming plans. And most often, that voice representative will live within the company's app, which you already have downloaded on your always-on, always-with-you smartphone.

The discoverability problem will be solved by eliminating it altogether. The entry point to voice experiences will be the apps and websites you use today. To arrange a picnic lunch, you won't ask Alexa or Siri to order one; you'll just pull up the app of your favorite food-ordering service and start speaking. In most cases, the app you already have on your phone, either as a customer or an employee, will be the starting point of your voice journey.

You'll get to have what you really want—the speed and convenience of expressing what you want through speech—while retaining a greater level of control over your consumer choices, the information you provide and receive, and your personal privacy. You'll also keep your one-on-one relationships with the companies and brands you like rather than having to channel your requests through a third-party intermediary. That means you'll continue to accumulate frequent-traveler points from the hotel chains and airlines you prefer; you'll order groceries from the services that carry the brands and products you favor; you'll refresh your summer wardrobe with T-shirts, shorts, and swimsuits from the sportswear company whose styles and sizing work best for you; and when packages are on their way to you, you'll track their arrival by speaking with an AI-powered voice agent from the delivery service. All of these companies will make it easy for you by providing voice interfaces that are convenient, smart, and fast.

For this reason, leaders who want to see their business benefit from the voice revolution must stop focusing on the stand-alone voice experience. Instead, they must set about incorporating voice into their existing legacy systems for key areas such as sales, customer service, and logistics. Voice will be the interface layer that sits between the human being and the device, the data, and the functionality the human being is trying to access. The integration of voice connections into systems that currently rely overwhelmingly on keyboards or touch screens will produce immediate benefits for customers and companies alike. It will provide customers with the seamless, fast, convenient, accurate, and custom-designed services they want. And eliminating third-party voice-bot agents will allow companies to retain their customers' loyalty, to keep control over the flow of marketplace data, to avoid having to share revenues with a voice-tech intermediary, and to tailor their voice tools to embody the branding characteristics that make their businesses unique.

Thoughtful observers of voice technology have foreseen this trend for quite a while. As far back as March 2019—an age ago in the fast-paced world of digital tech—Bret Kinsella, the publisher of Voicebot.ai and arguably today's leading commentator on the voice industry, predicted it in a column with the title "Why Alexa and Google Assistant Will Spawn Thousands of Assistants."[1] A year and a half later, Kinsella had to amend his prediction: "It now seems more likely there will be *millions* of assistants [emphasis added]. Most of those will essentially be voice assistants-as-applications for brands and enterprises. Don't believe me? Spotify, Pandora, BBC, Bank of America, Capital One, Charles Schwab, U.S. Bank, Comcast, Deutsche Telekom, Swiss Telecom, Telifonica, Ikea, BMW, Ford, GM, Mercedes, and many others have voice assistants as part of their products or mobile apps."[2]

In earlier chapters of this book, I've already described how industry leaders are integrating voice into both the activities of their daily business and their longer-term strategy—and thereby reducing or eliminating the role played by third-party voice intermediaries. Consider following their lead. Beginning the work of incorporating voice as a tool to activate and enhance your existing customer apps, rather than imagining that some future version of Alexa or Siri will do it for you, is a challenging and important job.

IDENTIFYING YOUR VOICE CASES

The work begins with *identifying your voice cases*: looking closely at every significant process within your business system. That includes interactions among your employees and interactions between your company and its customers. In each case, ask yourself how information and instructions are being transmitted. What modes of connection are being used? Where is friction apparent—instances where an interaction is time-consuming, awkward, error-prone, or simply annoying? And how can those interactions be streamlined, accelerated, made more accurate, reduced in cost, or otherwise improved?

Particularly in cases where a keyboard is the chief mode of communication—whether on a computer, a tablet, or a smartphone—there may be the opportunity to convert the communication to voice, achieving meaningful improvements in the process. There are six categories of interactions that are especially good targets for this sort of improvement:

- *Conveying information to devices*: Interactions involving extensive data-entry tasks—for example, filling out an insurance claim form, opening a checking account with a bank, submitting an expense-account report to human resources, or completing a customer-satisfaction survey.

- *Retrieving data*: Interactions aimed at retrieving specific information or solutions from the sea of data in which we are all immersed. Because users can easily say much longer search phrases than they can type, voice enables much more detailed and specific information search than traditional keyboarding.

- *Handling transactions*: Interactions largely focused on economic exchange—for example, purchasing a product or service from an online market, making a cash transfer between one person's account and another's, subscribing to an online publication, or paying a credit-card bill.

- *Operating hands-free and heads-up*: Interactions in environments such as warehouses and factories, or while engaging in activities such as driving, law enforcement, military operations, or engaging with customers, in which having both hands and eyes available and unoccupied is critical.

- *Gathering ambient information*: Interactions in which information from the surrounding ecosystem can be captured, analyzed, and responded to. Typical settings include hospitals and clinics, government and legal offices, and call centers.

- *Facilitating instant responses*: Interactions that enable direct navigation to an experience that was previously cumbersome, such as finding a show or responding to an ad.

Start by listing all the processes like these that are a routine part of the interactions your organization engages in. The users involved may include external customers (the people who buy your products or use your services); internal people in your offices, factory, warehouse, and out in the field; and external business partners such as retailers, vendors, and service suppliers.

Then review the list of processes with a team drawn from every department that touches the transactions. These might include sales, customer service, finance, production, marketing, logistics, and human resources. Brainstorm whether some or all of the keyboard-based communications you engage in with your users could be simplified by substituting voice communication. For each interaction, ask the question: Is it likely that users would find it easier, faster, and more convenient to handle this interaction, in part or in whole, through voice?

If your collective answer to that question is yes, then you've identified a process that can serve as one of your organization's initial voice cases—an opportunity to begin improving your operations. As you get started in incorporating voice technology, you may choose to focus on just one or two cases. The experience you gain from a couple of experimental projects will help you judge which voice cases work well for your organization, which ones are less compelling, and how you may want to expand your use of voice into other areas over time.

We spoke with an information-technology administration manager at a professional-services firm who described the way his company has gradually incorporated voice tech into a growing range of business activities.[3] (He requested anonymity for competitive reasons.) The firm first employed voice to help streamline its customer relations department. A voice bot with AI-powered links to various databases was developed to provide round-the-clock information service to client companies. Next, a voice bot was created to serve the company's own employees in the marketing department. While working offsite—for example, making presentations to clients at their headquarters—the marketing staffers could use the voice bot to get data and answers to questions at any time of the day or night.

Having discovered how useful these voice tools could be in helping the company connect effectively with customers, it began adapting such tools for internal purposes. For instance, the human-resources department now uses a specialized voice bot with access to the company's employee database to handle most of the questions formerly managed by HR professionals: "How much paid-leave time have I used so far this year, and how much time do I have left?" "I'm planning to take a graduate-level course in software design next fall. Will the tuition be covered by our educational benefits program?"

Today, the company is examining the possibility of adapting voice tools to facilitate automatic payment of invoices from outside contractors, suppliers, and others. The goal would be to eliminate the time-consuming process of generating and circulating paper forms when payments are due, instead allowing selected team members to process payments simply through voice messages. It expects to move carefully and deliberately on this front, for obvious reasons—when large sums of money are involved, safeguards against error, fraud, and security breaches are essential. They'll implement this next stage of voice adoption only when the systems appear practically impervious. That, of course, is the appropriate attitude to take.

FINDING VOICE-TECH CASES:
EXAMPLES OF THE PROCESS IN ACTION

Every company will of course choose its own path when it comes to identifying cases for implementing voice tech. Gordon Chu, manager of conversational AI at Cathay Pacific Airways, has been working with an internal team and a number of external developers to create voice-based tools (voice bots) to make the organization's customer-service processes easier and faster. So far, they've managed to automate the response to some 40 to 60 percent of the queries received from customers by telephone, including most routine questions such as flight delays and seat assignments. Currently, the Cathay Pacific voice bots must respond to some of the more complex requests (involving questions ranging from travel visas to insurance forms) by sending customers off to other self-service locations, such as the airline website or mobile app, or by engaging a human service agent. In the months and years to come, a key goal for Cathay Pacific is to gradually expand the number of customer-service use cases they can handle through voice technology. When 90 percent of customer calls can be fully managed through automated voice tools, they'll have reached a major milestone, providing both improved service and significant cost savings. Experts estimate that the average customer call converted to automated voice-tech response can save a company between five and eight dollars.

At the same time, Cathay Pacific is exploring other potential use cases beyond customer service. For example, the airline is developing plans for using voice tools to simplify and automate communications tasks for the aircraft-maintenance teams working in airport hangars and for cabin crews who service the planes between flights.[4] The centralized voice team led by Chu will continue to examine all of the airline's operations looking for opportunities to save time, money, and other resources. As their experience level rises, their knowledge and dexterity will increase, and the usefulness and value of voice to every department of Cathay Pacific will steadily grow.

Cathay Pacific's approach is a good example of how big companies with complex operations may want to proceed with voice tech. The airline started by "going big" with voice-powered customer service—an activity in which effective voice tools have already been widely used by a range of companies, and one where improved efficiency can produce significant gains in customer satisfaction. (Any traveler can testify to the frustrations engendered by service snafus—delayed flights, lost bags—and the enormous relief felt when such problems get resolved quickly.) Having established a strong foothold in customer service, and honing their expertise in the process, Cathay Pacific's voice team is now moving to explore ways to use the same technology to improve other organization processes. This is a sound voice strategy that should produce cascading benefits in the years to come.

A variety of factors can play a role in determining how and where you should begin incorporating voice into your systems. Van West is CEO of Vocalytics AI, a firm that helps companies develop tools for capturing and interpreting ambient sounds in order to enhance customer service. West talks about the powerful opportunities his company has discovered to make use of voice to improve the client experience in the world of health care. One reason for these abundant opportunities is the simple fact that hundreds of thousands of hospital beds are already equipped with microphones. Until now, they've been used almost exclusively for a single, low-tech purpose: to allow patients to ask nurses or aides for help. Now, with today's AI-powered voice tools, the same microphones can do much more. Vocalytics is using them to pick up sounds from the hospital room that can alert caregivers to problems that would otherwise go unnoticed—for example, patient coughs that may indicate an emergent respiratory problem, or voices raised in anger that could signal an out-of-control patient creating a safety threat against staff.[5]

The infrastructure of countless bed-based microphones, already in place in so many hospitals, gives these facilities a huge leg up when it comes to capturing the value inherent in the continual flow of sound. Does your industry offer similar opportunities? Examine the environment within which you do business. Your customers may already be using voice-based tools in a basic form to interact with your business— for example, through traditional customer-service phone lines. The same may be true of your employees—for example, you may have field service representatives or salespeople who stay in touch with the home office via phone or Zoom. As Vocalytics did, you can examine these basic uses of voice to determine whether the new voice technologies offer ways to expand the services provided or improve their efficiencies. Environmental features you take for granted may help you uncover a potential voice case from which your company can benefit.

Another important lesson from Cathay Pacific is that companies looking for possible voice cases should search both internal and external opportunities. I've described a number of cases in which voice tools are being used to make it easier for consumers to get information about products, place orders, track deliveries, request help, and access other services. Similar tools can provide support to your own employees as well.

For example, retail stores and the companies that provide them with goods are deploying voice systems throughout their facilities not just to serve customers but to empower sales staffs. A team of researchers from MIT describes how beacon-activated microphones in retail facilities are enabling employees to quickly reorder merchandise the moment a need is identified. "By capturing these demand signals earlier than cyclical ordering systems do," the researchers explain, "retailers and their suppliers will gain new insight into demand profiles to which they can tailor their supply operations. . . . This could help solve the 'phantom inventory' problem, in which unavailable items are mistakenly shown as available—a major cause of lost sales."[6]

One retailer using voice tech to empower its employees is the Container Store chain. The company had long used traditional walkie-talkies and overhead speakers to connect its employees with one another, but it wanted a system that would be faster, easier to use, more efficient, and ubiquitous. The Container Store worked in partnership with the voice-tech firm Theatro to custom-design a mobile communication platform using small, wearable mic-plus-speaker devices that every employee and manager can use. The Theatro device gives every team member immediate access to data regarding pricing, product specs, available inventory—including at nearby Container Store outlets—as well as status updates on in-store pickups. Other retailers such as Walgreens and Bass Pro Shops are using their own versions of the Theatro system.[7]

There are many other inefficient, costly, or underused organizational systems that can potentially benefit from the integration of voice technology. Consulting giant Accenture, for example, has a code of business ethics that is supposed to guide the behavior of all its employees. The code prescribes legal and ethical principles that should be applied to six fundamental areas of behavior:

- Making conduct count
- Compliance with laws
- Delivering for clients
- Protecting people, information, and the business
- Running the business responsibly
- Being a good corporate citizen

The code is frequently updated to address changing business and social conditions. It's a valuable tool for protecting both Accenture and the clients they serve, and the organization takes it very seriously.

But there's a problem. Accenture employees have not always consulted and followed the code as often as they should, partly because of its complexity and density. As a result, some business problems that would benefit from application of the code go unnoticed and unresolved.

To address this issue, Accenture's executive team in charge of compliance worked with their digital marketing division, called Fjord, to design a voice interface, accessible by computer or mobile device, that can provide quick responses to employees' ethical issues and concerns. Dubbed COBE (Code of Business Ethics), the tool uses AI capabilities to search the code of ethics for information and concepts relevant to an employee's question. This enables the system to provide quick, specific answers to most ethical dilemmas. When a problem is more serious, the voice system refers users to human experts who can provide further guidance, including internal legal counsel and, when necessary, government authorities. Both the identities of the users and the details of the issue are kept confidential, and information from the searches is never used to drive investigations or disciplinary actions against employees.

Since introducing the voice interface, employee inquiries about ethical challenges have reached over 2,000 a week, a twenty-fold increase over the former rate. It means that employees are taking advantage of the existence of COBE to get guidance on thorny ethical challenges directly from an authoritative source—which is exactly the response that Accenture's ethics team was hoping for.[8]

Are there activities, tools, or resources within your organization that are potentially valuable but underutilized? Providing access through voice tools may be a way of unlocking all that hidden value. Seeking such underutilized sources of value is another way to identify voice cases your organization may want to address.

APPLYING THE LONG TAIL PRINCIPLE

The *long tail* principle is an important factor to be top-of-mind when defining your list of voice cases. As we noted in Chapter 3, the concept of the long tail refers to issues critical to customer satisfaction but that occur relatively rarely. In the world of publishing, for example, a "long tail book" is a niche product that is unlikely to ever appear on a best-seller list, but that is highly valued by a specific audience and therefore may sell steadily, in modest numbers, for many years. Publishers specializing in books aimed at small but passionate audiences, from opera lovers to rock-climbing fans, can build very successful businesses based on serving long tail markets.

Many other businesses have their own long tail markets—customer groups with needs and interests that are important but relatively rare. Voice technology can make it easier to serve such markets, because

AI-powered voice technology enables a high degree of customization and personalization. This flexibility means that you can often use voice tools to serve customers and support employees even in regard to activities you think of as niche processes that are rarely used.

In financial services, for example, the majority of people who call their bank, visit its website, or click on its mobile app do so for a small handful of common reasons, such as to check on their account balance. That's the kind of information a bank user may need to access several times in a given month. By contrast, most people need to look up their bank's ABA routing number or SWIFT code very rarely, generally only when it's required to facilitate an interbank funds transfer. Because it's a highly unusual request, this falls into the category of long tail services.

For most customers, getting the bank's SWIFT code requires a call to a bank office. But now a number of banks have deployed voice assistants that can provide the code number instantly, saving customers time and aggravation while reducing service costs to the bank. And this is just one example of the long tail banking services being facilitated by voice. According to executive Richard Weeks, head of conversational experiences at U.S. Bank, his bank's voice-based mobile app can handle more than 300 different types of customer requests, some of them very unusual and rare.[9]

This is the kind of complex challenge that only voice tools can adequately address. No designer, no matter how talented, can find a user-friendly and efficient way to organize 300 features to be navigable and easily findable on a smartphone screen. A well-designed voice tool that has been trained to recognize and respond quickly to hundreds of different requests makes the process of discovering these kinds of long tail services very simple.

The cumulative impact on bank service centers is potentially enormous. A given bank with hundreds of thousands of customers may only need to handle 1,000 or so SWIFT code requests in a single month. But when you multiply 1,000 automated service calls by 300 different services, suddenly you are looking at hundreds of thousands of calls for which human support is no longer needed. The cost savings and the service benefits to customers are both significant.

The power of voice to provide customized services even in response to little-used or obscure requests helps to explain one important trend in marketing. Voice search via engines like Google or devices like Alexa and Siri is increasingly focused on highly customized local results—not just "plastic surgery" or even "plastic surgery in Columbus, Ohio" but "Which Columbus plastic surgeons specialize in men's body sculpting surgery?"[10] Recent statistics suggest that some 58 percent of voice-search users have discovered local businesses through this tool.[11] As highlighted in Part One of the book, the breakthrough that voice provides is to make detailed, multi-word searches much easier and therefore more common. Users find it cumbersome to type "Which plastic surgeons in Columbus, Ohio, specialize in men's body sculpting surgery?" into a search bar—but speaking it aloud is quick and easy, and users will happily do so if they believe it will give them more accurate search results.

The power of voice-based search engines to identify local providers to meet highly specific needs offers valuable benefits both to prospective customers and to the companies that want to serve them. Marketers and web designers cognizant of this trend have been modifying their search engine optimization (SEO) techniques to take full advantage of it. Short, one- or two-word keywords that were formerly the gold standard when crafting internet content are giving way to "long-tail keywords" that are highly descriptive, include localized descriptions and data, and mimic the language used by people in conversational speech.[12] These kinds of modifications greatly increase the odds that customers using voice search to find a product or service will find your company first—including a way to access your offerings in their own community.

It's another example of how voice technology can help you connect with the long tail of niche consumers—in this case, highly targeted groups of potential customers in a particular geographic location, who are valuable leads.

To take full advantage of the long tail principle, don't merely scratch the surface when you are searching for use cases for voice. Dig deep into the details of what your customers, employees, and business partners want to do with you. You're likely to uncover a surprisingly long list of ways that people would like to connect with you—many of which can be made easier, faster, and more efficient than ever through voice tech.

To identify long tail services that voice can help to supply, think about the niche customer groups you serve. It's likely that some of these groups have special needs that currently are poorly met or that require a significant level of customized human intervention, which can be both inefficient and costly.

For example, suppose you provide a product or service for older people. Voice technology can be a powerful way to make it easier, safer, and more convenient for them to take advantage of the benefits you have to offer. Older adults who find it difficult to use a keyboard (due to arthritis, for example), have trouble making out the tiny print on a smartphone, or never quite got the hang of using complex computer software often respond with delight and enthusiasm when given the opportunity to use voice commands to interact with technology.

When a retirement community in San Diego launched a project to help residents in using voice tools for tasks like playing music or controlling the lights and temperature controls in the home, the reaction was overwhelming. "They're simple things, but these simple things can have tremendous and dramatic implications for daily living," said Davis Park, executive director of the center. "It blew us out of the water at how really excited people were."[13] When your business incorporates a voice interface into its customer-facing services, you may be happily surprised by the increase in the number of older customers you attract.

The same applies to people with disabilities, who experts estimate make up close to a quarter of the adult population.[14] Their needs and preferences are often overlooked by product designers, service providers, and marketing teams, all of whom focus mainly on customers with mainstream capabilities. For many of these neglected individuals, well-crafted voice tools can quickly and economically expand the usefulness of countless products and services.

Robin Christopherson is visually impaired and the head of digital inclusion at AbilityNet, a UK-based nonprofit that has been working since 1998 to develop tools and services to help people with disabilities make better use of technology. For him, the arrival of voice tools has been life-changing. "What Siri can do in five seconds might take me five minutes, or sometimes ten!" he says. And Sam Berman, an accessibility consultant who has lost the use of one hand—which makes typing slow and laborious—can offer a long list of activities that are now faster and easier for him thanks to the use of voice tech, from setting a kitchen timer to scheduling medication reminders on his smartphone.[15] People like these may represent millions of potential customers who may be reachable for the first time through voice technology.

Groups like the elderly and the differently abled are often overlooked when companies design and market products and services. Or, there is the assumption that adapting a product to accommodate these groups would be too complicated and expensive. Take another look at this opportunity, and consider how voice technology, intelligently integrated into your business's overall systems, may be able to expand your customer base at modest additional cost.

WHAT LEVEL OF VOICE TECH DOES A PARTICULAR VOICE CASE DEMAND?

Much of the current buzz around voice technology centers on the gradual improvements being made in conversational AI—the increasing ability of algorithms to engage in quasi-human dialogues with people. Typical voice tools equipped with modern natural-language interfaces can generally recognize words and phrases drawn from a predefined lexicon of relevant terms. By contrast, tools with conversational AI capabilities can understand spoken language and the intent behind it even when non-standard words and phrases are used. They can also use sophisticated tools for analysis and search to respond appropriately to complex, open-ended statements and requests.

Thus, a simple voice app can easily handle a request like "Play 'I've Got a Feeling' from the Beatles rooftop concert" or "Order a small mushroom pizza from Domino's." By contrast, an app with conversational AI can also handle a request like "Play a few of my favorite songs by female artists" or "Find an Italian restaurant somewhere between my office and my sister's place and order two portions of fettucine alfredo for me to pick up this evening."

The widespread fascination with conversational AI is understandable. The idea of talking with a machine in almost the same way as we talk with other people has been an age-old fantasy, captured in tales of automatons, cyborgs, and robots as well as in the tantalizing concept of the Turing test from the earliest days of computing. First proposed in 1950 by computing pioneer Alan Turing, the Turing test suggested that the elusive concept of human intelligence could be defined by challenging a computer to conduct a dialogue, all in text, with a human being. If a neutral observer with access only to the text of the dialogue was unable to identify the computer, Turing proposed, one could conclude that the computer was, for all practical purposes, engaged in "thinking."[16]

In the decades since then, many have debated the validity of the Turing test, and countless software developers have tried to build conversational programs capable of engaging in plausibly human interactions. What's more, the last several years have seen some truly impressive breakthroughs in conversational AI, enabling machines to get closer and closer to human-like dialogue capabilities. As I've noted, the launch of ChatGPT 3.5 in 2022 received enormous media attention precisely because it represented a noteworthy step in the direction of turning the ancient dream of "a machine that can talk like a person" into a reality.

These AI developments are impressive, and there are certainly powerful business implications for the future of conversational AI. However, you should *not* automatically assume that this technology is the key to implementing voice tech effectively for your business. There are cases in which conversational AI is the gold standard to which you should aspire. But as I discussed in Chapter 7, in many cases, a bounded mode of interaction that limits the use of voice to predetermined words or phrases is more realistic. And for most use cases today, such bounded interactions are completely sufficient—as well as much easier, faster, and less costly to implement.

Bret Kinsella, the publisher of Voicebot.ai, has illuminated this distinction very clearly. He lists the most common ways in which voice assistants are currently used on smartphones or dedicated devices like Alexa. These uses include requesting a favorite song, checking the latest weather report, setting an alarm, asking for a piece of data, placing a phone call, and asking for directions. Nearly all of these, as Kinsella points out, "are simple interactions where the voice assistants can be trained for high success rates . . . requests followed by a simple response snatched from a database or simple task completion." None requires an extensive give-and-take between user and machine. In other words, none truly calls for conversational AI capability.[17]

What does this mean for companies that want to make the most of what voice has to offer? For now, they should be focused mainly on solving the simple problems that voice can help with—even *without* the full panoply of tools that conversational AI enables. Doing this will help millions more consumers to get used to using voice in countless practical ways. And this, in turn, will prepare them to embrace the use of conversational AI systems in the near future, when the technology has become more capable of tackling the complicated challenges that demand near-human levels of communication skill.

Having said this, there are a few cases even today in which conversational AI is a desirable capability. How can you decide whether the needs of your organization warrant this level of technological sophistication?

One key to determining the right level of voice technology lies in analyzing the business context for your voice application. In some circumstances, you can greatly improve the quality of service you provide by equipping a voice tool with access to data about the customer, their account, and the specific issues associated with both—all organized and analyzed using AI. When there's a strong case for incorporating information from the broad business context, then it may make sense to create a powerful voice tool with conversational AI capabilities.

An example comes from Truist, a bank that is using voice technology to pursue an idealistic vision of "designing for humans." Their goal is to eventually deploy automated voice tools that can help customers solve even complex financial challenges that today require the intervention of a live human being.

Peter Sutherland, Truist's director of innovation engineering, explains some of the many aspects of the business context that their software design team has learned to examine when creating software to serve customers in the fastest, easiest, and most intuitive way. They include not just the identity of the user and basic data such as the kind of bank account the user has but also more complex and subtle factors, such as what Sutherland refers to as "incident patterns" and user habits.

For example, a sophisticated financial voice bot equipped with conversational AI might respond to a request for a credit-card recommendation by analyzing the customer's typical spending patterns from recent bank statements. If much of the customer's money is spent on airline tickets and hotel accommodations, the voice bot might recommend a credit card that offers exceptional benefits for travel-related expenses. By contrast, if the customer's spending is largely dedicated to business expenses such as office equipment, a credit card offering special deals on business activities might be most appropriate.

Well-designed AI programs can proactively look at data like this and draw smart conclusions from them, thereby making lengthy Q&A exchanges with the customer largely unnecessary. It's a sophisticated and potentially powerful capability—and also one that should be deployed with care and mindfulness. "Being a steward of clients' data," says Sutherland, "isn't just about protecting that data and guarding client privacy. It's also about using that data so as to be helpful to clients—and doing so in a way that isn't perceived as creepy."[18]

Making the decision as to what level of voice tech your company should employ is an important one that requires input from an array of sources, including marketing and customer-service professionals, business-strategy team members, and potential users of your proposed voice tools. Try to figure out what users will really want and appreciate when it comes to voice tech, and start there. Over time, as user needs and interests evolve, your voice offerings can evolve with them.

WORKING WITH VOICE-TECH DEVELOPMENT PARTNERS

Because voice is a complex tool that incorporates elements of software development, design, AI, product design, marketing, customer service, branding, logistics, and many other disciplines, you'll almost certainly need to work with one or more outside companies when your organization is ready to dive into the voice pool. This is especially important given the fact that voice technology is continually and rapidly evolving, with new breakthroughs in usability, accuracy, speed, and efficiency happening on a monthly basis. Because voice is at the leading edge of current technology, specialized expertise in fields like automatic speech recognition (ASR), natural language processing (NLP), and voice biometrics is essential.

Fortunately, there are many companies that are building powerful tools in all these areas, some of which are likely to suit your purposes. Seek out advisors who can help you determine which recent technology breakthroughs can help your company, and make them members of your interface design team. For most companies, having a network of trusted advisors steeped in the changing world of voice is the only way to ensure you're up to speed on the latest developments. Working with such outside experts can also save you a lot of time, energy, and money. There are a growing number of off-the-shelf voice tools that are likely adaptable to the specific projects you'll decide to launch. Why reinvent the wheel when someone else has already done it for you?

Identifying, choosing, and working productively with the best outside suppliers of voice-tech tools offers its own challenges. Early in the process, you'll want to identify a *voice orchestrator*. This is an individual or a team who can lead your organization's process of incorporating voice, from identifying use cases and analyzing the needs that voice can address to architecting a voice system. Your voice orchestrator may be an internal leader if your organization has an individual with some voice-technology experience; in other cases, you may want to choose an outside consultant to fill this role. Thereafter, in concert with the voice orchestrator, you will select a variety of technologies to put together all the pieces of the voice experience while linking them into all the other user experiences your company offers, including your website, your mobile apps, your human customer-service reps, your in-store experiences, and so on. In selecting outside companies to help you develop your voice tools, seek out partners with the cultural grounding needed to produce tools that will work effectively with your core audience of users.

Mihai Antonescu is one of the most experienced veterans of the voice-tech arena. He led the team that developed Hey Mercedes, the voice assistant that has made Mercedes-Benz a leader in the automotive space. Mercedes found that it was important to partner with an array of outside organizations in order to get access to the best and latest insights and technology related to voice. The companies Mercedes chose to work with included firms from around the world, including SoundHound (based in the United States and serving Mercedes's operations in North America), Cerence (in Europe), and ECARX (in China). Each of these suppliers had a deep reservoir of specialized knowledge regarding factors such as language, cultural assumptions, consumer preferences, and driver behavior, all of which vary from one geographic region to another, and each of which has a powerful impact on the details of how voice tools should be designed and implemented.

Cathay Pacific Airlines offers another example of this principle. The airline's digital leader Gordon Chu has been working with a number of outside vendors on a range of customer-service tools and innovations, including voice tools. However, Cathay Pacific has also retained a local developer in Hong Kong to manage its conversational AI program, specifically in order to have a partner team that is steeped in both the linguistic and cultural environment of Asia. Other companies, especially those with an international footprint, should consider applying the same principle.

CHALLENGES YOU'LL FACE WHEN INCORPORATING VOICE INTO YOUR BUSINESS SYSTEMS

Depending on the specific environments in which you operate, you can generally expect to encounter some resistance to the use of any new technology—and that includes voice technology. So you need to identify where pockets of resistance are most likely to arise and plan ways to adapt and respond effectively.

Users vary from place to place. Voice-tech experts with global experience report that, in Asia, voice tools are more readily adopted than in the West. They theorize this may be, in part, because typing Asian languages, with their thousands of characters, is harder than typing Western languages—making voice input an especially attractive alternative.

Users also vary according to many other characteristics—age, professional background, education, economic status, work style, and depth of technology experience. Each of these may make voice either more or less attractive to the users your business interacts with. And, of course, the nature of the circumstances in which you most typically connect with users will greatly impact the usefulness of voice. When using a keyboard or scrutinizing a screen is difficult or impossible, voice technology will be especially welcome. In other cases, talking to a device may be problematic because of noisy conditions or lack of privacy, which may mean voice tools need to be specifically modified, supplemented with other modalities, or dropped altogether.

In an earlier chapter, you met Dr. Yaa Kumah-Crystal, the pediatrician and professor at Vanderbilt University Medical Center who is helping to pioneer the adoption of voice technology in health care. She understands better than most people the kinds of psychological and social pushback that tech innovators can expect. After all, health care is a high-stress environment, and its practitioners are highly trained experts who have mastered a particular, complex way of carrying out extremely difficult, high-stakes tasks. It's understandable that some of them resist calls to change their daily routines—even when the change may make their lives easier in the long run.

In seeking to encourage the use of voice tools by health-care professionals, Dr. Kumah-Crystal and her team of "clinical informatics" experts have found constructive ways of adjusting to the attitudes and biases of the potential users.[19] They realized early on that nurses were among those who could benefit most from voice tools. "Nurses have to do a lot of documentation," she observes, "noting vital signs, observations about patients, and other data. At the same time, their hands are always tied up with various activities. So voice could be the ideal modality for them."

Yet—surprisingly—in the real world of 2020–2021, Kumah-Crystal found that nurses were among the *most resistant* to adopting new technology. The unprecedented pressures created by a global pandemic were the core reason. "Things have been so crazy with COVID," she says, "that we're trying to avoid giving [nurses] anything new to tackle that could divert them from the care they need to provide to their patients and themselves."

By contrast, selected groups of physicians have been more willing to experiment with voice, even when the specific applications

Kumah-Crystal's team offers "aren't fully polished yet." This makes them ideal subjects for experimentation, yielding insights that can generate steady improvements in the voice tools and the algorithms that control them. (This is a common pattern that you can use when seeking to introduce voice into a large and diverse population. As voice expert Mihai Antonescu puts it, "Early adopters are more tolerant of failure. But they also push the system to try to achieve more and better things.")

The dividing lines between users who are eager to use the new technology and those who are reluctant are often hard to predict. Contrary to what you might assume, Kumah-Crystal found that some of the older physicians at Vanderbilt have been among the most avid adopters of voice tech, while some of the younger ones have been resistant. A bit of probing revealed the reason. "Some older physicians grew up using paper notes and never fully adjusted to working with the keyboard and the computer," Kumah-Crystal explains. "So when they try using voice, which lets them bypass the keyboard, they love it. But many of the younger doctors have always entered their notes electronically, and they're so fast with the keyboard that they don't see the voice system as a huge improvement." As a result, older doctors have become some of Kumah-Crystal's early voice adopters, somewhat to her surprise.

Kumah-Crystal also points out that, in health care as in other arenas, specific forms of activity may be more or less appropriate for early adoption of voice tech. User trials, experimentation, and surveys can help to uncover these differences and suggest ways for the tool developers to adjust. In one early set of clinical trials, a group of pediatric endocrinologists (practitioners of the same specialty as Dr. Kumah-Crystal herself) responded overwhelmingly positively to a voice app that made it quick and easy for them to order specific lab tests for a patient: "Please schedule a urine microalbumin screening for Tanya Cortez."

By contrast, other groups of physicians expressed concern over the use of voice to record information related to sensitive issues like mental health or sexually transmitted diseases. In this case, the specific work context proved to be very important. "If you're in a work room that's open only to providers," Kumah-Crystal says, "you probably feel comfortable talking out loud about a patient's condition. That's something we do among colleagues all the time. But if you're on the elevator or in the cafeteria, it's a totally different thing." Voice systems need to be designed, deployed, and tested with flexibility to fit these kinds of varying circumstances. Early results will help you figure out what further changes may be needed to win over potential users for whom the first version of your voice tool is not adequate.

In some cases, the appropriate adaptations required are not obvious. "We looked at some specific scenarios to figure out what users would be comfortable with," Kumah-Crystal recalls. "For example, you might need to make a note that a particular patient has a history of suicidal ideation" (that is, imagining self-harm during a period of severe depression). "That raises a privacy concern. Some of our doctors said they would want to be able to use the system to mark that data point as sensitive. But then others objected. 'Why should that be labeled as sensitive? Isn't that a way of stigmatizing the patient?' It's an ongoing issue that we're still working on resolving."

"Different physicians have different styles and different ways of communicating," Kumah-Crystal notes. "So designing a system that will serve all of them is quite challenging."

Finally, understand that your newly launched voice tools will not be perfect. Plan on gathering feedback from users that will help you begin the process of iteratively improving them. That means being prepared to acknowledge publicly that your tools are still in the process of development, and that user input regarding what does work, what doesn't, and what kinds of changes they'd like will be welcome.

It takes a degree of courage for business leaders to acknowledge their need for feedback and help in improving a system they've built and launched. But this attitude is essential if your long-term goal is to make your use of voice tech as powerful and valuable as possible. Yes, in the early stages of testing and deploying a new voice-tech system, you'll probably receive some criticism that may be painful and humbling to hear. But if you manage the process intelligently, you'll likely be pleased by the overall response from users and by their willingness to help you improve your offering.

In the words of Alex Misiaszek, senior vice president and experience design director for Truist, "Be transparent with users about what your voice tool can do—and what it can't do. Users are forgiving, so long as you set the right expectations and explain them forthrightly." Make users into your partners in the development process, and you'll achieve your goals more quickly and easily than would otherwise be possible.

In the chapters that follow, we'll dig more deeply into the specific steps to follow as you work on designing and implementing great voice-tech tools.

9

TRAINING VOICE TOOLS TO UNDERSTAND YOUR WORLD

A SIMPLE EXAMPLE ILLUSTRATES THE COMPLEXITY OF IMPLE-menting voice technology. I might tell my Domino's app, "Get me a pepperoni pizza—no, scratch that, let's make it sausage." Any five-year-old child would understand that sentence. But it's taken fifty years of voice-tech development to get computers to reach the level of a five-year-old. And even with that technological underpinning, it took a popular pizza chain six months to develop and train its own voice-driven ordering algorithm.

The voice-tech industry has created systems that are highly skilled at translating the sounds we make into words. What is much more diffi-cult is training computers to know what those words actually mean and what actions to take as a result. This is a complex technical task that requires the combination of several highly specialized skills. It's also a human-powered job that needs extensive input from people who deeply understand what a given user wants in a variety of circumstances.

Training a voice-enabled software model to interpret and respond to voice interactions unavoidably requires a significant element of human input—what many in the industry humorously call "artificial artificial intelligence." This training of models, which underpins multimodal interfaces, is a crucial technical battleground. Companies and organizations who begin that quest today will have a substantial advantage over laggards, just like the one that early movers on the web and mobile apps enjoyed.

A key point here is that every company should build its own models with its own data. Avoid trusting open models like ChatGPT, since their answers cannot be controlled or differentiated from those provided by the competition. A better solution will be to license an engine like the underlying GPT model, then train it with your own data and processes to solve your own problems in a controlled-output environment. In the world of generative AI, you want to remain firmly in control of the way your model responds to questions. That will be a major competitive advantage of tomorrow.

THE FIRST STEP IN TRAINING YOUR VOICE MODEL: IDENTIFYING JOBS TO BE DONE

AI is very good at figuring out how to do something, but not at figuring out what to do. That's where humans come in.

The previous chapter explained how to identify and target voice cases. The next issue on the agenda is creating a concrete, specific list of the "jobs to be done" in relation to each of those voice cases. The jobs-to-be-done approach is a way of discovering and prioritizing the unmet needs of customers, originated by the business strategy guru Clayton Christensen. (For this purpose, the term *customers* is defined broadly, including not just external consumers but also internal customers, including frontline employees, members of your production team, staff members, and financial managers.) Once the unmet customer needs are identified using the jobs-to-be-done method, you can set about the task of determining the best ways to meet those needs—which may involve deploying voice technology. The goal is to help customers handle their jobs-to-be-done with as much efficiency, speed, ease, and productivity as possible.

Notice that, at this stage in the process, you do *not* want to jump immediately into designing a voice tool. Rather than starting by looking for where to deploy a new technology, immerse yourself in the challenges faced by your customers and look for the friction points they face. Only after understanding exactly what makes their life and work difficult can you decide if a new technology, like voice, can help. It's important to continually remind yourself that now is the time to "fall in love with the problem"—that is, to focus on exploring the challenge as deeply and thoroughly as possible, rather than prematurely prescribing a solution.

You can begin creating the jobs-to-be-done list by analyzing data showing how the processes affecting your customers are currently managed using traditional communication methods. These could include any number of familiar technologies and tools, such as the company website, mobile apps, customer-service telephone lines, and internet sales and marketing platforms like Amazon.

For example, suppose that one of the voice cases you are considering is aimed at improving your customer-service department. As I've noted, this is a problem area for many companies. It's often expensive to run, difficult to manage (plagued by frequent staff turnover requiring continual recruitment, hiring, and training), and a source of customer unhappiness (due to long waits on hold and inconsistent service quality). The methods traditionally employed to fix these problems, such as measuring average call handle time, often increase efficiency but decrease customer satisfaction.

You are hoping to improve the situation by converting your customer-service department from human operators staffing a call center to handling more calls via voice technology before a human is required. Your goals in making this conversion include improving customer service by increasing the speed and accuracy with which problems get resolved, and freeing up staff members from handling purely routine questions so they can devote more time and energy to complex customer problems, which will save money while also improving morale.

Your first task is to "fall in love with the problem"—to get to know the issues surrounding customer service more deeply than ever before. Start by studying records of the customer-service calls handled by the department over the past six months. Get to know the kinds of questions they must handle, with a special focus on those that are most persistent and troublesome. Spend time interviewing customer-service-center reps, including those you've identified as high and low performers, in order to understand their problems and what differentiates the two. Based on this and other research, separate the calls into buckets, each containing a specific kind of question or challenge, and rank them by frequency.

You might end up with a list that includes entries like these:

Helping customer correct an error in their online account—11 percent

Answering a customer question about an upcoming sales promotion—9 percent

Answering a customer question about a product feature—8 percent

Responding to a customer complaint about a product—6 percent

This list can be the basis of your list of jobs-to-be-done by the members of your customer-service team. Working off this list, you can begin to analyze how these jobs-to-be-done are being handled now—and to determine whether introducing new tools, including voice technology, can help to get the jobs done more accurately, easily, and quickly.

In some cases, a valuable step in the work of determining user jobs-to-be-done is to create a *journey map* that uses a chronological format to capture the activities and thoughts of a user as he interacts with your organization through one or more of its systems. In the case of a customer-service department, the user would be a customer calling your service center with a question or a problem. In other cases, the user of a potential voice system might be an airline passenger seeking to confirm or change a flight reservation, a small business owner looking for information about the credit-card billing system she uses to handle customer accounts, or a utility customer needing to move her energy service from her current residential address to a new one. In each case, there will be a series of steps that the user typically moves through. Taken together, these steps constitute the journey map—and one or more of these steps may present an opportunity for improved efficiency, speed, accuracy, convenience, or some other beneficial change.

Figure 9.1 shows the journey map for customers of a company in the food-delivery business. It traces the user experience during five stages of the food-ordering process, from exploring restaurants for today's meal through tracking the delivery up to the moment when it arrives. At each stage, the journey map records the activities that the user may perform, the things the user may be thinking and feeling, and the perceived points of friction in the experience.

The journey map of the food delivery customer as illustrated here is somewhat simplified. A full journey map often breaks down what we think of as a simple process into dozens of steps and sub-steps, including the *triggers* that lead a user to start an action as well as the *reactions* the user might feel hours, days, or weeks later.

For example, take a company creating a journey map for a customer whose job-to-be-done is getting an electric vehicle (EV) charged at a charging station. The journey map might start with several different scenarios as to when and why a charge is needed, including how much range is left on the vehicle's battery. (Details specific to the user experience in a given industry are often crucially important. For example, it's well known that "range anxiety" is a critical issue for the EV

Figure 9.1. Journey Map: Ordering Food Delivery

	Explore Restaurants	Explore Menu	Socialize Order	Order	Track
ACTIVITIES	• Browse restaurants nearby • Explore restaurants by type of cuisine • Find a restaurant I haven't been to	• Review menu • Review prices • View photos of food • Determine what's popular	• Discover if any coworkers or friends want to order food with me	• Add menu item to basket • Modify order • Reorder what I got last time	• Locate delivery person • Modify order • Receive order!
THINKING	• How long is the delivery time for this restaurant? • What are the reviews like for this restaurant?	• What am I in the mood for? • Have I ordered anything here before?	• Does anyone else want to order with me? • Does anyone want to split a food item with me?	• What is my total cost? • How much am I paying in tip? • Is there a delivery fee?	• How is the delivery person progressing? • Where is the delivery person?
FEELING	TRIGGER: I'm hungry.	These items look tasty. I'm looking forward to eating!	Happy to find someone to eat with.	All ordered! Now I just need to wait.	Ugh, the delivery person doesn't know where I am.
FRICTION	• There's not an easy way to determine what the fastest option will be	• There aren't photos for all the food items • It's not clear to me if I can modify a menu item	• It's difficult to tell who else near me wants to get delivery	• Entering in my payment information each time is annoying	• I can't tell if the delivery person knows my address and building layout

industry; depending on how close a driver's vehicle is to running out of the energy needed to complete her journey, the driver's needs and her initial state of mind may be quite different.)

Next, the user might use one of a number of methods, including a smartphone app and/or a web page, to identify the nearest charging locations along their current travel route. The user might want stations sorted by distance, cost, brand, or other factors. And depending on her level of range anxiety, she might or might not be willing to backtrack or go off route to find a station. All these scenarios are likely to play a role in the user's reactions to the existing system for finding a charging station—as well as the organization's ability to improve the system through the use of voice technology.

Next, there are numerous steps the user will go through during charging, including the thirty minutes to be spent at the charging station. Finally, there are a number of possible reactions the user might have to the entire experience, from highly satisfied or even delighted to very dissatisfied, disappointed, and perhaps angry. These, too, should be part of the journey map.

Crafting a complete, accurate journey map for a typical user is very detail-oriented work, where the biggest insights usually come from understanding every nuance. It requires a thorough knowledge of your user's world as well as her needs, interests, fears, concerns, and desires. You'll probably want to enlist the help of a team of colleagues to brainstorm every detail that should be included in the journey map. For example, when working on the journey map of a typical customer of your company, draw on the knowledge of team members from a range of disciplines, including marketing, sales, service, and product design.

Once the journey map is completed, you're ready to take on the next task—creating a *jobs-to-be-done map*, which grows naturally out of the journey map.

As you trace each stage in the journey map, you will identify jobs-to-be-done that the user is tackling in turn. A chronological list of these jobs will form the basis of the jobs-to-be-done map. For each job, seek a real-life user's response to two key questions:

- How important is this job to you?
- How satisfied are you with the current ways of tackling this job-to-be-done?

The relative importance and current satisfaction level of any particular job-to-be-done are important data points for your organization. When a job-to-be-done is important yet has a low satisfaction level, we say it has a *high opportunity score*. This means there may be an opportunity to create a better solution—perhaps one that implements the use of voice technology.

Figure 9.2 shows a jobs-to-be-done map based on the journey map in Figure 9.1. You can see that a few jobs receive high opportunity scores based on the sizable gap between importance and satisfaction. For instance, customers ranked the job "Explore restaurants by delivery time" as important, and they were unsatisfied with currently available solutions to this challenge. The high opportunity score earned by this job suggests the possibility of creating a solution using voice technology. It also indicates that, if you can create such a solution, it has the potential to be quite popular among users.

Margo Bulka, principal product strategist for WillowTree, has guided many of our clients through the work of discovering jobs-to-be-done by their customers and figuring out better ways to help get those jobs done. Bulka has a favorite quotation that she likes to share with clients that captures the mindset behind this process. It's from an award-winning user experience designer named Cliff Kuang:

All the nuances of designing new products can be reduced to one of two basic strategies: either finding what causes us pain and trying to eliminate it, or reinforcing what we already do with a

Figure 9.2. Jobs-to-Be-Done Map: Ordering Food Delivery

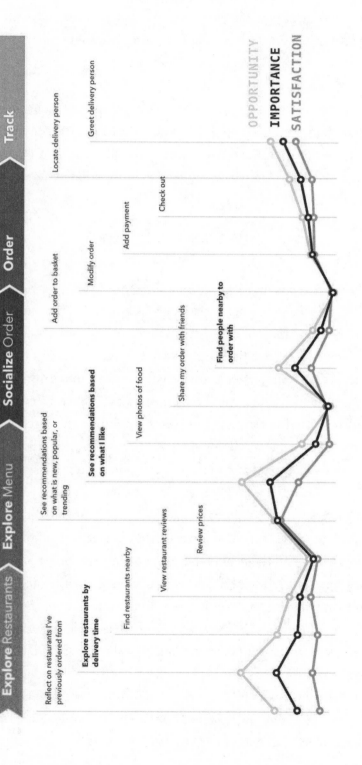

new object that makes it so easy it becomes second nature. The truest material for making new things isn't aluminum or carbon fiber. It's behavior.[1]

If you want to discover how to make your organization more valuable to users than ever, become deeply knowledgeable about their behavior— and then provide them with tools that will make that behavior easier and more enjoyable. Voice can help to make it happen.

STEP TWO: STUDYING USER INTERACTIONS TO DESIGN A VOICE SYSTEM PROTOTYPE

The next step is to design a prototype of your voice system that is capable of helping users tackle their jobs-to-be-done. This is a low-tech outline or simulation of the voice system, using words and diagrams on paper rather than actual coding of software, that shows how users will interact with the system once it is up and running. If an operational voice system is like a motion picture that has been filmed and edited, and is ready for viewing, the prototype is like the screenplay. It will serve as a useful guide for the software developers who will actually create the coding that makes your computerized voice system run.

To create the prototype, you need to have a clear understanding of how users will want to interact with your system—the activities they'll want to undertake, the information they'll need, the problems they may experience, and the results they want to achieve. Some of this information may be readily available to you, especially after the work you've done in mapping the user journey. But if you don't currently have sufficient data about the interactions you are considering upgrading using voice, you may need to conduct additional research into the needs and preferences of users.

Whenever possible, observe users in their real-life context. When our WillowTree team began working on developing the Vocable app that enabled the paralyzed Anastasia Soule to communicate with her family and caregivers, we knew we had to understand the jobs-to-be-done of people experiencing serious paralysis as a result of illness or accident. As I explained in the prologue, we gained this knowledge by working with experts from the speech pathology departments at Duke University Hospital and WakeMed Hospital to identify issues likely to affect people experiencing paralysis, as well as the language they might want to use to describe those issues. We then tested what we learned through experiments with potential users of our voice app—paralyzed individuals and their caregivers. This work with real people was invaluable to making sure that our app handled their jobs-to-be-done in ways that were practical and effective rather than confusing and frustrating.

Let's consider a different example. Michael Freenor is a principal data scientist at WillowTree. He describes the work involved in developing a prototype for a voice tool designed to help users of a dental flossing device. The goal was to create a voice-driven app, accessible via smartphone, that would help new customers master the use of their devices during the first fourteen days after an initial purchase. (Research had shown that new customers who use the device successfully for two weeks straight usually become lifetime users—and therefore valuable customers.) The hope was that a voice app could easily and conveniently answer users' questions about the device—including some that live customer service employees might struggle with—thereby helping to convert first-time users into permanent fans.

To create the prototype design for such an app, Freenor and his team began by analyzing all the information available about the flossing device, drawn from the preexisting customer manual, the company website, a compiled list of frequently asked questions, the engineering specs for the device, and similar internal sources. They also studied archives of phone calls to customer service to identify the kinds of questions and complaints most often raised by new users of the device. Gradually, they sorted the conversations into a collection of buckets that represented the issues they knew the app would have to address. Each bucket captured a specific job-to-be-done by users of the flossing device.

Traditionally, this task—compiling a data set of topics to be covered—has been one of the most laborious and time-consuming stages in the design process. Freenor estimates that, for a typical project like the flossing device job, this work would have taken an average of four weeks. However, the process has been dramatically streamlined by recent improvements in AI. Freenor reports that, using an AI tool from OpenAI, the creators of ChatGPT, WillowTree has now reduced the time required for creating such a data set to a single afternoon—a remarkable example of how technology breakthroughs continue to shatter once-formidable practical barriers.[2]

Now the team had to figure out how a voice app might be able to help users tackle these jobs-to-be-done. Having seen the kinds of questions and complaints people using the product were raising when they called the company's customer-service department, the team decided to create a voice-enabled experience that could address those issues effectively through dialogues with customers.

To develop a prototype for the system, the team set about developing a series of flowcharts showing how conversations around these jobs-to-be-done would usually be launched as well as the various directions into which the dialogue should be channeled. For example, Freenor's team learned that new flossing-device customers often wondered about the sounds created by the unfamiliar machine. They created a bucket for questions that asked about these sounds using various spoken words—"noise," "buzzing," "clicking," "vibration"—and even oral sound effects like "zzzz" and "brrrr." This bucket led to a number of follow-up questions to be asked by the system—"Is the sound steady or intermittent?" for example. The answers would help to sort the issue into one of eight or nine categories depending on whether a noise was a symptom of a problem or simply an ordinary feature of the device. Eventually, the flowchart would lead to a resolution for the user's issue—for example, "You need to replace the hose on your flossing device. We can send you one at no charge." Often, the most efficient way to respond to the user was via a multimodal screen, but sometimes it was a voice response. Optimizing these interactions is all part of multimodal experience design.

If the information provided by the user turned out to be self-contradictory or if the problem was too complex or unusual for the system to handle, the prototype design would pass the user on to a live customer-service representative. Of course, the goal was to make the voice app as flexible and comprehensive as possible so that it would rarely be necessary to make this handoff to a live staff member.

In the process of designing this voice-system prototype, Freenor and his team leaned heavily on documentation provided by the sponsoring company—specifically, the user manual describing the features of the flossing device and walking users through the steps to take in the event of a problem. That's an approach that can work well for many use cases. Most companies already have such manuals, in which frequently used information has been compiled for reference purposes by customer-service personnel. The information to be used by a voice app can often be drawn directly from the manual.

For example, here's a typical excerpt from the user's manual for the same kind of flossing device:

> Hard water deposits may build up in your unit, depending on the mineral content of your water. If left unattended, this can hinder performance by reducing water pressure. Cleaning internal parts: add 2 tablespoons of white vinegar to a full reservoir of warm water. Point the handle and brush head into sink. Turn Water Flosser ON and run until reservoir is empty. Rinse by repeating with a full reservoir of clean warm water. This process should be done every 1 to 3 months to ensure optimal performance.

This information would be used as raw material for a dialogue between a user of the flossing device and the system. The artificial-intelligence system driving the app would be trained to recognize terms like "low water pressure," "not enough pressure," or "weak water flow" when mentioned by the user. These terms would then trigger a dialogue that might begin as follows:

> **USER:** I'm not getting much water pressure from the flosser.

> **VOICE RESPONSE:** It sounds as though your device may have built up some hard water deposits. That's a common problem. Have you cleaned the water reservoir in the last three months?

This voice response would be accompanied by a screen image of hard water deposits with the text, "Hard water deposits are often the problem. Is this what you are seeing?"

> **USER:** Hmm, I guess so.

> **VOICE RESPONSE:** That could be the cause of the problem. You can clean the reservoir using a mixture of white vinegar and water. It takes about fifteen minutes. Would you like me to walk you through the process now?

During this response, the user's screen would show an image of cleaning solution being poured into the device with a bottle of vinegar visible in the background. The accompanying text reads, "Cleaning the reservoir takes about 15 minutes."

Depending on the user response to the last question, the system could either describe the cleaning process, step-by-step, or offer an alternative. For example, if the user responded, "Now is not a good time for me. I don't have any vinegar on hand," the system could respond with, "Okay. I recommend you get some white vinegar and find a good time to clean the reservoir. When you're ready, call me back and I'll walk you through the cleaning process. Meanwhile, you may want to hold off on using your flossing device."

As you can see from this example, a multimodal response often allows for much more information to be transmitted to the user in a faster response cycle.

A second key step in designing a prototype for developing your voice tool is to engage in *conversation-modeling exercises*. In this process, you ask pairs of people—they could be members of your development team, for example—to improvise the kinds of dialogue that might take place between a user and a tool. The rest of the team is asked to watch and take notes, observing the variations in vocabulary and sentence structure that the user might employ, ambiguities in the user's statements and questions, whether structured or unstructured prompts from the system are more helpful, and points in the exchange when the user would benefit from additional guidance or an explanation.[3]

Start the exercise by asking your dialogue improvisers to model the shortest route to completion of the job-to-be-done. Then imagine dialogues that include more complexity and variations. As you build these varying dialogues, you can capture the kinds of challenges your voice system will need to deal with when it is operating under real-world circumstances.[4] Be careful *not* to allow the team to default to the common call-and-response approach. And push very hard toward building a multimodal solution.

To illustrate, here is a sample dialogue that represents the shortest route to completion for one typical job-to-be-done—namely, booking a room at a hotel. For each step in the interaction, we provide both a voice response and a screen response.

> **USER:** Book me a room at the Sleepy Inn for next Saturday.
>
> **VOICE RESPONSE:** How many nights?
>
> **SCREEN RESPONSE:** Select number of nights.
>
> **USER:** One night, please.
>
> **VOICE RESPONSE:** I found the lowest price standard room for $200. Would you like me to book it, or shall I list other options?
>
> **SCREEN RESPONSE:** Image of the prices available and a spoken prompt, "Say which room you would like."

> **USER:** I'll take the standard room for $200.
>
> **VOICE RESPONSE:** Shall I charge your card on file?
>
> **SCREEN RESPONSE:** Tap confirm to charge your card on file.
>
> **USER**: Yes.
>
> **VOICE RESPONSE**: Okay, you're all set. A confirmation email will arrive shortly.
>
> **SCREEN RESPONSE**: Image of confirmation and note it has also been emailed.

Again, note that, in most circumstances, the multimodal interaction with an app will be much faster than a voice-to-voice interaction.

Now here is a sample dialogue that captures one possible set of variations on the shortest route, in which the user offers responses that are incomplete or require further clarification. (In this scenario, we are modeling a voice-to-voice experience. A multimodal experience, as per above, would likely avoid this level of required clarification because multiple room types could be shown on the response screen. This is an excellent example of the limitations of voice-to-voice interfaces, and the promise of multimodal.)

> **USER:** Book me a room at the Sleepy Inn.
>
> **VOICE BOT:** Okay, when would you like to visit the Sleepy Inn?
>
> **USER:** Next weekend.
>
> **VOICE BOT:** On what day would you like to arrive?
>
> **USER:** Saturday.
>
> **VOICE BOT:** And how many nights will you stay?
>
> **USER:** Just the night, please.
>
> **VOICE BOT:** I found a standard room for $200. Would you like me to book it?
>
> **USER:** I was hoping for a suite with two queen-size beds.

> **VOICE BOT:** I'm sorry, there are no suites with two queen-size beds available. There is a suite with one king-size bed available. Would you like me to book it?
>
> **USER:** No, I need two beds.
>
> **VOICE BOT:** There is a standard room with two queen-size beds. Would you like me to book it?
>
> **USER:** Yes.
>
> **VOICE BOT:** Shall I charge your digital wallet?
>
> **USER:** Yes.
>
> **VOICE BOT:** Okay, you're all set. The confirmation email will arrive shortly.

It's easy to imagine further complications that could arise: the user might want to ask the price of the room with two beds before agreeing to book it, she might want to provide a credit-card number rather than using a preselected digital wallet, and she might have additional questions to ask, like "Does the hotel have an on-site restaurant?" or "What is the check-in time?" All of these variations, and the best ways for the voice bot to respond to them, would be noted by the team as they develop their model dialogues.

Insights drawn from exercises like these can be used in creating the prototype design for your multimodal or voice-only tool, prior to any actual coding. Voice-technology companies such as Sayspring (a division of Adobe) and PullString offer software tools that can be used to help guide the prototyping process for a voice application.

In addition, advanced AI tools like GPT from OpenAI can also be used to help draft a preliminary version of the prototype tool for your app. Existing apps that serve similar or parallel purposes can be used to train GPT in the basic structure needed—often referred to as the *wireframe* for the app. You can then ask GPT to generate a wireframe along the same lines for the new app you are creating. The rough version GPT creates can then be edited, refined, and improved by your team. Chances are good that the complete process will be much faster and easier than if you'd labored to create the prototype design completely from scratch.

Once you've developed a prototype design for your voice tool, you can use similar exercises to test it. Again, two participants are required—one playing the role of the voice system, the other playing the user. To add a touch of verisimilitude, the user might sit at a desk or on a sofa with a smartphone or laptop in front of them, while the person playing the system is behind a screen, out of sight. The user then asks questions or seeks information, and the individual playing the role of the system must respond strictly according to the rules and frameworks dictated in the prototype design. A dialogue flowchart to be followed by the system-simulator will be helpful.

This kind of simulation, often referred to as *Wizard of Oz testing*, can uncover points where the interaction is prone to breakdown due to failed communication, helping your team identify ways to improve the design of the system while it is still in the prototype phase.

STEP THREE: DEFINING THE LANGUAGE NEEDED TO HANDLE YOUR USERS' JOBS

Once a prototype for basic voice interactions has been created, you're ready to begin training your voice NLP model (like GPT) to communicate effectively with real-world users of your system. This requires you to identify the most common words, phrases, and expressions used in handling each of the user's jobs-to-be-done, and specifying what the appropriate response should be.

For instance, you might need to identify the language that customers are likely to use when asking about a product feature—phrases such as "How do I adjust the bicycle seat?" and "Is the bike available in different colors?" To respond to such questions, the voice app will need access to a database with specific, useful information about each notable product feature, so that the customer will be able to find the answer she wants with relative ease.

Let's return to the Vocable example. The research we did with paralyzed individuals and their caregivers, as well as with medical experts who work with patients like Anastasia Soule, helped us develop a set of vocabulary lists reflecting the challenges faced by paralyzed people as well as the clinicians working with them. Each vocabulary list dealt with a specific topic and included an array of vocabulary words and phrases that our multimodal system needed to be able to understand and use. For example, the topic of "Temperature" generated a vocabulary list that included varied, idiomatic phrases like "I am cold," "I am sweaty," "I want more blankets," and "I need a jacket." We used these lists in training the Vocable app to be able to communicate effectively with our target users.

As these examples suggest, the job of training your voice interface is likely to be a complicated, detail-driven one. Don't try to rush through it or shortchange the resources required.

In March 2016, Capital One launched its first voice assistant in the form of an Alexa skill. In the early days, its capabilities were limited—in part because the bank wanted to be cautious about handling sensitive financial data. Users found it could do a few things with great reliability and accuracy—for example, reporting a current account balance, confirming a recent transaction, and getting the due date for their next credit-card bill. They found it quick and convenient to use the voice assistant for these few tasks, and they understood that more complex banking tasks required them to use the traditional problem-solving methods, such as speaking to a live customer-service agent in person or by phone.

But the Capital One team wasn't finished with its work of training its voice assistant. Even as the initial version of the assistant was being used by bank customers, the Capital One team was developing the information and capabilities needed to allow the voice tool to tackle a broader array of tasks. One by one, these new tasks were added to the capabilities of the skill. For example, by the end of 2016, the skill had been trained to recognize and pronounce the names of some 2,000 widely used merchants, enabling it to answer a user question like "How much did I spend at Starbucks in October?"[5]

Thus, Capital One took a measured, step-by-step approach to developing, refining, and then implementing the vocabulary and other resources needed to handle a wide array of tasks using its voice interface. That's a smart approach.

Another financial-services company has followed a similar arc. Bank of America's highly successful Erica voice tool was launched in June 2018. It was immediately lauded as the best interactive voice interface in banking. But Christian Kitchell, the bank's executive in charge of AI solutions, wisely declared, "We're only in the first mile of a marathon." The company has continued expanding, enhancing, and improving Erica's talents. As of this writing, in addition to being able to execute most online banking tasks, like transferring money, adding users to accounts, and paying bills, Erica is able to understand more than 60,000 often-used phrases and answer more than a million different finance-related questions. These are the kinds of capabilities that can't be developed overnight—and that enable the bank to provide valuable benefits to its customers, in the form of quick, easy, and convenient information regarding an almost limitless array of banking topics.

DATA ARCHIVES AND DIVERSE INSIGHTS: THE BIG BUSINESS EDGE AND WAYS TO OVERCOME IT

As we've noted, one of the ways to develop insights into the kinds of jobs-to-be-done your users face and the vocabulary needed to handle those jobs is to closely study archives of past interactions with those users. Here is where big businesses currently have a distinct advantage over start-ups or small competitors. Fortune 500 companies have vast archives of data drawn from customer interactions and other processes that can be used as the basis for training their voice-interface models. The information embedded in these data archives offers powerful insights into customer behavior, interests, and needs, including some that are counterintuitive.

For example, large banks already have many thousands of hours' worth of recorded telephone conversations with their customers. One surprising fact among many that can be derived from these archives: more than 50 percent of the calls placed by customers at many banks are simply to check their account balances. All by itself, this single data point offers powerful evidence of the money-saving potential of voice technology since each of those millions of simple balance-checking calls costs the bank about one US dollar when it's handled by today's typical interactive voice response (IVR) technology—while an online system that uses a voice-activated app to provide the same information without a phone call reduces the cost by over 90 percent, to about seven cents. Banks armed with this kind of data can tailor their interface modeling process to take full advantage of what they know.

Large companies and organizations, based on their vast experience and data sets, have a distinct advantage when it comes to understanding and analyzing user needs. Does this mean that smaller businesses will be unable to claim their share of the benefits from the coming world of voice? Not necessarily. There are R&D programs underway that are making real progress at overcoming the data advantage that giant organizations currently enjoy. One of the findings of this movement is that *synthetic data* generated from a relatively tiny amount of real-world information may be just as powerful for training purposes as the vast archives that giant companies own.

The Open Virtual Assistant Lab (OVAL), a project housed at Stanford University and supported in part by a grant from the Alfred P. Sloan Foundation, is working to produce a set of open-source voice tools that any organization can use. The overarching goal of OVAL: "to enable every organization to provide voice-based assistance to their services as easily as creating a website."[6] The resources available to companies through OVAL include GenieScript, a software language that lets developers create voice tools using only a high-level script charting the desired interaction flow and access to a company database of information. It's designed to be *sample efficient*, which means that only a small amount of real-world data is needed to begin the tool development and learning process. Another resource from OVAL is Thingpedia, an open-source repository of voice interfaces that can be adapted by any business or organization for a wide range of uses, from apps and web services to IoT (internet of things) devices.

On another front, a number of for-profit companies have developed tools to create synthetic data that can be used in creating voice systems and other AI-driven projects. This is data that closely simulates the kind of user information embedded in the vast data archives that big companies often maintain. In addition to enabling small organizations to overcome the data advantage enjoyed by giant companies, synthetic data offers other advantages. Perhaps the most significant is the improvement of data security: when synthetic data is used for model-training purposes, the privacy of real customer information does not need to be compromised.[7]

The existence of resources like OVAL and the burgeoning array of data-synthesizing tools makes it easier for even small businesses with limited customer bases and modest budgets to benefit from voice technology. Using such resources, a neighborhood credit union or a nonprofit organization offering microfinance services for low-income consumers can develop a customized voice-driven customer-service app that might come close to rivaling Chase or Citibank. Continuing breakthroughs like these will bring the power of voice within the reach of more and more companies in the years to come.

Another way that organizations of *every* size—not just the giant industry-leaders—can improve their ability to design and train the most effective voice models is by making sure that the team building and training these models is as diverse as possible. The needs, interests, preferences, passions, biases, blind spots, and behaviors of users vary widely from one person to another. And these variations are inevitably impacted by demographic and social differences of all kinds—gender, ethnicity, age, income, education, professional background, and political perspectives. If you want to create voice tools that will work for the widest possible assortment of human beings, your chances of succeeding will go way up if you assemble a working team that also varies across as many of these characteristics as possible. And as the process continues, with testing, evaluation, and improvement of the model, including a sample of users that is also extremely diverse will help ensure that issues important to specific subgroups are not overlooked. Early facial-recognition tools, for example, proved much worse at recognizing the faces of people of color, because so few were on the teams that developed this technology and the early prototypes. The lesson: "You cannot create the world's best products if everyone in the room looks the same."[8]

Smart organizations have taken this message to heart. They are recruiting people with widely varying demographics, skills, and perspectives to work on voice-interface projects, and a whole industry has emerged around AI annotation. It's projected to grow into a $3.6 billion market by 2027, led by players such as Appen, Oracle, and TELUS International (the parent company of WillowTree).[9]

Ken Dodelin of Capital One notes that the team the bank assembled to design and train their assistant Eno embraced not only people of varying ethnicities, genders, and ages but also a wide range of professional backgrounds, including "a former Pixar filmmaker, an anthropologist, a journalist and one of the original engineers for IBM's Watson." Dodelin explains, "Eno is a product for everyone, and so Eno needs to be able to understand the wide variety of ways people talk about money."[10] One of the best ways to produce tools capable of serving diverse users is to invite diverse participants into the development process.

STEP FOUR: PRE-TESTING AND IMPROVING THE MODEL

Pre-testing and improving the model before it is formally launched are essential steps if you hope to move beyond the level of rudimentary usability.

John Kelvie is CEO of the voice development company Bespoken, which conducts testing of newly developed voice tools for its clients. His team watches an array of users interacting with the tool and observes the success or failure of each interaction. A number of voice-specific metrics are used to measure specific aspects of the tool's performance. For example, the measurement *word error rate* calculates the numbers of words spoken by users that the system misunderstands or misinterprets.

Similarly, it's important to calculate how well the intent of users is matched with the capacities of the system. The *intent match rate* is high when most users request information or activities that are within the domain of the system and when the request is understood and acted upon correctly. By contrast, the intent match rate is low when users mistakenly request information or activities beyond the scope of the system, or when the system fails to understand the user's intent correctly.

During testing, it's important to pose a wide range and variety of challenges to the voice system, thereby reflecting the diversity of real-world issues that are likely to come up once the system goes live. For example, the Bespoken team likes to test the question-answering capabilities of a voice assistant by using sample questions drawn from ComQA, a data set of over 11,000 questions created by WikiAnswers, a community website where anyone can ask a question for other users to answer. ComQA takes these real-life questions and organizes them into clusters that ask for the same information using different language with varying degrees of clarity. For example, one sample cluster contains these three questions:

- US president during Vietnam conflict?
- Who was the president of the US during Vietnam War?
- Who was the US president during the war of Vietnam?[11]

A good assistant, like ChatGPT, will answer all of these questions accurately—and similarly—despite their varying wordings. The ability of a voice assistant to answer a question consistently no matter how it may be worded is one valuable predictor of how well it will serve actual users. Other tools are available for use in testing other attributes of voice systems.

Kelvie reports that it's typical to see error rates of 20 percent or higher during the first rounds of testing of a particular voice system. This would be considered unacceptably high by any standard. Thankfully, the test results themselves often allow you to identify the most common causes of errors, and then to introduce modifications to the voice tool that can alleviate the problems.

Often, the needed modifications are surprisingly simple. When Bespoken was working with a marketing-services firm known as the Mars Agency to create a voice tool to provide customer service for a cosmetics company, a high rate of errors was caused by the speech-recognition system's failure to correctly interpret key words and phrases. For example, one of the company's products had a brand name that included the word "Ageless"—but when customers spoke the word, the speech recognition system repeatedly interpreted it as "age list." Result: the voice bot became confused and was unable to help the customer with her product request.

Fixing this problem turned out to be relatively easy. Because the phrase "age list" is a very unusual one that is unlikely to be used in ordinary English speech, the programming team simply instructed the algorithm to consider "age list" a synonym for "Ageless." Compiling a list of other commonly made mistakes and feeding appropriate corrections into the algorithm's memory reduced the voice bot's error rate by more than 80 percent. This kind of improvement isn't unusual—Kelvie reports that similar techniques typically produce error-reduction rates of between 75 and 95 percent.[12]

In other cases, errors may be triggered not by vocabulary problems but by small flaws in the system design. For example, experience shows the importance of keeping statements by a voice bot as brief and simple as possible. It's difficult for users to understand, remember, and respond correctly to a lengthy sentence delivered orally. When complex content needs to be conveyed, the communication method must be adjusted to make it easier for the user.

One rule of thumb: when asking the user to make a choice, no more than three options should be presented at a time.[13] Again, note that the ability to display multiple options on a screen is a significant advantage of the multimodal interface. Let's return to the customer seeking a room at the Sleepy Inn. It's possible the hotel might have many different kinds of rooms available: single rooms with one or two beds of various sizes, suites with the same range of bed options, apartments with kitchenette facilities, and so on. If the voice bot were to rattle off a list with all these possibilities, the user would likely be confused, and the error rate for user responses would probably soar. Instead, the options should be broken down into a series of choices: First, single room or suite? Second, number of beds? Third, size of bed? And so on.

The more efficient way of alleviating the same problem is to take advantage of multimodal design possibilities. Thus, if the prospective hotel guest is accessing the reservation system through a smartphone, tablet, or laptop, a screen can be provided that lists the ten or twelve room options available for the selected night. Visually scanning such a list is much faster and easier than trying to absorb it through hearing. The user can glance at the choice, ask questions as needed, and then tell the app which room she would prefer.

In certain scenarios, such as when driving, multimodal experiences are not possible, but when they are, they typically offer a much better user experience.

In still other cases, errors can be caused by a failure to anticipate possible user statements and to prepare appropriate system responses. For example, a voice-driven email-writing system might ask a user who has finished dictating a message, "Do you want to send it or change it?" The objective is to have the user choose one of the two options mentioned. But a user who is slightly distracted might instead say, "Yes." This could trigger an error message from the system ("Sorry, I don't understand what you said"), which might lead to further confusion and frustration.

Two small tweaks in the system design could fix the problem. First, the wording of the question could be changed to emphasize the either/ or choice: "What would you like to do—send it, or change it?" Second, if the user still answers, "Yes," the system could be trained to move forward by saying, "Okay, you can change the email and then send it. Tell me what you'd like to change."[14]

During system testing, useful information can be gathered from sources other than objective counts of system errors. Your team can also glean useful insights into the power of the voice tool simply by observing and analyzing user reactions during and after the tests. Listening to recordings of sample interactions can help you detect signs of satisfaction and happiness—or frustration and annoyance—on the part of users. There are also voice-analysis tools that can automatically gauge such emotional reactions for larger collections of test interactions. User surveys and feedback can also help you recognize whether the early version of a tool is performing up to par.

Of course, even after you've tested your voice model and used the results to improve it, you can't expect to reduce the error rate to zero. After all, the smartest and most experienced human assistants make occasional mistakes; we can't yet expect AI to outperform such experts. Therefore, one of the most important aspects of your system design will be the way it handles errors—a craft known as *error flow handling*.

WillowTree's Michael Freenor has seen the importance of excellent error flow handling time and time again. He points out that a lot of the challenge of creating voice tools lies in things that we are not in control of—things like background noise that interferes with understanding, or a user who speaks very softly or with a unique accent. There are so many ways people can miscommunicate, and it's impossible for a development team to anticipate them all.

Therefore, great error flow handling is key to creating a great voice interface. And, unfortunately, lack of it is one of the most common reasons some people sour on voice. Freenor recalls hearing about a friend's experience with one of the first automotive voice systems back in the 1990s. It sometimes had trouble understanding what the driver was trying to say, partly because the tool was brand new, partly because of built-in challenges: the car might be bouncing along on a bumpy road, or background noises from city streets might be interfering. And whenever this happened, the system would stop the interaction and kick the user all the way back to the front of the activity menu, forcing him to restart the whole process from scratch. It was an exercise in frustration. No wonder people with that kind of experience sometimes conclude that voice systems are just terrible, and decide never to use them again.[15]

Avoiding such problems and dealing with them successfully requires thoughtful attention to the details of user/system interactions, as well as sophisticated understanding of the nuances of human speech. For example, imagine someone using a voice tool to buy tickets for a movie. In the middle of the interaction, the user might confuse the system by suddenly shifting gears, perhaps with a sentence like "Give me two tickets to *Star Wars* at 7:30 p.m.—no, wait, make that 8:15." The natural language processing tool in this case needs to be trained to understand that the phrase "no, wait" usually serves as a signal that the most recent previous piece of information (in this instance, the time of the movie showing) is to be discarded and replaced by a new piece subsequently supplied by the user. (Other colloquial phrases, like "Hold on," "Just a sec," and, as I mentioned earlier in this chapter, "Scratch that," have similar meanings and would also need to be part of the vocabulary list provided when training the system.)

Equally important, "no, wait" normally does *not* mean that the user wants to discard the entire contents of the interaction and start the conversation all over again. It's crucial for the system to understand this difference and act accordingly. The system needs to have what's sometimes called a *conversational repair mechanism*. And that requires accurately sorting a huge number of different utterances—phrases like "no, wait," and thousands more—into a limited set of buckets, and then giving the system clear instructions about how to handle each bucket.

Here, too, sensitivity to the conversational context is essential. For example, suppose your voice system is walking the user through the series of steps needed to complete an order form—name, address, credit information, and so on. If a particular item as provided by the user can't be understood by the system, it should avoid defaulting to a generic error response like "Sorry, I didn't get that." Instead, the system should be trained to specify exactly which item has been missed, and clear instructions to provide the needed data should be given, ideally with an example: "Sorry, I didn't get your phone number. Please speak or enter your ten-digit phone number, starting with the area code— for example, 555-678-1414." This eliminates any possible confusion or doubt on the user's part.

It's also useful to create a "Help" option, accessible either by a button on the device or by a spoken command, that users can select when confused about how to use your voice tool. (It's particularly important to offer this support in these early days of voice adoption, when a fairly large number of users may be unfamiliar with voice tech. A few years from now, this option may no longer be necessary.) Your help offering should explain the basics of using the voice tool, providing advice such as "Touch the microphone icon. When it lights up, speak your request in a normal tone of voice," or "When entering data such as address and phone number, you may either speak to the app or use the keyboard on your device." You may want to train your system to proactively recommend use of the help option whenever the user commits the same error twice.[16]

Make sure the help option can be activated without shutting down any conversation the user may already be engaged in. Otherwise, the system may add to the user's frustration by forcing him to start the interaction all over again.

As you can see, creating an effective conversation repair mechanism is complex, painstaking work that demands the help of experts with training and experience in natural language processing, where the sciences of linguistics and computer programming meet.

Sometimes an error arises that is too complex for your voice system to resolve. If the system is well designed, this should be rare. But when it does happen, there must be a channel that quickly and courteously guides the user to an alternative source of help—most often a live human being. Even the most powerful technical systems can't do everything. When they fall short, we owe it to users to provide them with an alternative way to handle their jobs-to-be-done.

CONTINUOUS IMPROVEMENT: LEARNING FROM YOUR VOICE EXPERIENCE

At a certain point in the process of development, testing, and improvement, you will decide that your voice interface is ready to be made available to users. Making this decision is a judgment call. You'll need to consider factors such as the potential impact of errors on users of the specific tool you are designing. If you're working on an app that will help people suffering from chronic diseases interpret changes in their symptoms, failed interactions may carry an unacceptably high level of human risk. You probably won't want to make the app available until it has passed an intensive testing regimen. By contrast, an app created to facilitate fun activities like a trivia guessing game or a musical sing-along involves no such risk. You could release an early version of this app knowing that possible errors can be corrected without causing any serious harm to anyone.

To minimize error risk while avoiding long delays in the release of a new voice tool, some organizations, including Capital One, have used the technique of staging a gradual rollout of their new voice interface, providing access initially to a limited number of customers, then making it more widely available as the early experience proves successful.

Once you've concluded that your model works well enough to provide value-adding service to users, and that potential errors are unlikely to cause any harm to users or to seriously alienate them, you can go live with it. But this doesn't mean that the model training process is done. You should think of it as an iterative process, rather than a one-and-done exercise.

As Michael Freenor says, "The best way to get data on a system is to put it in the wild and see how it performs." The initial testing you've done has improved your voice tool to the point where it can provide an acceptable level of service to users. However, it's likely that during the first several months after the tool goes live, new errors that didn't arise during initial testing will crop up.

This happens for several reasons. Over time, as more people become aware of the availability of the voice tool, the numbers of users will steadily increase—and the rising volume of interactions will naturally uncover error types you didn't encounter previously. An expanding user base is also likely to be more varied than the limited collection of individuals you engaged for initial testing. That means more diverse styles of speaking—various accents, dialects, word preferences, speed, intonation, and other changes that the voice algorithm will need to learn to handle. Varying background environments may also increase the challenges faced by the speech-recognition algorithm.

What's more, the passage of time is likely to bring other changes to which the voice tool must adjust. A voice-enabled app designed to provide customer service may be thrown off when the company introduces a new product variation, or when users begin to use new terms in response to shifts in fashion, culture, or customer preferences.

For all these reasons, you should plan on continual monitoring of real-world results whenever you launch a new voice tool. Commercially available tools can help you set up a regular testing process for a voice interface that is in use. Track error rates to quickly identify new trouble spots that are reducing the effectiveness of your voice tool. In addition, count the percentage of times when users abandon the system without having successfully completed their jobs-to-be-done. And invite users to provide feedback on their experiences with the system, for example through user surveys or by allowing them to post comments and ratings on your website. You can use the information you gather as the basis for updates and improvements to your voice model.

Great voice experiences are built the same way any great user experience is built. Start by looking for the problems users are having, not places to apply voice. Then develop and explore those problems with diverse, cross-functional teams that bring to bear a wide variety of business, technical, and design capabilities. Finally, using the core teachings of the agile mindset, design a tool that solves the users' biggest problems. Start simple, and then iterate, iterate, iterate.

10

DESIGNING AND REDESIGNING THE MULTIMODAL USER EXPERIENCE

PROJECT VOICE IS ONE OF THE LARGEST CONFERENCES focused exclusively on the voice industry. After a two-year COVID hiatus, it returned in April 2022. Many of the world's leaders in the voice arena traveled from Silicon Valley, Boston, Austin, and other tech centers across the US, Europe, and as far away as India to attend the gathering in Chattanooga, Tennessee. Technology gurus, software developers, customer-service specialists, marketing and sales professionals, and business strategy experts shared their experiences around incorporating voice into a wide range of applications.

Just after lunch on the first day of the conference, we heard an impressive presentation by Bala Maddali, head of conversational AI experiences with the telecom giant Verizon. As a small demonstration of how Verizon is using conversational AI to improve its customer service, Maddali played an audio recording of a voice assistant helping a customer perform a relatively simple business transaction—changing the due date on her monthly bill from the first day of the month to the fifteenth. The whole process was quick, easy, and routine. In fact, the recording would have seemed absolutely ordinary were it not for the fact that all of us in the audience knew that the voice on the line was not human but was driven purely by a computer algorithm.

When the recording was finished, Maddali said, "Notice how simple that was." Audience members nodded. Then Maddali dropped his punch line. "That simple conversation represented the culmination of a two-year development process that included fifty-three iterations of our software!"

Maddali's experience in working on voice tools for Verizon is far from unique. The third step in the development process is the most complex, challenging, and important of all. It's about designing your user interface to be as simple, useful, and pleasant as possible—and then redesigning it as often as necessary to continue to achieve those goals in a world in which customer expectations and business needs are constantly evolving.

In such a world, fifty-three iterations of software design may only be the beginning.

This doesn't mean that the first fifty-two iterations of Verizon's software were all "failures" and valueless to customers and the company—far from it. Each iteration was a necessary, valuable step in a process of continual learning and improvement, and each contributed to the creation of a better user experience. The message for all of us is that voice-tool development is never a "once-and-done" activity. Instead, like any important element of your business, it should be viewed as an arena for constant, unlimited growth. And the sooner you get started on the process, the higher your ceiling of achievement.

THINKING MULTIMODALLY:
ONE KEY TO EFFECTIVE USER EXPERIENCE DESIGN

Designing your user experience builds on the work of Step Two of the voice development process—training your voice interface model. The job now is to make the actual interface—the combination of aural, visual, and tactile elements that users will use to participate in your business process—as easy and pleasant to use as possible. In many cases, as we've seen, achieving this goal is likely to involve a multimodal interface, which uses a variety of modes of interaction to make every step in the communication process as fast, easy, and natural-feeling as possible.

In fact, I'm so convinced of the importance of multimodal thinking that I would propose this rule: *When designing for voice, start with the assumption that people will talk, while devices will listen.* In any interaction, once the human users have provided their input in the most convenient way—usually by speaking—the device can respond with text, graphics, sounds, or haptics, whichever is most efficient. In some cases, two or three forms of response can be combined; for example, while the device speaks, a screen can simultaneously display a list, table, map, or text that summarizes and reinforces the key information being presented. In this way, your users will be well served, no matter what mode of communication best suits their personal style and the overall circumstances.

You should program an application to use voice responses alone *only* in circumstances when the evidence makes it clear that voice is the best and most naturally desired option. All other things being equal, assume that multimodal is the way to go.

The multimodal interface solves the biggest problem with voice-only interfaces—namely, the fact that the efficiency gains from being able to speak to Siri are lost when we have to listen to her, especially when the data we must absorb is long or complicated. It's much better for us to receive information in text or graphic form, because, as we've seen, people can read about three times as fast as they can listen.

When a multimodal interface is intelligently designed, it maximizes speed and ease of use at every point in the user experience. It also provides a number of other benefits to users. For example, one reason for the relatively small number of applications that most users access on devices like Alexa is the lack of a visual interface. This leads to the discoverability problem I described in Chapter 9. On a smartphone, the screen display serves as a "constantly rotating billboard" of app suggestions—which is one reason why smartphone owners use an average of forty-six different apps every month. They are constantly being reminded which apps they have by simply scrolling around their phone, and all of those tools are easily available via a single tap. By contrast, Alexa users, who have no such billboard to scan, report using an average of just 3.5 voice apps during their entire history with the device.[1] In this case, a multimodal interface that creates numerous, varied opportunities for users to discover ways of connecting with their devices leads to a much richer array of value-creating experiences. This highlights why, in the future, the vast majority of users will start their voice experiences on a website or an app, not through a stand-alone digital assistant like Alexa or Siri.

Notice the difference between this example and the case of the U.S. Bank app, with its 300 "long tail" service applications. When it comes to banking, users generally turn to the app with a specific financial activity in mind—transferring funds, paying a bill, monitoring an account balance. Allowing customers to simply use their voices to name what they want to do makes much more sense than, for example, providing an on-screen list of 300 tasks for users to scroll through laboriously—which is why U.S. Bank manages its discoverability challenge purely through voice. By contrast, Alexa hosts an array of interesting and enjoyable applications created by various sponsors, most of which are unknown to casual users. In this case, a screen display listing the voice-based apps and perhaps recommending specific ones based on user interests would be a valuable feature likely to increase awareness and use of these many apps. The difference between these cases vividly illustrates the kind of thoughtful analysis of the user experience that's needed to make best use of the potential of voice and the multimodal interfaces that are possible.

The good news is that recognition is growing of the value of multimodal communication and combining two or more modalities in their interactions with users. Some companies that formerly connected with customers strictly through keyboards and screens, whether via websites accessed on laptops, tablet features, or smartphone apps, are now using microphones and speech-recognition tools to empower users to provide input that is fast and hands-free. The subsequent response often includes words or images on a screen, in combination with spoken words, other sounds, or haptics like device vibrations.

ChatGPT is incredibly powerful and impressive, but as of the spring of 2023, it's purely a text-based tool. In time, designers and engineers will turn it into a multimodal tool, in which users dictate questions or commands to ChatGPT with their voices, and the output is returned in a multimodal format. That evolution will start unleashing the true effectiveness of NLP and generative AI tools like ChatGPT.

As multimodal communication becomes more widespread, new technologies to facilitate it are being developed. In November 2022, the voice-tech company SoundHound unveiled a new system called Dynamic Interaction, a patented multimodal interface that combines real-time natural language processing with visual cues and input through voice and touch screen. The company's demonstration video shows a user ordering food using the Dynamic Interaction system. As the user mentions each food item, an image and a verbal description appear on the screen of his device. When modifications and additions are made ("Delete the milkshake, change the fries to onion rings, make it a pretzel bun") they are reflected almost instantaneously on the screen. And when the user needs to be cued to select from a menu of options, the list appears on the screen the moment it is needed—so when the user says, "I'd like a side," a list of seven side dishes immediately pops up. All the information is presented, captured, and updated faster than even the most adept human waiter could manage.[2]

As I write, Dynamic Interaction is just making its way to the marketplace; the jury is still out on its overall effectiveness. But it represents one vivid example of the kind of multimodal efficiency that will soon become the gold standard for most forms of human-machine interaction. Not only are we not listening to machines, but we have stepped away from the age-old call-and-response paradigm of communication. Instead, we are entering a new world of simultaneous communication where the device is conversing with us while we are still talking.

In some cases, multimodal connections are emerging as organizations that formerly used voice alone diversify their systems to include other communication modes. Dr. Yaa Kumah-Crystal reports that V-EVA, the Vanderbilt University Medical Center voice assistant that provides caregivers with a summary of basic information about a particular patient in response to a voice command, has been adapted to offer multimodal display options. Thus, rather than speaking aloud the details about a patient case, which can be difficult for a busy physician to track, V-EVA can display the information on a screen for the doctor to take in at a glance. Providing this kind of option to meet real-world user needs is a perfect illustration of the multimodal advantage.[3]

Joel Sucherman is the vice president of audio platform strategy for National Public Radio (NPR), the nonprofit media network that provides news, entertainment, and public affairs content to public radio stations across the United States. NPR has always been an early adopter of new communication technologies, including voice. In fact, the very first promotional video released by Amazon to publicize the brand-new Alexa Echo device featured a link to NPR (ironically, without NPR's prior permission).[4]

Sucherman recalls thinking that the arrival of Alexa portended "a new kind of radio," and he and his colleagues immediately set about planning how NPR could capture a significant space in the evolving voice landscape. Among the innovations they've created are an hourly newscast for Alexa that includes visual content—for example, photos and videos that bring breaking news stories to life. NPR is also producing what Sucherman calls "video assets" for TikTok, Instagram, and YouTube. This is "a better way to reach younger audiences," he says, even as the network remains primarily audio-centered, true to its radio roots. And there is NPR (formerly NPR One), an app for smartphones that offers a steady, on-demand stream of news, stories, and podcasts curated by NPR editors.

Thus, the movement to a multimodal interface can work in more than one direction: Voice can be added to systems that formerly lacked it, while voice-only systems (like radio, in the case of NPR) can be made more attractive and powerful by adding non-audio components.

Christophe Couvreur is vice president of core technologies and hybrid platforms at Cerence, a voice-tech company that specializes in developing voice tools for use in automobiles and other vehicles. Couvreur has one of the longest track records in the field, having been working with voice-tech tools (as of 2022) for some twenty-five years. He earned his PhD in the late 1990s with a research study into what would today be called machine learning. He then spent years working with ScanSoft, then the leader in speech technologies, with brands that included Dragon and Dictaphone. In time, ScanSoft purchased Daimler Research, an arm of Mercedes-Benz, which is how Couvreur got involved in bringing voice tech to the automotive space.

Couvreur has also become deeply versed in how the power of the multimodal interface can be applied to the automotive arena, thanks in part to his long-term view of the evolution of voice tech. "The first killer app for voice in the car," Couvreur recalls, "was Phone Daddy. It was an app that let you safely use your phone while driving, hands-free and eyes-free. In effect, Phone Daddy let you use your voice to push buttons. A very simple application, but at the time a very powerful one."

Today, as I've already discussed, drivers have been given a wealth of ways to use their voices to manage activities in their cars. Voice agents in cars can understand a large number of words and phrases, interpret their meanings in the automotive context, and take appropriate actions in response. For example, whether a driver says "It's hot in here," "Lower the temperature, please," or "Increase the air conditioning," smart car companions, like those in new Mercedes models, will comprehend what's intended and adjust the climate controls accordingly.

Now Cerence is going several steps further, in many cases developing multimodal interface elements that make the in-vehicle user experience even more intuitive and responsive. Infrared cameras are being installed with links to software systems that can interpret visual cues derived from live video images of the driver. Powered by AI, these systems can recognize when a driver appears to be drowsy or distracted—for example, by noticing when the driver's gaze remains fixed for an extended period of time, which is generally a sign of sleepiness. The system can respond in various ways to remedy the situation. For instance, it might activate its synthetic voice to arouse the driver by offering to chat, play a game, or provide some music. Smartly, the system is trained *not* to react in a way that could be perceived as unpleasant, intrusive, or negative—for instance, with a harsh buzzer or words of warning. Cerence has learned from experimentation and user experience that some drivers are prone to respond to this kind of stimulus by shutting down the system, thereby defeating its purpose. So gentler, more positive solutions are employed first. However, in an extreme case, as when the driver continues to fall deeper into sleep, the AI system can temporarily take over the controls of the automobile when necessary to avoid an accident.

The Cerence in-car tools are evolving way beyond the simplistic voice-only model of a Siri or an Alexa. Sounds, visual cues, active physical controls—all are combined in appropriate ways to maximize the benefits to users as conveniently and comfortably as possible. It's another example of the power of multimodal design to take full advantage of what voice tech and other new communications technologies have to offer.

OPTIMIZING THE USER EXPERIENCE DESIGN PROCESS

Multimodal interface design is by definition a complex emerging field. Knowing how and when to shift from one communication mode to another requires a deep understanding of user needs, habits, and preferences.

Shadiah Garwell works with me and my colleagues at WillowTree as a senior product designer. She is part of a team of experts from many disciplines who collaborate on designing apps and tools for clients in a range of industries, often with voice as a key component. Before joining WillowTree, Garwell's professional experience was largely focused on the graphic elements of website design, a discipline that is closely related to app development. Knowing how to use elements such as typography, images, buttons, links, shapes, and colors to communicate clearly and effectively is a major aspect of both web design and app development. But when asked about her work, Garwell downplays her strong background in graphic design. "The design part of my work—which people typically assume is most of what a product designer does—ends up being the *smallest* part of what I do. In reality, the product designer's role is to be a facilitator of conversations—to ask questions and get everybody's input into them."

Aesthetic choices are important when designing the user experience. But even more important is uncovering the insights into user needs and preferences—often unexpressed and little-understood—that must be appreciated before smart design decisions can be made.

Here are important elements in tackling the work of user experience design that I've found to be crucial to developing insights essential to the success of your interface.

It takes a cross-functional team to tackle the multimodal design challenge. Don't give in to the temptation to ask one group—your marketing team, say—to create a "wish list" of interface features, then hand the list to engineers or app designers to execute. That's a formula for misunderstanding, confusion, and disappointment. Instead, teams from *every* relevant department should join forces collaboratively to explore the key customer needs and develop plans to meet them most effectively. Input from users themselves is also vitally important. Give and take among professionals with varied backgrounds, combined with feedback from test users, is likely to generate a better design than one created by people drawn from any single discipline.

Design all of the system's communication modes—voice, visual elements, sounds, and haptics—simultaneously and collaboratively. Don't make the mistake of having one set of designers—those on the visual side, for example—take a first crack at modeling your system, and then turning the draft design over to the voice experts to add their contributions. Remember that all the components of a multimodal conversation must fit together seamlessly and support one another. That means it's essential for your entire design team to collaborate on the project from start to finish.[5]

Plan on continual, iterative conversations and collaborations among people with varying kinds of expertise. Get everyone around a table to brainstorm, experiment, and swap ideas. Those who will use your tech interface—consumers, employees, and others—will have diverse perspectives and experiences. If you hope to satisfy all or even most of them, you need a similarly diverse group to participate in designing your interface. Go beyond "mainstream" populations to gather feedback from people of various ages, genders, ethnic backgrounds, languages, education levels, and economic status.

Make sure at least one high-level executive is engaged in the effort. Like other leading-edge technological challenges, voice adoption can be complex, costly, and time-consuming. It also involves variables that are impossible to predict with perfect accuracy. For this reason, your voice project needs the involvement of a high-level company leader who can provide the necessary level of long-term support—in terms of money, staffing, flexibility, and organizational commitment. The payoff from voice is likely to be big—but it's also likely to take longer and be more difficult to achieve than you might imagine. Keeping your organization's top leaders informed and involved is crucial.

Assume that your interface design will need continual updating and improvement. As voice technology continues to improve, your ability to offer users a seamless, enjoyable experience will continue to rise—and so will user expectations. Think about the great multimodal interface you will design and launch in year one of your voice integration project as a starting point—a launching pad for the even better versions that you will create in year two, in year three, and beyond.

GETTING THE DESIGN DETAILS RIGHT

As with any design project, there are dozens of small details that need to be managed correctly in order to produce the desired outcome for your voice-tech project—a simple, efficient, easy, and enjoyable experience for the user. Fortunately, you and your team don't need to invent approaches to make sure all the details are right. You can lean on the experience of other organizations who have created powerful tools for communication and control—including voice-based tools. By studying what they've done, consulting with the people who helped them do it, and listening closely and empathetically to the needs, interests, and wishes of your own users, you can develop a design that works as well as any other in the field—and maybe better.

Blake Sirach, WillowTree's chief product officer, has written extensively about voice design, and his teammate Shadiah Garwell has worked with him to create a kit that companies can use when designing their own voice interface.[6] The kit provides a checklist that can help ensure you are not overlooking any key question you need to answer or any crucial element you need to include when designing a voice tool for any purpose.

For example, take the seemingly simple task of designing the interface for a conversational tool that will use AI to allow users (external customers or internal employees, for instance) to get responses to questions delivered orally.[7] It's the kind of tool that might be housed in a smartphone app or as part of a website to be accessed by laptop or tablet, and which could ultimately eliminate most of the customer-service phone calls your company now handles through human staff members.

Designing such an interface is more complex than you might assume. In fact, it requires a thoughtful understanding of how users experience the process of posing a question to a voice-based communication tool and then absorbing the response. During this process, the interaction passes through a series of conditions or states, each of which should be considered, defined, and appropriately reflected in the interface design. A well-designed interface guides the user effortlessly through each state, making it clear what is happening and how the user needs to respond. The states in this example would unfold as follows:

> State 1: *Inviting the question.* A design tool to mark this state for the user may be as simple as an on-screen icon (such as the image of a microphone) that lets users know they have the option of using voice to ask for information. But deciding exactly what the icon should look like, what words (if any) to include, and where to locate it on the app or web page are important decisions that require the design team to carefully consider the attitudes and background knowledge of likely users as well as the organization's goals. What fraction of users are likely to use the voice tool? How many will recognize and understand a particular icon? Are there some categories of questions that should be directed toward the voice option—and are there some that should *not*? Answers to questions like these will help you design your voice app to handle this first state of the process most effectively.
>
> State 2: *Receiving the question.* When two people engage in conversation, one typically is talking, the other person indicating that she is listening through verbal, visual, or physical cues—for example, nodding or murmuring "Mm hmm." So when a person speaks to a device, it's helpful for the device to mimic this kind of human behavior—for

example, by having the microphone icon change color or flash repeatedly during the "listening" phase. Otherwise, the user may wonder whether anything is happening at all. Even a very brief period of such uncertainty may cause the user to become confused or impatient and perhaps abandon the process.

State 3: *Acknowledging the question.* It's very helpful for the user to receive a clear signal that the device has understood the question being asked—especially when the user is someone for whom voice technology is a new experience. The acknowledgment could be delivered in any of a number of ways—for example, it could be provided visually by showing on screen a handful of key phrases from the question asked, or by having the tool offer a visual or verbal statement like "Thanks for your question" or "I get it, you want to know about X."

State 4: *Preparing a response.* It may take a few seconds for the device to gather and organize the information needed to respond to the user's question—for example, to look up the bank-balance data requested by the user, or to find an alternative airline flight for a passenger seeking to change his reservation. If there is no cue provided to show that the device is processing the response, the user may become anxious, fearing that the device is malfunctioning or that the connection has been lost. The user interface can address this problem by using a visual, aural, or other cue to communicate that the device is "thinking"—for example, a blinking dot or a spoken message like "Give me a minute to check that for you."

State 5: *Providing the response.* The final step is actually delivering the response, which could take any of several forms, depending on the content. In some cases, it may be ideal to respond to the question using two or more communication modes—for example, having the device speak the answer aloud at the same time that the key information is presented visually on the screen. This will make the response easier for the user to understand and absorb under a range of circumstances—for example, if the user is visually impaired, if the sound volume on the device has been turned down, or if ambient noise in the environment makes listening difficult.

Notice that, if a user experience design team overlooks, ignores, or mis-designs any one of these five states, the result is likely to be an interface that is confusing or annoying for some users. When you remember that it only takes a few seconds for users to become impatient and irritated with malfunctioning technology, you realize that even a single error of this kind will probably cause a significant number of users to abandon the interface in frustration. That means lost sales, unhappy customers, and a reputational black eye for your business.

As this example shows, even a relatively simple voice-based activity is likely to include a number of specific details, each of which is important and has the potential to make or break the success of a user interaction. To ensure that each of these details is considered thoughtfully in the user-experience design process, work closely with an experienced design team, use checklists and other design tools to guide the process, and, of course, expect to test and retest your interface reiteratively with a range of users to catch any bugs or glitches that need to be corrected.

TAILORING A VOICE-BASED USER EXPERIENCE TO FIT YOUR BRAND

Voice will increasingly become required table stakes for any digital user experience in the coming years.[8] It's part of the process of integration and naturalization that every successful new technology goes through. In the earliest days of the internet, having a web page was a distinctive feature for tech-savvy, progressive companies; today, even the smallest mom-and-pop organization has an internet presence that probably includes a vibrant e-commerce component. When smartphones were new, many companies regarded having a mobile app as a nice luxury; today, with smartphones having become both ubiquitous and the dominant mode of computing, a great mobile app is essential for almost every business.

A similar phenomenon is taking place with voice. Today, a car company like Mercedes can point to its industry-leading voice interface as a competitive advantage over other luxury automakers. Within the next decade, every car company will offer a similar array of voice tools.

This means that—whatever industry you are in—over time, it will become both more difficult and more important to differentiate your voice offerings from those of your competitors. One of the key challenges, then, will be making your voice-based user experience into a natural extension of your company's brand.

A number of forward-thinking companies are working to meet this challenge. One piece of the puzzle is thinking about voice as part of a *sonic branding* strategy that includes music, sound effects, electronic tones, and even a "sonic logo" that instantly conjures up the image of your brand. (For classic examples, think of the three tones that have represented the NBC television network for decades, or the dramatic music/sound effect combination that accompanies the visual logo for the TV drama *Law and Order*.) Today, such sonic logos are being developed and used in a wide range of applications, including mobile apps, websites, and many electronic devices that have built-in sound capabilities.

Audrey Arbeeny is the founder of Audiobrain, a firm that has helped companies like Microsoft, Virgin Mobile USA, and McDonald's define their suites of signature sounds. When working with companies she points to research indicating that brands with strongly aligned sonic-branding strategies are 98 percent more likely to be remembered by consumers. The reason? For Arbeeny, it's "the connection between music, emotion, and memory," which branding experts believe can be used to imprint a brand's identity deeply in the unconscious mind of a consumer.[9]

Increasingly, synthesized voices like those used in mobile apps, websites, and electronic tools built into devices are an important part of a company's sonic branding strategy. A growing number of consulting and development firms can work with companies to define and create the kind of synthetic voice that embodies the identity of their brand.

Cindy Hamer and Ricardo Garza are business-development executives with one of these firms, ReadSpeaker North America. They report that their business clients are increasingly seeking more varied, emotional, customized, and brand-specific speaking styles for their voice tools. "If Pepsi and Coke are going to speak to their customers, they shouldn't sound the same," Hamer says. "And in the same way, Schwab and Bank of America shouldn't sound the same either."

To meet this need, neural text-to-speech (TTS) technology can be used to craft a distinctive speaking voice that can serve as the brand ambassador for a particular product or service. The synthesized voice can answer questions, present information, and solve problems for customers, all while speaking in a distinctive voice that quickly becomes associated with the brand.[10] ReadSpeaker uses its version of TTS technology to analyze and clone the voice of celebrities and other well-known figures. For example, it analyzed the voice of cartoon character Hello Kitty (most often depicted in videos by Japanese voice actress Megumi Hayashibara) and created a synthesized version of the voice to participate with users in a game called Hello Kitty's Room, accessible via Google Assistant.[11]

Even more challenging, the ReadSpeaker tool can also transfer specific voice characteristics to some forty languages, which means the same voice can serve as a brand spokesperson worldwide—without requiring the time and talents of native speakers from many different countries.

Other companies are also using their own AI systems to clone familiar voices and make them available for appropriate uses. VocaliD, acquired in mid-2022 by the voice-tech development company Veritone Voice, has developed an array of synthetic voices based on those of such personalities as Brooklyn and Los Angeles Dodgers announcer Vin Scully and legendary newscaster Walter Cronkite. Companies can arrange to use these and other voices for advertisements, voice-over announcements, and other brand-enhancing purposes.[12] (Of course, when a voice modeled on that of a celebrity or a fictional character like Hello Kitty is to be used, a legal and financial agreement with the individuals involved or the organizations that control the rights to their images and voices must be reached.)

When it comes to an iconic global character like Hello Kitty, it's crucial that the aural brand identity be consistent across all applications and geographies. But in other cases, it's desirable for a brand identity to be flexible and diverse. This is especially true in a world where organizations are under increasing pressure to treat people of every background fairly and equitably. Members of groups that have traditionally been undervalued and disempowered are demanding the right to speak for themselves and to be heard with respect—which means that the way your organization deploys voice for commercial purposes can be a sensitive issue. The voice you use should represent your brand in a way that everyone can appreciate and enjoy.

There has been a rightful outcry that "female" voices are so often used for digital assistants like Alexa, Siri, Bank of America's Erica, and many others. The companies claim that these voices were designed based on the customer preferences revealed through pre-testing, and I take them at their word. However, the practice of "feminizing" voice assistants reinforces the age-old stereotype of a woman as a subservient helpmate. Others have complained that the synthesized voices of these bots generally speak with what mainstream culture regards as a "neutral" accent—one that vaguely resembles the speech of a college-educated female from Northern California or perhaps the northeastern US. This, too, is felt to reinforce stereotypes that are limiting and potentially exclusionary. Just because a particular design choice tests well doesn't mean it's the right thing to do.

To combat this problem—and the negative public-relations impact it has had on the tech industry as a whole—many companies have taken steps to offer more diverse and varied choices among synthesized voices. For example, in 2013, Apple introduced a male-sounding voice as an optional alternative for Siri. Then, in 2021, Apple introduced two new optional voices for Siri that were based on the recorded speech of African American voice actors—one male, one female. At the same time, the company altered the traditional protocol by which a female-sounding voice represented the default option for Siri. Instead, new users were required to make a deliberate choice among the available voices for Siri, thereby undermining the notion that Apple is promoting the assumption that women should automatically be slotted into the role of assistant.

Most recently, in 2022, Apple announced plans to introduce a new voice for Siri in iOS 15.4 that would be explicitly gender-neutral (neither male nor female). The company has dubbed the new voice "Quinn," designed to be both a gender-neutral name and a reference to the fact that this will be the fifth voice available in the Siri repertoire. Apple stated that the synthesized voice was built from one recorded by a member of the LGBTQ community (though the identity of the voice actor was not revealed).[13]

Obviously companies are investing a lot of time, thought, and money in choosing and designing voices that will represent their brands appropriately. Research suggests that the subtly varied voices used by different voice assistants have a powerful unconscious impact on the ways users perceive them.

For example, researchers at the University of Waterloo had ten men and ten women interact with Amazon's Alexa, Apple's Siri, and Google Assistant; they then asked the users to describe the appearance and personality of each voice assistant as they perceived it. The results were striking. Despite Google Assistant's lack of a personal name, users found it easy to anthropomorphize the bot, even offering opinions regarding the color of its hair and the clothes it might wear. The test subjects also reported strongly contrasting impressions of the personalities behind the synthetic voices. Alexa struck them as "genuine" and "caring," while Siri seemed to be "disingenuous" and "cunning."[14]

In my own household, my youngest son Max (nine years old) starts talking to our Google Assistant's female voice as we make breakfast every morning. He's typically asking for sports scores or game highlights, the weather, and an occasional joke. But the way he speaks to the female assistant voice is fully disrespectful. "Please" and "thank you" are completely out of the question, and rudeness is the norm if Max doesn't get what he wants. He often tells the assistant, "You're stupid," or worse.

My wife and I are put in the somewhat comical position of asking our son to be polite to the electronic assistant. "Why do I need to do that?" he asks. "It's not a real person."

He's right, of course. But we're concerned that Max may be developing a pattern of interaction he'll bring to his real-world relationships.

The message is clear: the greater the role played by voice tech in representing your organization to the world, the more important it is to design the voice interface to embody the best traits of your brand—even as you also strive to provide consistently excellent, value-enhancing services to everyone who uses the voice tools you provide.

MEETING USER CHALLENGES WHEN YOU IMPLEMENT VOICE TOOLS

Getting users to feel comfortable using a new technology is often a challenge—even when the technology itself has been thoughtfully designed, painstakingly tested, and continually enhanced. Voice tech is no exception.

Doug Lilly has been a firefighter and an emergency medical technician (EMT) in a suburb of Cincinnati for twenty-one years.[15] He recently lived through the transition from traditional communications technologies to voice tech in handling emergency calls. Lilly's account illustrates some of the subtle nuances that can be involved in successfully managing the introduction of voice technology.

Through most of Lilly's career, emergency calls received by the local 911 dispatch center were handled in the same way. An operator would field the call, gather the basic information, and launch the process of dispatching emergency services by making a radio call to the appropriate fire house: "There's a fire at 783 Main Street. Engine Five respond." Bells would ring in the station where Lilly and his colleagues were on duty, and they would get into their gear and rev up the fire truck. While they were performing these familiar rituals, the operator at the dispatch center would be gathering additional details from the caller: "Is anyone trapped in the house? How many children? Which rooms do you think they are in? Any signs that the fire is spreading?" When new information emerged that could affect the firefighters and their work, the operator would put the call on hold, get back on the radio, and transmit the news to the crew. This back-and-forth process might last several minutes.

Today, this traditional system has been transformed by the introduction of voice technology. When you call 911, you still speak to a human being in the dispatch center. But she no longer needs to jump on the radio to contact the fire house. Instead, while remaining on the 911 phone line, she types the address and the basic nature of the emergency on a keyboard attached to what's called the mobile dispatching computer (MDC) system. The information is immediately transmitted to the fire house via a new, AI-enhanced voice system created by a company called Locution. A clear robotic voice speaks to the firefighters through speakers located throughout the facility: "Fire 783 Main Street. Engine Five respond."

As always, the firefighters immediately jump into action. But now, the operator in the dispatch center is already communicating additional information from the 911 call using her keyboard. As these new details arrive, they are being sent to the firefighters via the robotic voice. They are also being sent in text form to a video screen mounted on the fire truck. (The same screen also displays a map of the emergency site showing crucial details like the location of nearby hydrants.) So even as the firefighters are roaring through the streets on their way to the blaze, they are being automatically fed fresh information via the Locution system.

To the average civilian, the improvements offered by the new Locution system are all but invisible—but to Doug Lilly, they are significant.

The robotic voice that now delivers the initial notification of an emergency is reliably loud, clear, and consistent—unlike the voices of the various dispatch operators, which vary in accent, pronunciations, speed, and clarity. "I can always understand what the robot is saying," Lilly says. "With an operator who may be rushed or excited, that's not always the case."

The fact that the operator can enter information into the system via keyboard rather than having to shift repeatedly between the phone line and a radio system means that vital data reaches the firefighters more quickly than ever. It also drastically reduces the amount of radio messaging being sent via the relevant frequencies. Lilly recalls, "Under the old system, when we needed to get on the radio to ask the dispatch center a question or send them some information, we were often cut off because of the sheer volume of calls that were on the line at one time. We might have to repeat the same message several times before we could be sure it got through. Now that rarely happens. When we do need to use our radio, the connection is always clean and clear."

The upgraded voice communication system has also brought other, even more subtle benefits. The speaker system in the fire house was formerly antiquated, unreliable, and hard to hear—especially in the bays for storing the trucks and other equipment, where the sound was generally echoey and unclear. The conversion to Locution included the installation of modern speakers calibrated to work well with the acoustic conditions in each location, so important details about a given emergency are no longer missed or misheard.

In addition, Locution has replaced the loud clanging bell formerly used to signal an emergency call with a series of tones that gradually increase in volume over a period of nine seconds. Why does that matter? Those alarm signals often wake the firefighters out of a deep sleep (they live in the firehouse, responding to calls, for several days at a time). "You'd be surprised to learn about the physical shock to the system that people experience when they are jolted out of REM sleep by a loud noise," Lilly says. "When that happens to you repeatedly over a period of years, it can do some real damage. The rising tones system is a lot more friendly to our bodies."

Most important, Lilly reports that the new Locution system has trimmed between ninety seconds and two minutes off the average time it takes to respond to an emergency. That's a big deal, given the fact that a house fire can spread significantly in that much time. The same time period can make a meaningful difference in the degree of harm suffered by a victim of stroke or heart attack—two other common calls that Lilly and his colleagues must respond to.

The switch to a voice-tech system for emergency calls has helped Doug Lilly and his fellow firefighters enormously. But it didn't happen easily—and it might not have happened at all if not for careful planning and implementation by the Locution team and the local officials they partnered with.

First, Locution had to make a convincing case for the benefits to be offered by their new technology. The company's twenty-five years of work in the field of fire-alerting automation—and the strong track record of its voice-based tools—provided them with the data they needed to make such a case. Over a period of several years, they presented proposals and information to the twenty-eight separate local fire departments in Hamilton County, Ohio, which all share the same 911 dispatch center. All twenty-eight departments had to sign on to the new voice-tech plan—and they also had to agree on a fair system for allocating the costs among departments with very different sizes, rates of emergency calls, staffing levels, and budgets. Furthermore, the staff of the dispatch center had to be convinced that they, too, would benefit from the change, and that the transition would not result in mass layoffs or firings. Managing this process took time and patience on all sides.

Once the plan to upgrade the Hamilton County emergency dispatch center was in place, actually implementing it presented other challenges. Firefighter culture was one of the biggest. Doug Lilly explains, "Firefighters are very proud of our traditions. We've served our communities for generations, and the way we do things in the firehouse has become something we're comfortable with. It's funny— we pride ourselves on being able to cope with almost any unpredictable disaster . . . but at the same time, we hate the idea of changing our daily routines! So convincing us to accept the new alert system wasn't easy."

Having worked with fire departments for many years, the Locution team was sensitive to these cultural realities. They implemented the new system in Hamilton County using a gradual approach. First, they installed the enhanced speaker systems, which produced immediate dividends in the form of clearer communications. Then they helped the firefighters get used to the new dispatch system a little bit at a time. "The first week," Lilly recalls, "they told us we'd be getting the new robotic alerts only for one category of calls—auto accidents. That meant we'd only hear the new voice once or twice a week. After a couple of weeks, they added another category of calls to the list, then another and another. After about three months, the transition was complete. The new alert system was now being used for all of our calls, and by then we were all comfortable with it."

This is not to say that the transition was totally painless. Doug Lilly told us that, at first, he had trouble adjusting to the change from a loud clanging bell to a rising series of tones. "The first night of that switch," he said, "I slept through three wake-up calls—something I never do!"

But after that night, his brain adjusted to the new system, and he hasn't missed a call since then.

Lilly is sold on the benefits of the new voice-based alert system. Not only does it help him and his fellow firefighters do their work better, but it also has helped the team in the dispatch center. Not a single dispatcher lost their job when the Locution system was installed. Rather than making the dispatchers dispensable, the system has made their lives easier. It enables them to focus better on gathering crucial data from the stressful, emotional calls they receive, rather than having to jump between phone calls, keyboard entry, and radio messaging.

Technological shifts, like all organizational transformations, can be difficult to manage. People and teams are often resistant to change. The transition to voice tech by the Hamilton County emergency-dispatch system illustrates some of the key strategies to use when managing such changes: Get to know the culture of the people you hope to serve. Design systems—such as voice systems—with their goals, needs, and problems in mind. Introduce any changes to work systems and communication styles gradually, giving people time to adapt. And make sure the people affected by the new systems are fully informed about the reasons for the change and the concrete benefits they can expect to enjoy.

SUCCESSFUL NEW TECHNOLOGY IS ABOUT MEETING BASIC HUMAN needs. In Part One of this book, we laid out how voice meets a wide range of human needs in ways few if any new technologies have ever done before. In some ways, the disruptions caused by the internet and then mobile technology may end up being just a preview of the dislocations and opportunities that voice technology will offer.

Designing a voice-driven user experience that people consider to be as easy as talking with a human being might be described as the business equivalent of passing the famous Turing test, which originally proposed measuring the success of AI by whether human beings would be fooled into thinking that the software they were interacting with was actually another person. This Turing test isn't about whether we can fool users into thinking we're human; it's about whether we can perform tasks better than humans (or current devices) can. And the outcome isn't just of philosophical interest; instead, it will determine which companies are the next generation's winners and losers.

For every business, the design of the user experience, for both customers and employees, is today's primary competitive battleground, where design-forward firms consistently outgrow user-experience laggards in revenues and shareholder returns.[16] In the user-experience battles of tomorrow, voice will be the differentiating weapon of choice.

Acknowledgments

THERE ARE MANY PEOPLE WITHOUT WHOM THIS BOOK WOULD not have been possible.

Top of the list is Karl Weber, my coauthor and partner in this endeavor. He had the extraordinary gift of being able to tease apart the many concepts and examples that define the voice-technology wave and organize them into a coherent story. He dived in and conducted many interviews directly, ultimately himself becoming an expert in the space. His writing was excellent, but most important, he did it all with infectious enthusiasm that made the project a pleasure.

My agent, Carol Franco, believed in this book and this story from the time she saw the first concept. Her relentless focus on making the proposal excellent was a critical step in getting us to this point. Carol's ability to cut to the salient points and ensure we landed those brilliantly is unparalleled.

The publishing team at PublicAffairs has been wonderful. Our editor, John Mahaney, was another partner who pushed Karl and me out of our comfort zone in the pursuit of excellence. His team also believed in this book from the first time they heard about it. John's experience and that of his team has been invaluable.

Shena Redmond and her team in charge of copyediting, composition, proofreading, and indexing provided invaluable support. For me as a first-time author, it was a refreshing experience to receive such a high level of professional help.

I'd like to thank the team that has helped get out the word about this book, including publicist Mark Fortier—the best of his profession—and the team of Dan Rovzar and Lisa Barnes. Jamie Leifer and Lindsay Fradkoff at PublicAffairs played an equally important role, as did our amazing marketing team at WillowTree, including Keith Miller, Adams Paschal, and Amanda Horner.

Salil Rao, chief of staff at WillowTree, played a vital role in wrangling all the moving parts in the writing and publishing process, from data and chapter drafts to interview management. More important, he was a sounding board and thought partner who helped me discover how to formulate and present the key ideas in this book.

There were other team members who helped launch the project in its early days. Ted Kinni, my first writing partner, initially proposed that we had something here that was material for a publishable book. He helped us distill our ideas into the concepts and stories that ultimately make up the book today.

I'd also like to acknowledge John Butman and his son Henry, who were wonderful writing partners until John's untimely death in March 2020. He left us much too young.

Thank you to all those who took the time to be interviewed for this book and share their ideas and experiences related to the coming voice wave. These include Mihai Antonescu, Lauren Becker,

Gordon Chu, Ken Dodelin, Darren Hudgins, Bret Kinsella, Dr. Yaa Kumah-Crystal, Doug Lilly, Arte Merritt, Danielle Ralston, Jon Stine, and Joel Sucherman.

In particular, I'd like to thank Adam Cheyer for sharing his amazing experiences in the earliest days of the voice revolution—starting Siri, interacting with Steve Jobs, selling Siri to Apple, and launching the voice ecosystem we know today.

Bret Kinsella has been at the center of voice and AI for a decade, and his perspectives, connections, and vision for voice have been an invaluable source of insight for me, along with his Voicebot.ai and Synthedia sites. Pete Erickson of Modev played an important role in connecting me and my team to industry leaders.

The Voice Innovation Team at WillowTree, a TELUS International company, is as talented as they come. Thank you to current and previous team members Daniel Atwood, Emily Banzhaf, Margo Bulka, Michael Freenor, Shadiah Garwell, Kylie Kalik, and Matt Kubota. I've learned a lot from each of these professionals, and I'll always value their contributions to our organization.

The leadership team at WillowTree and TELUS International has embraced a "voice is the future" mentality, and I want to thank my extraordinary partner Mike Moore, TELUS International CEO Jeffrey Puritt, as well as Jarrod Cady, Alex Shafran, Will Mayo, Blake Sirach, Jamie Timm, and Patrick Wright for embracing voice and making it a critical part of our client conversations.

My world-class executive assistant Trina Clark bore the brunt of managing countless important details: organizing meetings and interviews, making connections, and especially organizing my time to get the book project over the finish line.

Thanks to my father Ottmar, who taught my brother and me a combination of respect for others and hard work from a young age that has served us well.

Finally, eternal gratitude to my wife, Lynn, and our four children—Lucas, Willem, Max, and Anna—for all their patience and understanding. They allowed me to sneak off to the office on nights and weekends to keep pushing this project forward. Their love and support make it all possible.

Tobias Dengel
Charlottesville, Virginia
October 2023

Notes

PROLOGUE

1. "New App Can Help People Communicate with Head-Tracking Technology," *Digital Accessibility* (blog), Bureau of Internet Accessibility, April 21, 2020, www.boia .org/blog/new-app-can-help-people-communicate-with-head-tracking-technology.

2. "WillowTree Releases Free Head Tracking App to Help Speech-Impaired Individuals Communicate with Caregivers & Loved Ones," WillowTree, March 20, 2020, www.willowtreeapps.com/insights/willowtree-releases-free-head-tracking -app-to-help-speech-impaired-individuals-communicate-with-caregivers-loved-ones.

3. Kylie Kalik, interview with author, January 31, 2022.

4. Chris Kubota, interview with author, January 25, 2022.

5. Damjana Alverson, "Guiding Innovation," Newsroom, Shepherd Center, April 14, 2021, https://news.shepherd.org/guiding-innovation/.

6. Jack Frederick, "'I Was Paralyzed': A Marathoner's Worst Nightmare Turns into a Miracle," Media Hub, University of North Carolina at Chapel Hill, November 16, 2018, https://mediahub.unc.edu/paralyzed-marathoners-worst-nightmare -turns-miracle/.

INTRODUCTION

1. Chris Silver Smith, "Are Yellow Pages Toast? Four Years Later We Review Ad Value," Search Engine Land, March 26, 2012, https://searchengineland.com /are-yellow-pages-toast-four-years-later-we-review-ad-value-116199.

2. Almar Latour, "BellSouth, SBC Plan Web Service for Yellow Pages," *Wall Street Journal*, November 4, 2004, www.wsj.com/articles/SB109952307835064161.

3. "Movie Upturn: Attendance Is Gaining After Four-Year Drop, Theater Men Think," *Wall Street Journal*, February 14, 1951.

4. Peter Newman, "The Smart Speaker Report: Smart Speakers Could Be the Fastest-Growing Digital Platform Ever—Here's How to Engage with Customers Through the Devices," Inside Intelligence, *Insider*, January 10, 2020, www.business insider.com/smart-speaker-report.

5. Masahiro Mori, "The Uncanny Valley," trans. Karl F. MacDorman and Norri Kageki, *IEEE Spectrum*, June 12, 2012, https://spectrum.ieee.org/the-uncanny-valley.

6. "Into the Uncanny Valley: Bridging the Gap Between Cartoon Avatars and Digital Likeness," *Possible Reality* (blog), May 3, 2018, https://medium.com /@possiblereality.co/into-the-uncanny-valley-bridging-the-gap-between-cartoon -avatars-and-digital-likeness-2f4479e48680.

7. Stephanie Zacharek, review of *The Polar Express*, directed by Robert Zemeckis, *Salon*, November 10, 2004, www.salon.com/2004/11/10/polar_express/.

8. Amy Webb, *The Signals Are Talking: Why Today's Fringe Is Tomorrow's Mainstream* (New York: PublicAffairs, 2016).

9. *The Smart Audio Report*, National Public Media, June 2022, www.nationa lpublicmedia.com/insights/reports/smart-audio-report/.

10. Christi Olson and Kelli Kemery, *Voice Report: From Answers to Action; Customer Adoption of Voice Technology and Digital Assistants*, Microsoft, 2019, https:// advertiseonbing-blob.azureedge.net/blob/bingads/media/insight/whitepapers/2019 /04%20apr/voice-report/bingads_2019_voicereport.pdf.

11. Ying Lin, "10 Voice Search Statistics You Need to Know in 2022," Oberlo, February 12, 2022, www.oberlo.com/blog/voice-search-statistics.

12. "Smart Talk: How Organizations and Consumers Are Embracing Voice and Chat Assistants," Capgemini, September 5, 2019, www.capgemini.com/us-en/news /smart-talk-how-organizations-and-consumers-are-embracing-voice-and-chat -assistants/.

13. Meaghan Yuen, "Chatbot Market in 2022: Stats, Trends, and Companies in the Growing AI Chatbot Industry," Insider Intelligence, April 15, 2022, www .insiderintelligence.com/insights/chatbot-market-stats-trends/.

14. "Number of Voice Assistant Devices in Use to Overtake World Population by 2024, Reaching 8.4bn, Led by Smartphones," Juniper Research, April 28, 2020, www.juniperresearch.com/press/number-of-voice-assistant-devices-in-use.

15. Derek Thompson, "Breakthroughs of the Year," *Atlantic*, December 8, 2022, www.theatlantic.com/newsletters/archive/2022/12/technology-medicine-law-ai-10 -breakthroughs-2022/672390/.

16. Kevin Roose, "The Brilliance and Weirdness of ChatGPT," *New York Times*, December 5, 2022, www.nytimes.com/2022/12/05/technology/chatgpt-ai-twitter .html; Kelsey Piper, "ChatGPT Has Given Everyone a Glimpse at AI's Astounding

Progress," *Vox*, December 15, 2022, www.vox.com/future-perfect/2022/12/15/23509014/chatgpt-artificial-intelligence-openai-language-models-ai-risk-google.

17. H. Holden Thorp, "ChatGPT Is Fun, but Not an Author," *Science*, January 26, 2023, www.science.org/doi/10.1126/science.adg7879.

18. Hasan Chowdhury, "It's Too Late, Google. AI Is Already Running Wild," *Insider*, January 19, 2023, www.businessinsider.com/google-fears-ai-running-wild-but-it-is-too-late-2023-1.

CHAPTER 1: SPEED

1. W. J. Baumol and W. G. Bowen, "On the Performing Arts: The Anatomy of Their Economic Problems," *American Economic Review* 55 no. 1/2 (March 1965): 495–502, www.jstor.org/stable/1816292.

2. Kristen Baker, "11 Website Page Load Time Statistics You Need [+ How to Increase Conversion Rate]," HubSpot, updated June 13, 2022, https://blog.hubspot.com/marketing/page-load-time-conversion-rates.

3. Aarti Shahani, "Voice Recognition Software Finally Beats Humans at Typing, Study Finds," *All Tech Considered*, NPR, August 24, 2016, www.npr.org/sections/alltechconsidered/2016/08/24/491156218/voice-recognition-software-finally-beats-humans-at-typing-study-finds.

4. "Occupational Employment and Wages, May 2020: 43-9022 Word Processors and Typists," US Bureau of Labor Statistics, last modified March 31, 2021, www.bls.gov/oes/2020/may/oes439022.htm.

5. Rina Diane Caballar, "Programming by Voice May Be the Next Frontier in Software Development," *IEEE Spectrum*, March 22, 2021, https://spectrum.ieee.org/programming-by-voice-may-be-the-next-frontier-in-software-development.

6. Emily Shea and Ryan Hileman, "Voice Coding," in *Google Cloud Platform Podcast*, hosted by Brian Dorsey and Mark Mirchandani, www.gcppodcast.com/post/episode-223-voice-coding-with-emily-shea-and-ryan-hileman/.

7. Matt Wiethoff, "How to Code with Your Voice (No Typing Required)," August 3, 2021, in *Learn to Code with Me*, hosted by Laurence Bradford, podcast, https://podcasts.apple.com/au/podcast/s8e6-how-to-code-with-your-voice-no-typing-required/id1106620664?i=1000530846436.

8. Tom Warren, "'Hey, GitHub!' Will Let Programmers Code with Just Their Voice," *The Verge*, November 9, 2022, www.theverge.com/2022/11/9/23449175/hey-github-voice-copilot-code-programming-system.

9. Alicia Kelso, "How Becoming 'a Tech Company That Sells Pizza' Delivered Huge for Domino's," *Forbes*, April 30, 2018, www.forbes.com/sites/aliciakelso/2018/04/30/delivery-digital-provide-dominos-with-game-changing-advantages/?sh=492cff8f7771.

10. Ryan Owen, "Artificial Intelligence at McDonald's—Two Current Use Cases," Emerj Artificial Intelligence Research, last updated January 26, 2022, https://emerj.com/ai-sector-overviews/artificial-intelligence-at-mcdonalds/.

11. Katie Deighton, "Restaurants Send More Customer Calls to Voice Bots amid Staffing Shortages," *Wall Street Journal*, August 24, 2022, www.wsj.com/articles /restaurants-send-more-customer-calls-to-voice-bots-amid-staffing-shortages -11661335202.

12. Ben Gran and Daphne Foreman, "How Banking Virtual Assistants Can Improve Your Banking Experience," *Forbes*, last updated April 5, 2022, www.forbes .com/advisor/banking/banking-virtual-assistants/.

13. Candace Widdoes and Joe Abi Akl, "Talking the Talk: The Voice-Recognition Disruptors Looking to Outsmart Big Tech," Global Future Council on Consumption, World Economic Forum, August 21, 2019, www.weforum.org/agenda/2019/08 /voice-recognition-disruptors-big-tech/.

14. Rehana Begg, "Voice Command: Multilingual Speech Recognition for the Shop Floor," *Machine Design*, August 10, 2021, www.machinedesign.com/automation -iiot/article/21171928/voice-command-multilingual-speech-recognition-for-the -shop-floor.

15. Tom Ward, Ashley Hubka, and Janey Whiteside, "Hey Siri, Add to Walmart: Introducing a New Shortcut for Online Grocery," Walmart, November 11, 2019, https://corporate.walmart.com/newsroom/2019/11/11/hey-siri-add-to-walmart -introducing-a-new-shortcut-for-online-grocery.

16. Sarah Perez, "Walmart Launches Its Own Voice Assistant, 'Ask Sam,' Initially for Employee Use," *TechCrunch*, July 29, 2020, https://techcrunch.com/2020 /07/29/walmart-launches-its-own-voice-assistant-ask-sam-initially-for-employee-use/.

17. Carla E. Small et al., "What Will Health Care Look Like Once Smart Speakers Are Everywhere?," *Harvard Business Review*, March 7, 2018, https://hbr .org/2018/03/what-will-health-care-look-like-once-smart-speakers-are-everywhere.

18. Nina Achadjian, "Voice + AI Is Coming to the Workplace Loud and Clear," *Forbes*, June 25, 2020, www.forbes.com/sites/ninaachadjian/2020/06/25/voice--ai -is-coming-to-the-workplace-loud-and-clear/.

19. Susan Kreimer, "Amazon's Alexa Is Now a Healthcare Provider," Medscape, February 17, 2022, www.medscape.com/viewarticle/968719.

20. Kyle Wiggers, "Why Salesforce Is Killing Off Einstein Voice Assistant," *VentureBeat*, July 21, 2020, https://venturebeat.com/2020/07/21/why-salesforce-is -killing-off-einstein-voice-assistant/.

CHAPTER 2: SAFETY

1. Andrea May Sahouri, "After Vehicle Plunges into Freezing Iowa River, Driver Uses Siri to Call 911," *Des Moines Register*, December 13, 2019, www.desmoinesregister .com/story/news/2019/12/13/man-uses-siri-call-911-after-his-vehicle-plunged-into -winnebago-river-cerro-gordo-mason-city/2636537001/.

2. Chris Porteous, "Cybercrime Could Cost the World $10.5 Trillion Annually by 2025," *Entrepreneur*, February 24, 2021, www.entrepreneur.com/business-new s/cybercrime-could-cost-the-world-105-trillion-annually-by/364015.

3. Rina Karnaukh, "How Technology Helps Save Lives: Smartphones, Wearables, and Voice Assistants," Alternative Spaces, accessed February 17, 2023, https://alternative-spaces.com/blog/how-technology-helps-save-lives-smartphones-wearables-and-voice-assistants/.

4. "'Hey Siri, Call 911!': Single Dad Paralyzed in Car Crash Credits Apple's Siri with Saving His Life," *Daily Mail*, January 12, 2019, www.dailymail.co.uk/news/article-6584643/Hey-Siri-call-911-Single-dad-paralyzed-car-crash-credits-Apples-Siri-saving-life.html.

5. Shelby Rogers, "Three Fishermen Claim Siri Saved Their Lives at Sea," *Interesting Engineering*, May 9, 2017, https://interestingengineering.com/three-fishermen-claim-siri-saved-their-lives-at-sea.

6. "Meet Our Newest Angel: Alexa!," Visiting Angels Living Assistance Services, accessed December 8, 2022, www.visitingangels.com/office-locator-alexa.

7. "Charles Schwab, Chase, Wells Fargo, and Others Use New Voice IAM Biometrics Technology," Abstract Forward Consulting, accessed February 17, 2023, www.abstractforward.com/charles-schwab-chase-wells-fargo-and-others-use-new-voice-iam-biometrics-technology/.

8. Kim Martin, "How Liveness Detection Would Have Foiled the Sneakers Movie Plot," ID R&D, accessed February 17, 2023, www.idrnd.ai/how-liveness-detection-would-have-foiled-the-sneakers-movie-plot/.

9. Chris Isidore, "Boeing's 737 Max Debacle Could Be the Most Expensive Corporate Blunder Ever," Business, CNN, November 17, 2020, www.cnn.com/2020/11/17/business/boeing-737-max-grounding-cost/index.html.

10. Dave Davies, "'Flying Blind' Author Says Boeing Put Profit Ahead of Safety with the 737 Max," *Fresh Air*, NPR, November 29, 2021, www.npr.org/2021/11/29/1059784424/flying-blind-author-says-boeing-put-profit-ahead-of-safety-with-the-737-max.

11. Woodrow Bellamy III, "Rockwell Collins Rapidly Advancing Cockpit Voice Recognition Technology," *Aviation Today*, November 13, 2014, www.aviationtoday.com/2014/11/13/rockwell-collins-rapidly-advancing-cockpit-voice-recognition-technology/.

12. Ramil Sitdikov, "Russia's MiG-35 to Be Equipped with Voice Assistant Helping Pilot in Tough Situations," Sputnik International, June 10, 2020, https://sputniknews.com/20200610/russias-mig-35-to-be-equipped-with-voice-assistant-helping-pilot-in-tough-situations-1079572763.html.

13. Thomas Pallini, "Siri and Alexa Are Coming to Airplane Cockpits. Here's How Engineers Are Working to Take Voice Tech from Sci-Fi to Reality," *Insider*, May 10, 2021, www.businessinsider.com/how-engineers-are-working-to-make-voice-controlled-aircraft-reality-2021-5.

14. "Urban Air Mobility and Advanced Air Mobility," Federal Aviation Administration, last updated June 1, 2022, www.faa.gov/uas/advanced_operations/urban_air_mobility.

15. "eVTOL Aircraft Market Size, Trend Analysis & Forecast to 2028," The Insight Partners, June 2022, www.theinsightpartners.com/reports/evtol-aircraft-market.

16. Pallini, "Siri and Alexa Are Coming."

17. Gabrielle N., "US Army Creates AI Natural Language Voice-Command for Tanks, Robots; Uses Tech for Search and Rescue," *Tech Times*, April 21, 2021, www.techtimes.com/articles/259348/20210421/us-army-ai-natural-communication-devcom-us-apple-siri-amazon-alexa-ai-us-army-ai-usa-china-ai.htm; Michael Peck, "'Siri, Find Me a Russian Submarine,' U.S. Navy Asks," *Forbes*, February 10, 2021, www.forbes.com/sites/michaelpeck/2021/02/10/siri-find-me-a-russian-submarine-us-navy-asks/?sh=21c1606e79e8.

18. Will Knight, "As Russia Plots Its Next Move, an AI Listens to the Chatter," *Wired*, April 4, 2022, www.wired.com/story/russia-ukraine-war-ai-surveillance/.

19. Jen Monnier, "What Was the Deepwater Horizon Disaster?," *Live Science*, April 19, 2021, www.livescience.com/deepwater-horizon-oil-spill-disaster.html.

20. Konrad Konarski, in "Innovation Minute: How AI Is Being Applied in Oil & Gas Fields," V-Soft Consulting, uploaded June 25, 2020, www.youtube.com/watch?v=Owof439fZYw.

21. Crispin Chatar, Zhe Huang, and Peter Hadrovic, "A Voice Interface for Drilling Systems" (paper presented at IADC/SPE International Drilling Conference and Exhibition, Galveston, TX, March 4, 2020), https://onepetro.org/SPEDC/proceedings-abstract/20DC/2-20DC/D091S008R004/447222.

22. Joann Muller, "Improved Voice Controls Could Increase Car Safety," *Axios*, March 29, 2019, www.axios.com/2019/03/29/autonomous-vehicles-safety-voice-controls.

23. Mihai Antonescu, interview with author, February 22, 2022. Thanks to Mihai Antonescu, project manager at Google and formerly group product manager at Mercedes-Benz Research & Development North America Inc., for his insights into the Mercedes voice-technology story.

24. Matt Richtel and Bill Vlasic, "Voice-Activated Technology Is Called Safety Risk for Drivers," *New York Times*, June 12, 2013, www.nytimes.com/2013/06/13/business/voice-activated-in-car-systems-are-called-risky.html.

25. Nils Schanz, head of User Interaction Voice Control at Daimler AG-Mercedes-Benz, quoted in Alisa Priddle, "Hey, Mercedes Is Making Upgrades to Its MBUX Infotainment System," *MotorTrend*, May 22, 2020, www.motortrend.com/news/mercedes-mbux-upgrades/.

26. "Cerence Raises the Bar for Mobility with the Introduction of Cerence Co-Pilot, a Deeply Integrated, Ultra-Intelligent In-Car Assistant," AiThority.com, December 20, 2021, https://aithority.com/technology/mobility/cerence-raises-the-bar-for-mobility-with-the-introduction-of-cerence-co-pilot-a-deeply-integrated-ultra-intelligent-in-car-assistant/.

27. Nor'adila Hepburn, "How Smart Motorcycle Helmets Can Change Your Ride," *SlashGear*, August 11, 2022, www.slashgear.com/961343/how-smart-motorcycle-helmets-can-change-your-ride/.

CHAPTER 3: KNOWLEDGE

1. Jeff Desjardins, "How Much Data Is Generated Each Day?," World Economic Forum, April 17, 2019, www.weforum.org/agenda/2019/04/how-much-data-is -generated-each-day-cf4bddf29f/.

2. Eric Hall Schwartz, "US Bank Launches Mobile App Voice Assistant Built to Mimic Human Bank Teller," Voicebot.ai, July 28, 2020, https://voicebot.ai/2020 /07/28/u-s-bank-launches-mobile-app-voice-assistant-built-to-mimic-human -bank-tellers/.

3. Tom Sullivan, "Vocera Unveils Smartbadge Combining Mobile Phone and Clinical Communications Features," Healthcare IT News, January 7, 2019, www .healthcareitnews.com/news/vocera-unveils-smartbadge-combining-mobile-phone -and-clinical-communications-features. The name "Sarah Goldberg" and the specific details of her story are fictitious, but the capabilities of Smartbadge are accurately described.

4. Mandy Oaklander, "Linking Health Care Workers: Vocera Smartbadge," Best Inventions of 2020, *Time*, November 19, 2020, https://time.com/collection/best -inventions-2020/5911335/vocera-smartbadge/.

5. "Voice Search Statistics and Emerging Trends," DBS Interactive, accessed February 17, 2023, www.dbswebsite.com/blog/trends-in-voice-search/.

6. Yaniv Leviathan and Yossi Matias, "Duplex Is Getting Smarter and Making Life a Little Easier," The Keyword, Google, October 15, 2020, https://blog.google /technology/ai/duplex-helpful-updates/.

7. See, for example, the model for digital government released by the Obama administration: "Digital Government: Building a 21st Century Platform to Better Serve the American People," Obama White House (archived website), accessed February 17, 2023, https://obamawhitehouse.archives.gov/sites/default/files/omb/egov /digital-government/digital-government.html.

8. Eric Hal Schwartz, "IBM Offers States Free Watson Virtual Assistant to Answer Voter Election Questions," Voicebot.ai, September 17, 2020, https://voicebot .ai/2020/09/17/ibm-offers-states-free-watson-virtual-assistant-to-answer-voter -election-questions/.

9. Darren Hudgins, interview with author, April 21, 2022.

10. Eric Hal Schwartz, "The US Navy Wants a Virtual Assistant to Help Hunt Submarines," Voicebot.ai, February 10, 2021, https://voicebot.ai/2021/02/10 /the-us-navy-wants-a-virtual-assistant-to-help-hunt-submarines/.

11. Arte Merritt, interview with author, May 11, 2022.

12. Bret Kinsella, "SoapBox Labs Lands Deal with McGraw Hill for Voice-Enabled Learning," Voicebot.ai, January 25, 2022, https://voicebot.ai/2022/01 /25/soapbox-labs-lands-deal-with-mcgraw-hill-for-voice-enabled-learning/.

13. Eric Hal Schwartz, "SoapBox Labs Will Augment Popular Lexile Reading Test with Voice AI Assessment," Voicebot.ai, March 22, 2022, https://voicebot

.ai/2022/03/22/soapbox-labs-will-augment-popular-lexile-reading-test-with-voice
-ai-assessment/.

CHAPTER 4: INCLUSION

1. "Look to Speak: Everything You Need to Know About Google's Novel App," *Deccan Herald*, last updated March 29, 2022, www.deccanherald.com/business /technology/look-to-speak-everything-you-need-to-know-about-googles-novel-app -1095792.html.

2. "Blindness and Vision Impairment," World Health Organization, October 13, 2022, www.who.int/news-room/fact-sheets/detail/blindness-and-visual-impairment.

3. Carole Martinez, "13 Must-Have Apps for Blind or Visually Impaired People in 2022," Inclusive City Maker, Okeenea, last updated December 28, 2021, www .inclusivecitymaker.com/apps-blind-visually-impaired-people/.

4. Hugh Langley, "Inside Google's Top-Secret Project to Give You Superhuman Hearing. Code Name: 'Wolverine,'" *Insider*, March 4, 2021, www.businessinsider .com/google-x-alphabet-hearing-project-wolverine-codename-augmented-reality -2021-3.

5. "Adult Literacy in the United States," National Center for Education Statistics, US Department of Education, July 2019, https://nces.ed.gov/pubs2019/2019179 /index.asp.

6. "Literacy Rate by Country 2023," World Population Review, accessed February 17, 2023, https://worldpopulationreview.com/country-rankings/literacy-rate-by -country.

7. Moussa Doumbouya, Lisa Einstein, and Chris Piech, "Why AI Needs to Be Able to Understand All the World's Languages," *Scientific American*, February 1, 2021, www.scientificamerican.com/article/why-ai-needs-to-be-able-to-understand-all -the-worlds-languages/.

8. Ayushman Baruah, "Oracle Sees Uptick in Adoption of AI-Enabled Chatbots in India," *Mint*, last updated July 5, 2020, www.livemint.com/companies/news /oracle-sees-uptick-in-adoption-of-ai-enabled-chatbots-in-india-11593937775357 .html.

9. Shiori Zinnen, "Listen and Learn: How Audiobooks Can Support Literacy Development," Reading Partners, October 27, 2021, https://readingpartners.org /blog/audiobooks/.

10. Zinnen, "Listen and Learn."

11. John Boitnott, "This Immigrant Founder Taught Himself English—Then Made an App That Helps Others with His Disability (and Speed Readers)," *Inc.*, August 29, 2017, www.inc.com/john-boitnott/how-one-founder-turned-his-dyslexia -into-an-app-th.html; Cliff Weitzman, "How I Overcame Dyslexia with Text to Speech, Audiobooks & Speechify," speech accepting Hamilton Life Achievement Award, Wheeler School, Providence, RI, March 20, 2019, www.youtube.com/watch ?v=yvzw4gj4AFU.

12. Boitnott, "This Immigrant Founder."

13. Eric Hal Schwartz, "Indian Government Service Voice Assistant Set for Release," Voicebot.ai, April 6, 2022, https://voicebot.ai/2022/04/06/indian -government-service-voice-assistant-set-for-release/; "Unified Mobile Application," GeeksforGeeks, last updated November 3, 2022, www.geeksforgeeks.org/unified -mobile-application/.

14. Timothy Obiezu, "Nigerian Language Advocates Seek Inclusion of African Languages in Tech Devices," *Voice of America*, January 26, 2022, www.voanews .com/a/nigerian-language-advocates-seek-inclusion-of-african-languages-in-tech -devices-/6413038.html.

15. Doumbouya, Einstein, and Piech, "Why AI Needs to Be Able to Understand All the World's Languages."

16. Eric Hal Schwartz, "Amazon Unveils Speech Datasets for Alexa Skill Development in 51 Languages," Voicebot.ai, April 20, 2022, https://voicebot.ai/2022/04 /20/amazon-unveils-speech-datasets-alexa-skill-development-in-51-languages/.

17. Kathleen Siminyu, "AI in Africa—Voice & Language Tools," February 9, 2022, in *Practical AI*, Changelog, hosted by Chris Benson, Joyce Nabende, and Daniel Whitenack, podcast, https://changelog.com/practicalai/167.

18. "Data and Statistics About ADHD," Centers for Disease Control and Prevention, last reviewed August 9, 2022, www.cdc.gov/ncbddd/adhd/data.html.

19. Danielle Ralston, interview with author, October 12, 2022.

20. Lauren Becker, interview with author, October 12, 2022.

CHAPTER 5: ENGAGEMENT

1. Ingrid Lunden, "Spotify Is Acquiring Sonantic, the AI Voice Platform Used to Simulate Val Kilmer's Voice in 'Top Gun: Maverick,'" *TechCrunch*, June 13, 2022, https://techcrunch.com/2022/06/13/spotify-is-acquiring-sonantic-the-ai-voice -platform-used-to-simulate-val-kilmers-voice-in-top-gun-maverick/.

2. Dalvin Brown, "AI Gave Val Kilmer His Voice Back. But Critics Worry the Technology Could Be Misused," *Washington Post*, August 18, 2021, www.washington post.com/technology/2021/08/18/val-kilmer-ai-voice-cloning/.

3. "Hear Val Kilmer's AI Voice," Sonantic, uploaded August 9, 2021, www .youtube.com/watch?v=OSMue60Gg6s.

4. Sascha Segan, "The IBM PC's Killer Apps: Where Are They Now?," *PCMag*, August 12, 2021, www.pcmag.com/news/the-ibm-pcs-killer-apps-where-are-they-now.

5. Donald Buckley, "Voice Technology Is the Next Big Thing in Media and Entertainment," *Variety*, August 5, 2021, https://variety.com/vip/voice-technology -is-the-next-big-thing-in-media-and-entertainment-1235031704/.

6. Bret Kinsella, "Clubhouse Surpasses 10 Million Users After Musk, Zuckerberg, Rogan, and MrBeast Join and Starts Drawing More Scrutiny," Voicebot.ai, February 23, 2021, https://voicebot.ai/2021/02/23/clubhouse-surpasses-10-million-users -after-musk-zuckerberg-rogan-and-mrbeast-join-and-starts-drawing-more-scrutiny/.

7. Wilson Chapman, "Spotify Greenroom Rebranded to Spotify Live," *Variety*, April 12, 2022, https://variety.com/2022/digital/news/spotify-greenroom-live-1235231178/.

8. "Social Audio Innovator Gimme Radio Raises $3 Million, Inks Media Partnership with iHeartMedia to Amplify Reach Across New Communities and Creators," Gimme Radio, press release, January 27, 2022, www.prnewswire.com/news-releases/social-audio-innovator-gimme-radio-raises-3-million-inks-media-partnership-with-iheartmedia-to-amplify-reach-across-new-communities-and-creators-301469894.html.

9. Mark van Rijmenam, "What Is Synthetic Media: The Ultimate Guide," The Digital Speaker, July 27, 2022, www.thedigitalspeaker.com/what-is-synthetic-media-ultimate-guide/.

10. Helen Rosner, "The Ethics of a Deepfake Anthony Bourdain Voice," *New Yorker*, July 17, 2021, www.newyorker.com/culture/annals-of-gastronomy/the-ethics-of-a-deepfake-anthony-bourdain-voice.

11. Eric Hal Schwartz, "AI-Powered Andy Warhol Voice Reads His Diary in New Netflix Documentary," Voicebot.ai, February 24, 2022, https://voicebot.ai/2022/02/24/ai-powered-andy-warhol-voice-reads-his-diary-in-new-netflix-documentary/.

12. Ellen Gamerman, "The Rise of the Robo-Voices," *Wall Street Journal*, October 7, 2021, www.wsj.com/articles/the-rise-of-the-robo-voices-11633615201.

13. Tom Simonite, "Synthetic Voices Want to Take Over Audiobooks," *Wired*, January 27, 2022, www.wired.com/story/audiobooks-synthetic-voices/.

14. "Every Book Deserves to Be Heard. With Apple Books Digital Narration, Now Yours Can Be," Apple Books for Authors, Apple, accessed January 6, 2023, https://authors.apple.com/support/4519-digital-narration-audiobooks.

15. Bret Kinsella and Voicebot.ai, "Mathbox.io and Question of the Day Acquired by Volley in Multimillion Dollar Transaction—Voice Insider 135," Patreon, March 8, 2022, www.patreon.com/posts/matchbox-io-and-63552697; Eric Hal Schwartz, "Volley Scores Exclusive License for Jeopardy and All Sony Pictures Television Voice Games," Voicebot.ai, March 17, 2022, https://voicebot.ai/2022/03/17/volley-scores-exclusive-license-for-jeopardy-and-all-sony-pictures-television-voice-games/.

16. Steve Kovach, "Mark Zuckerberg's 'Metaverse' Business Lost More Than $10 Billion Last Year, and the Losses Keep Growing," CNBC, February 2, 2022, www.cnbc.com/2022/02/02/meta-reality-labs-reports-10-billion-loss.html.

17. Shirin Ghaffary, "Mark Zuckerberg Wants to Build a Voice Assistant That Blows Alexa and Siri Away," *Vox*, February 23, 2022, www.vox.com/recode/22948097/mark-zuckerberg-voice-assistant-metaverse-ai-announcement.

18. Ghaffary, "Mark Zuckerberg."

19. Janko Roettgers and Nick Statt, "In the Metaverse, Everyone Can Sound Like Morgan Freeman," *Protocol*, January 21, 2022, www.protocol.com/newsletters/entertainment/metaverse-spacial-audio.

20. Roettgers and Statt, "In the Metaverse."

21. Eric Hal Schwartz, "Children's Bedtime Robot Startup Snorble Raises $10M," Voicebot.ai, April 20, 2022, https://voicebot.ai/2022/04/20/childrens-bedtime-robot -startup-snorble-raises-10m/.

22. Tanya Basu, "A Voice Game Boom Is Giving Kids a Break from Screen Time," *MIT Technology Review*, March 27, 2021, www.technologyreview.com/2021 /03/27/1021270/voice-game-kids-screen-time/.

23. Jenny Medeiros, "From Storytelling to Settling Arguments: Voice Technology for Kids," Modev, May 18, 2018, www.modev.com/blog/from-storytelling-to -settling-arguments-voice-technology-for-kids.

24. Eric Hal Schwartz, "Disney Appoints Metaverse Chief to Blend Physical and Digital Worlds," Voicebot.ai, February 16, 2022, https://voicebot.ai/2022/02 /16/disney-appoints-metaverse-chief-to-blend-physical-and-digital-worlds/.

25. Eric Hal Schwartz, "Lego and Epic Games Unveil Metaverse for Children Plans," Voiecbot.ai, April 7, 2022, https://voicebot.ai/2022/04/07/lego-and-epic -games-unveil-metaverse-for-children-plan/.

26. Gaea Vilage, "Voice AI and the Metaverse Shopping Experience," Read-Speaker AI, May 31, 2022, www.readspeaker.ai/blog/metaverse-shopping -experience/.

27. Julia Russell, "Metaverse, Social Commerce—What's Next in Digital Retail?," SmartBrief, April 22, 2022, https://corp.smartbrief.com/original/2022/04 /metaverse-social-commerce-whats-next-for-digital-retail.

28. Nick Heethuis, "How the Metaverse Will Reshape E-Commerce Forever," Forbes Councils, January 24, 2022, www.forbes.com/sites/theyec/2022/01/24/how -the-metaverse-will-reshape-e-commerce-forever/?sh=342cc9a669d9.

29. Russell, "Metaverse, Social Commerce."

30. Vilage, "Voice AI."

CHAPTER 6: TRANSFORMATION

1. Tim Johnson, "When Customers Forget Their Passwords, Business Suffers," McClatchy Washington Bureau, June 20, 2017, Phys.org, https://phys.org /news/2017-06-customers-passwords-business.html.

2. "Voice and Speech Recognition Market Worth $53.66 Billion by 2030," Grand View Research, May 2022, www.grandviewresearch.com/press-release/global-voice -recognition-industry.

3. Jefferson Graham, "Hate Being on Hold? Google Introduces 'Hold for Me' Feature, but It's a Mixed Bag," *USA Today*, October 14, 2020, www.usatoday .com/story/tech/2020/10/14/googles-hold-me-feature-pixel-phones-how-works /3638626001/.

4. Shaun Cooley, August 13, 2020, and Dominik, September 7, 2020, and Mike Vande Ven Jr., September 2, 2020, comments on "Holds vs Callbacks: A Customer Service Observation," Stonemaier Games, August 13, 2020, https://stonemaiergames .com/holds-vs-callbacks-a-customer-service-observation/.

5. Yaniv Leviathan and Yossi Matias, "Google Duplex: An AI System for Accomplishing Real-World Tasks over the Phone," Google Research, May 8, 2018, https://ai.googleblog.com/2018/05/duplex-ai-system-for-natural-conversation.html.

6. Clint Boulton, "Customers Bank on BofA Chatbot amid Pandemic," CIO, June 29, 2020, www.cio.com/article/193662/customers-bank-on-bofa-chatbot-amid-pandemic.html.

7. "Alexa, Ask TD Ameritrade: Amazon Skill Reads Market Updates, Quotes and More," TD Ameritrade, accessed February 17, 2023, https://tickertape.tdameritrade.com/tools/alexa-td-ameritrade-15897.

8. "Garanti BBVA Interacts with More Than 650,000 Customers a Month with Its Smart Assistant Ugi," BBVA, December 30, 2021, www.bbva.com/en/tr/garanti-bbva-interacts-with-more-than-650000-customers-a-month-with-its-smart-assistant-ugi/.

9. Aaron Byrne, "How FIs Can Reinvent Their Business Models with Financial Ecosystems," EY, September 22, 2020, accessed October 12, 2022, www.ey.com/en_us/financial-services/how-fis-can-reinvent-their-business-models-with-financial-ecosystems.

10. Jamie Grill-Goodman, "IoT Wearables Revolutionize the Container Store Experience," Retail Info Systems, January 7, 2018, https://risnews.com/iot-wearables-revolutionize-container-store-experience.

11. Damian Radcliffe, "From Search to Smart Speakers: Why Voice Is Too Big for Media Companies to Ignore," InContext, Digital Context Next, June 28, 2018, https://digitalcontentnext.org/blog/2018/06/28/from-search-to-smart-speakers-why-voice-is-too-big-for-media-companies-to-ignore/.

12. Claire Fanning, "Voice Technology Is Changing the Future of Audio Advertising," Partner Experts, Adweek, accessed February 17, 2023, www.adweek.com/partner-articles/voice-technology-is-changing-the-future-of-audio-advertising/; Ashley Carman, "Pandora Wants You to Talk to Its Ads," *The Verge*, July 23, 2020, www.theverge.com/2020/7/23/21334484/pandora-interactive-voice-ads-voice-mode.

13. Sarah Perez, "Alexa Can Now Pay for Gas at Over 11,500 Exxon and Mobil Stations in the US," *TechCrunch*, September 1, 2020, https://techcrunch.com/2020/09/01/alexa-can-now-pay-for-gas-at-over-11500-exxon-and-mobil-stations-in-the-u-s/.

14. Eric Hal Schwartz, "TCL Picks TV AI Startup Disruptel to Bring Visually Aware Voice Assistants to Smart TVs," Voicebot.ai, January 12, 2022, https://voicebot.ai/2022/01/12/tcl-picks-tv-ai-startup-disruptel-to-bring-visually-aware-voice-assistants-to-smart-tvs/.

15. Dr. Yaa Kumah-Crystal, interview with author, March 8, 2022.

16. Jenni Spinner, "Vocal Biomarkers Enable Unique Diagnosis, Monitoring Capabilities," Outsourcing-Pharma, March 2, 2021, www.outsourcing-pharma.com/Article/2021/03/02/Vocal-biomarkers-enable-diagnosis-monitoring-capabilities.

17. "Record Your Voice to Help AI Beat COVID!," COVID Voice Detector, Carnegie Mellon University, accessed February 17, 2023, https://cvd.lti

.cmu.edu; "COVID-19 Sounds App," University of Cambridge, accessed February 17, 2023, www.covid-19-sounds.org/en/; "How to Develop a Voice-Based COVID-19 Test!," Audeering, accessed February 17, 2023, www.audeering.com /products/covid-19/.

18. "This Is the Place to Predict Alzheimer's," This Is the Place: Startup Stories, University of Toronto, accessed February 17, 2023, www.utoronto.ca/entrepreneurs /winterlight; Janet Morrissey, "Looking to Technology to Avoid Doctors' Offices and Emergency Rooms," *New York Times*, February 21, 2019, www.nytimes.com /2019/02/21/business/medical-technology-ai-tests.html.

19. Emily Anthes, "Alexa, Do I Have COVID-19?," *Nature*, September 30, 2020, www.nature.com/articles/d41586-020-02732-4.

20. "New HHS Study Shows 63-Fold Increase in Medicare Telehealth Utilization During the Pandemic," Centers for Medicare & Medicaid Services, US Department of Health and Human Services, December 3, 2021, www.hhs.gov/about /news/2021/12/03/new-hhs-study-shows-63-fold-increase-in-medicare-telehealth -utilization-during-pandemic.html.

21. "SYPDK—What Happens When Tele-Health Visits Explode," Voicebot.ai, December 29, 2020, paywall post, accessed May 2022.

22. Elizabeth Wallace, "Voice Tech Becoming Indispensable to Healthcare," RTInsights, October 4, 2021, www.rtinsights.com/voice-tech-becoming -indispensable-to-healthcare/.

23. Nawar Shara et al., "Voice Activated Remote Monitoring Technology for Heart Failure Patients: Study Design, Feasibility and Observations from a Pilot Randomized Control Trial," *PLoS ONE* 17, no. 5 (May 6, 2022), https://journals.plos.org /plosone/article?id=10.1371/journal.pone.0267794.

24. Karen Brown, "Something Bothering You? Tell It to Woebot," *New York Times*, June 1, 2021, www.nytimes.com/2021/06/01/health/artificial-intelligence -therapy-woebot.html.

25. Brown, "Something Bothering You?"

CHAPTER 7: FALLING BARRIERS

1. Material in this section is drawn from an author interview with Adam Cheyer, March 24, 2022.

2. "Apple's 1987 Knowledge Navigator Video," uploaded April 8, 2007, www .youtube.com/watch?v=HGYFEI6uLy0.

3. "Consumer Intelligence Series: Prepare for the Voice Revolution," PwC, accessed October 1, 2022, www.pwc.com/us/en/advisory-services/publications /consumer-intelligence-series/voice-assistants.pdf.

4. Veronica Combs, "Survey: Voice Tech Is at a Tipping Point with 31% of Respondents Using It Daily," TechRepublic, July 21, 2021, www.techrepublic.com /article/survey-voice-tech-is-at-a-tipping-point-with-31-of-respondents-using-it-daily/.

5. Adam Cheyer, email to author, February 3, 2023.

6. Oleg Bestsennyy et al., "Telehealth: A Quarter-Trillion-Dollar Post-COVID-19 Reality?," McKinsey & Company, July 9, 2021, www.mckinsey.com/industries/healthcare-systems-and-services/our-insights/telehealth-a-quarter-trillion-dollar-post-covid-19-reality.

7. Kelley A. Wittbold et al., "How Hospitals Are Using AI to Battle Covid-19," *Harvard Business Review*, April 3, 2020, https://hbr.org/2020/04/how-hospitals-are-using-ai-to-battle-covid-19.

8. Ken Labbe, "Capital One AI VP Discusses AI Assistant Eno," TechTarget, March 29, 2019, www.techtarget.com/searchenterpriseai/feature/Capital-One-AI-VP-discusses-AI-assistant-Eno.

9. Example from Andrew Mauboussin, "A Visual Introduction to Language Models in NLP," Surge AI, November 4, 2021, www.surgehq.ai/blog/an-introduction-to-language-models-in-nlp-part-1-intuition.

10. "SYPDK—Stanford OVAL Says You Can Now Train an NLU with 99% Less Data," Voicebot.ai, October 26, 2020, paywall post, accessed May 2022.

11. "Albert Mehrabian," Management Thinkers, British Library, accessed January 5, 2023, www.bl.uk/people/albert-mehrabian.

12. "Advanced Voice User Interface Design," in Cathy Pearl, *Designing Voice User Interfaces: Principles of Conversational Experiences* (Newton, MA: O'Reilly Media, 2017).

13. David Priest, "'Hey, Google' No More: The Nest Hub Max Is Getting a Workaround," CNET, May 11, 2022, www.cnet.com/home/smart-home/hey-google-no-more-the-nest-hub-max-is-getting-a-workaround/.

14. Jonathan Vanian and Aaron Pressman, "How Amazon, Apple, Google, and Microsoft Created an Eavesdropping Explosion—Data Sheet," *Fortune*, August 8, 2019, https://fortune.com/2019/08/08/gogole-amazon-microsoft-listen-conversation-siri/.

15. Mike Pearl, "The ChatGPT Chatbot from OpenAI Is Amazing, Creative, and Totally Wrong," *Mashable*, December 10, 2022, https://mashable.com/article/chatgpt-amazing-wrong.

16. Jon Stine, interview with author, May 16, 2022.

17. See, for example, Dave Lee and Michael Pooler, "Travis Kalanick Expands 'Dark Kitchens' Venture Across Latin America," *Financial Times*, September 6, 2022, www.ft.com/content/162460f3-5707-4857-9676-70aa1d9df203.

CHAPTER 8: MAKING VOICE AN INTEGRAL PART OF YOUR EXISTING BUSINESS SYSTEMS

1. Bret Kinsella and Voicebot.ai, "Why Alexa and Google Assistant Will Spawn Thousands of Assistants," Patreon, March 1, 2019, www.patreon.com/posts/voice-insider-28-25062829.

2. Bret Kinsella and Voicebot.ai, "99 Problems but Voice Tech Ain't One," Patreon, November 3, 2020, www.patreon.com/posts/43499836.

3. Interview with author, October 11, 2022.

4. Gordon Chu, interview with author, March 17, 2022.

5. Van West, "The Growing Role of Edge Computing Within Conversational AI" (panel discussion at Project Voice 22, Chattanooga, TN, April 26, 2022).

6. Brian Subirana et al., "Can Your Supply Chain Hear Me Now?," *MIT Sloan Management Review*, May 7, 2018, https://sloanreview.mit.edu/article/can-your-supply-chain-hear-me-now/.

7. "Retail Communication Platform," Theatro, accessed November 23, 2022, www.theatro.com/solutions/retail/; Payton Potter, "Walgreens Adopts Dallas-Based Theatro's SaaS Solutions for Nearly 10,000 Stores," *Dallas Innovates*, July 26, 2019, https://dallasinnovates.com/walgreens-adopts-dallas-based-theatros-saas-solutions-for-nearly-10000-stores/.

8. Samuel Rubenfeld, "Accenture Tries Chatbot for Code of Conduct," *Wall Street Journal*, January 24, 2018, www.wsj.com/articles/accenture-tries-chatbot-for-code-of-conduct-1516819919; Michael Blanding, "Ethics Bots and Other Ways to Move Your Code of Business Conduct Beyond Puffery," Working Knowledge, *Harvard Business Review*, May 14, 2019, https://hbswk.hbs.edu/item/ethics-bots-and-other-ways-to-move-your-code-of-business-conduct-beyond-puffery.

9. Bret Kinsella, "When Adding Voice Assistants to Mobile Apps, Consider the Long Tail," Voicebot.ai, February 15, 2022, paywall post, accessed May 2022.

10. "How Long Tail Key Words, and Voice Search, Are Connected," Sevell+Sevell, accessed August 10, 2022, www.sevell.com/news/how-long-tail-keywords-and-voice-search-are-connected.

11. Purity Muriuki, "How Does Voice Search Technology Dominate SEO in 2022?," Startup.info, February 16, 2022, https://startup.info/how-does-voice-search-technology-dominate-seo/.

12. "How Alexa Is Making Long-Tail Keywords Essential," Helium 10, August 9, 2022, www.helium10.com/blog/alexa-making-long-tail-keywords-essential/.

13. Randy Rieland, "Alexa? How Voice-First Technology Helps Older Adults," Next Avenue, May 4, 2018, www.forbes.com/sites/nextavenue/2018/05/04/alexa-how-voice-first-technology-helps-older-adults/.

14. "Disability Impacts All of Us," Centers for Disease Control and Prevention, accessed August 19, 2022, www.cdc.gov/ncbddd/disabilityandhealth/infographic-disability-impacts-all.html.

15. Jenny Medeiros, "Voice Assistants Are Changing How Users with Disabilities Get Things Done," Modev, April 19, 2018, www.modev.com/blog/voice-assistants-are-changing-how-users-with-disabilities-get-things-done.

16. "The Turing Test, 1950," The Alan Turing Internet Scrapbook, accessed February 17, 2023, www.turing.org.uk/scrapbook/test.html.

17. Bret Kinsella, "Is the Near Future of Voice Assistants a Step Backward?," Voicebot.ai, March 8, 2022, paywall post, accessed May 2022.

18. Peter Sutherland, "Achieving Financial Wellness with Conversational AI" (presentation at Project Voice 22, Chattanooga, TN, April 25, 2022).

19. Content of the next several paragraphs drawn from author interview with Dr. Yaa Kumah-Crystal, March 8, 2022.

CHAPTER 9: TRAINING VOICE TOOLS TO UNDERSTAND YOUR WORLD

1. Cliff Kuang, *User Friendly* (New York: Picador, 2020), 96.

2. Michael Freenor, interview with author, March 3, 2023.

3. Jennifer Wise, *How to Design Digital Voice Experiences*, Forrester Research, March 27, 2019, www.forrester.com/report/how-to-design-digital-voice-experiences /RES146079.

4. This recommendation and the following sample dialogs are adapted from Darek Bittner, "Designing a Voice User Interface Is Easier Than You May Think," User Experience Center, Bentley University, accessed November 25, 2022, www .bentley.edu/centers/user-experience-center/voice-design-blog.

5. Zoey Collier, "The Story of the Capital One Alexa Skill," Alexa Blogs, Amazon, December 16, 2016, https://developer.amazon.com/blogs/alexa/post/c70e3a9b -405c-4fe1-bc20-bc0519d48c97/the-story-of-the-capital-one-alexa-skill.

6. "Stanford Open Virtual Assistant Lab," Open Virtual Assistant Lab, accessed September 16, 2022, https://oval.cs.stanford.edu.

7. Pritesh, "15 Best Synthetic Data Generation Tools," Squeeze Growth, December 2, 2021, https://squeezegrowth.com/synthetic-data-generation-tools/.

8. Margo Bulka, in "VOICE Talks: Caitlin Gutekunst & Margo Bulka Give Tips for the Transition from Mobile to Voice," VOICE & AI, uploaded April 1, 2021, www .youtube.com/watch?v=q7Ju0fvlXDY.

9. "Appen (Australia), Oracle (US) and TELUS International (Canada) Are Leading Players in Data Annotation and Labeling Market," MarketsandMarkets, accessed February 17, 2023, www.marketsandmarkets.com/ResearchInsight/data-annotation -and-labelling-market.asp.

10. Ken Dodelin, "5 Common Misconceptions About Intelligent Assistants," Capital One, October 29, 2018, www.capitalone.com/tech/machine-learning/five -common-misconceptions-about-intelligent-assistants/.

11. "ComQA: A Dataset for Complex Factoid Question Answering with Paraphrase Clusters," Database & Information Systems Group, Max Planck Institute for Informatics, 2019, https://qa.mpi-inf.mpg.de/comqa/.

12. John Kelvie, "Understanding Is Crucial for Voice and AI: Testing and Training Are Key to Monitoring and Improving It," Voicebot.ai, October 24, 2020, https://voicebot.ai/2020/10/24/understanding-is-crucial-for-voice-and-ai-testing -and-training-are-key-to-monitoring-and-improving-it/.

13. Ditte Hvas Mortensen, "How to Design Voice User Interfaces," Interactive Design Foundation, accessed November 25, 2022, www.interaction-design.org /literature/article/how-to-design-voice-user-interfaces.

14. Cathy Pearl, "Basic Principles for Designing Voice User Interfaces," O'Reilly Online Learning Platform, November 21, 2016, www.oreilly.com/content /basic-principles-for-designing-voice-user-interfaces/.

15. Comments in this section drawn from author interviews with Michael Freenor, January 7, 2022, and February 2, 2022.

16. Marc Ericson Santos, "Design Guidelines for Voice User Interfaces," UX Collective, May 29, 2019, https://uxdesign.cc/design-guidelines-for-voice-user-interfaces -3c3b73982f4c.

CHAPTER 10: DESIGNING AND REDESIGNING
THE MULTIMODAL USER EXPERIENCE

1. Bret Kinsella, "No Discovery but No Intent to Find Voice App Discovery," Voicebot.ai, February 21, 2022, paywall post, accessed May 2022.

2. Keyvan Mohajer, "How New Voice AI Breakthrough Will Change Human-Computer Interaction Forever—Starting with How You Order Takeout," SoundHound, November 17, 2022, www.soundhound.com/voice-ai-blog/how-new -voice-ai-breakthrough-will-change-human-computer-interaction-forever-starting -with-how-you-order-takeout.

3. Dr. Yaa Kumah-Crystal, interview with author, March 8, 2022.

4. Joel Sucherman, interview with author, May 13, 2022.

5. Cathy Pearl, "Basic Principles for Designing Voice User Interfaces," O'Reilly Online Learning Platform, November 21, 2016, www.oreilly.com/content/basic -principles-for-designing-voice-user-interfaces/.

6. The WillowTree voice user interface design kit is available for download at https://www.willowtreeapps.com/services/voice.

7. Shadiah Garwell, interview with author, January 24, 2022.

8. Mihai Antonescu, interview with author, February 22, 2022.

9. David John Farinella, "Companies Seek Signature Sound," *Variety*, December 1, 2009, https://variety.com/2009/digital/news/companies-seek-signature-sound -1118012189/; Audrey Arbeeny, "Connecting Beyond Voice Through Sonic Branding," Voicebot.ai, March 1, 2019, https://voicebot.ai/2019/03/01/connecting-beyond -voice-through-sonic-branding/.

10. Cindy Hamer and Ricardo Garza, "From AAA Gaming on the Nintendo Switch to Education with Moodle: Augmenting Customer Experience Through Synthetic Voice" (presentation at Project Voice 22, Chattanooga, TN, April 25, 2022).

11. Nate Murray, "Voice-Enabled 'Hello Kitty's Room'" Game on Google Assistant Uses ReadSpeaker," ReadSpeaker AI, November 23, 2021, www.readspeaker.ai /blog/hello-kitty-voice-by-readspeaker/.

12. Jeff Hyatt, "Veritone Acquires Artificial Intelligence Voice Creator VocaliD," MESA Technology, June 17, 2022, www.mesaonline.org/2022/06/17/veritone-acquires -artificial-intelligence-voice-creator-vocalid/.

13. Eric Hal Schwartz, "Apple Will Introduce a Gender-Neutral Siri Voice in iOS Update," Voicebot.ai, February 22, 2022, https://voicebot.ai/2022/02/22/apple -will-introduce-a-gender-neutral-siri-voice-in-ios-update/.

14. Bret Kinsella, "University of Waterloo Study Found Consumers Believe Siri Is Disingenuous and Cunning Compared to Alexa as Genuine and Caring," Voicebot.ai, January 5, 2020, https://voicebot.ai/2020/01/05/university-of-waterloo-study-found -consumers-believe-siri-is-disingenuous-and-cunning-compared-to-alexa-as -genuine-and-caring/.

15. Doug Lilly, interview with author, September 23, 2022.

16. See, for example, Benedict Sheppard et al., "The Business Value of Design," *McKinsey Quarterly*, October 15, 2018, www.mckinsey.com/capabilities/mckinsey -design/our-insights/the-business-value-of-design.

Index

SARAH CRAMER SHIELDS

Tobias Dengel is president of WillowTree, a global leader in digital product design and development, with headquarters in Charlottesville, VA, and offices throughout North America, South America, and Europe. WillowTree, now part of TELUS International, has been named by *Inc.* magazine to the Inc. 5000 list of America's fastest-growing companies, with clients that include major companies and large government agencies.

MARY-JO WEBER

Karl Weber is a writer and editor who specializes in topics from business, politics, current affairs, and social issues. He has worked with authors including former president Jimmy Carter, 2006 Nobel Peace Prize laureate Muhammad Yunus, and a number of leading CEOs, consultants, and business experts.

PublicAffairs is a publishing house founded in 1997. It is a tribute to the standards, values, and flair of three persons who have served as mentors to countless reporters, writers, editors, and book people of all kinds, including me.

I. F. STONE, proprietor of *I. F. Stone's Weekly*, combined a commitment to the First Amendment with entrepreneurial zeal and reporting skill and became one of the great independent journalists in American history. At the age of eighty, Izzy published *The Trial of Socrates*, which was a national bestseller. He wrote the book after he taught himself ancient Greek.

BENJAMIN C. BRADLEE was for nearly thirty years the charismatic editorial leader of *The Washington Post*. It was Ben who gave the *Post* the range and courage to pursue such historic issues as Watergate. He supported his reporters with a tenacity that made them fearless and it is no accident that so many became authors of influential, best-selling books.

ROBERT L. BERNSTEIN, the chief executive of Random House for more than a quarter century, guided one of the nation's premier publishing houses. Bob was personally responsible for many books of political dissent and argument that challenged tyranny around the globe. He is also the founder and longtime chair of Human Rights Watch, one of the most respected human rights organizations in the world.

•   •   •

For fifty years, the banner of Public Affairs Press was carried by its owner Morris B. Schnapper, who published Gandhi, Nasser, Toynbee, Truman, and about 1,500 other authors. In 1983, Schnapper was described by *The Washington Post* as "a redoubtable gadfly." His legacy will endure in the books to come.

Peter Osnos, *Founder*